Captain Kidd

Captain Kidd

The Hunt for the Truth

Craig Cabell, Graham A Thomas and Allan Richards

Pen & Sword
MARITIME

First published in Great Britain in 2010 by
Pen & Sword Maritime
an imprint of
Pen & Sword Books Ltd
47 Church Street
Barnsley
South Yorkshire
S70 2AS

ISBN 978 1 84415 961 1

A CIP catalogue record for this book is available from the British Library

Printed and bound in UK by
MPG Books UK

Pen & Sword Books Ltd incorporates the Imprints of
Pen & Sword Aviation, Pen & Sword Maritime, Pen & Sword Military,
Wharncliffe Local History, Pen and Sword Select, Pen and Sword Military Classics,
Leo Cooper, Remember When, Seaforth Publishing and Frontline Publishing.

For a complete list of Pen & Sword titles please contact
PEN & SWORD BOOKS LIMITED
47 Church Street, Barnsley, South Yorkshire, S70 2AS, England
E-mail: enquiries@pen-and-sword.co.uk
Website: www.pen-and-sword.co.uk

Contents

This book is dedicated to our ex-colleague at MoD *Focus* David Barlow
– a brilliant graphics designer, artist and great friend

Acknowledgements

There are many people we would like to thank for their guidance and perception concerning Kidd's story. The tracking down of certain documents, in research for this book was the easy part, understanding the background was another. The authors would like to thank the following people whose contribution to the evolution of this book has been important: the staff of the National Archives at Kew, especially Geoff Baxter for his help and inspiration, Mary Brazil and her colleagues at the National Maritime Museum, Ian and Mavis Dow, David Barlow and Rupert Harding.

The sources of some of the illustrations are not known. If anyone has any information regarding images which are not credited please contact the publisher.

Sincerely, many thanks to all.

CC, GT, AR, December 2008

Preface

I believe the world is convinced that no conquests of importance can be made without us; and yet, as soon as we have accomplished the service we are ordered upon, we are neglected . . . all we get is honour and salt beef. (Lord Nelson, HMS *Agamemnon*, September 1793)

Captain Kidd. The name conjures up images of buried treasure and swashbuckling pirates, adventures on the high seas plastered across the pages of a boy's own storybook.

But what of the true story of Captain Kidd? So much of it is surrounded in myth and legend. It is very difficult to disprove a myth because people wallow in the romance of the fantasy and prefer their own perception to historical fact. And what is that historical fact?

The belief that has lasted for centuries is that Captain Kidd was given a commission by the King to act as a privateer and capture and plunder pirate ships as well as French ships. France was the enemy and any opportunity to damage her on the high seas was something that England would take. But then he turned pirate and plundered several ships. Although, to the end, he claimed he was innocent.

This view comes from a variety of sources, many of which we have used in writing this book. Primarily the facts in the Kidd case come from the testimonies and depositions of the men who sailed with Kidd, from his own account, from letters written by highly influential men such as Lord Bellomont as well as from reports written by the East India Company about Kidd's behaviour in India. All of this was used by Captain Charles Johnson who wrote an account of Kidd in his book *A General History of the Most Notorious Pirates* which was published some twenty years after Kidd died.

This account is said to be fairly accurate as Johnson is the closest author to the time of Kidd. He painted Kidd as a pirate who turned away from his privateering commission and committed many acts of piracy.

Today, many historians base their work about pirates in general and Kidd in particular on Johnson's work. But what many fail to realize is that past historians – and play-wrights – wrote to please their public and political masters. When Johnson published his book about pirates they were public enemy number one, so painting them in a sympathetic way was not an option.

This concept is difficult for a modern-day audience to appreciate, because of the way earlier accounts colour our view of the past. A classic case is William Shakespeare's wonderfully horrific tale of King Richard III. In the play Richard is portrayed as a psychopathic serial killer, disfigured in body and mind, dressed in black, who we can't wait to see murdered on the fields of Bosworth at the play's climax. Unfortunately, there is much strong evidence to suggest that Richard III was not a wicked hunchback but quite a weak king. The fact that Queen Elizabeth I's grandfather defeated Richard and Shakespeare was writing to please his queen may well have influenced his interpretation of the character! But nowadays most people accept Shakespeare's interpretation of Richard III as the authentic one – and there lies the rub: the myth persists and history is forgotten.

Another example of this distortion of history is the life of the Roman Emperor Gaius Caesar. Through the account by Seneca, we are led to believe that Caligula (to give Gaius his popular title) was a raving lunatic; but he wasn't. The historical facts suggest that he was a great leader and soldier who was killed by the Senate because they feared that he was getting too powerful and would do away with them once and for all. They assassinated him and, the same day, tried to restore the Republic but were thwarted by the Praetorian Guard who had already proclaimed Claudius the new emperor. Seneca wrote for Claudius who needed to hide the truth of what happened to Caligula but, because many knew the basic facts about his death, the more obscure facts had to be overblown/misrepresented to justify the assassination.

So now we come onto Captain Kidd: the most infamous pirate who ever sailed the high seas or a privateer doing the business for the King of England? Ultimately the answer to this comes from you, the reader. In this book, we – the authors – are merely placing the facts before you. Our aim is to show you the legend of Kidd and to search for the truth of the man. But at the end of the day we leave the decisions about him to you.

However, there is one interesting fact that we must bring to light here. In all of our sources and all our research there is no single person who is able to confirm Kidd's account from beginning to end. At his trial no one really stood for him and confirmed everything he said. He was alone.

We can look at this in a number of ways. One is that Kidd was guilty of turning pirate and when he wrote his account much of it was embellished, some of the key facts were left out and some of it was completely untrue. Another is that all the people from whom the authorities gathered evidence were coached on what they should say, even under oath. Conspiracy theorists would probably agree here. But so many people testified against him on a wide variety of issues from all over the world that it seems hard to believe such a case could have been so entirely fabricated.

But perhaps it was. The prosecution had two years to prepare their case while Kidd had only two weeks and he didn't get all the documents he needed to build his case. As we shall see, these documents may not have helped him anyway.

Craig Cabell and Graham A Thomas
London, September 2009

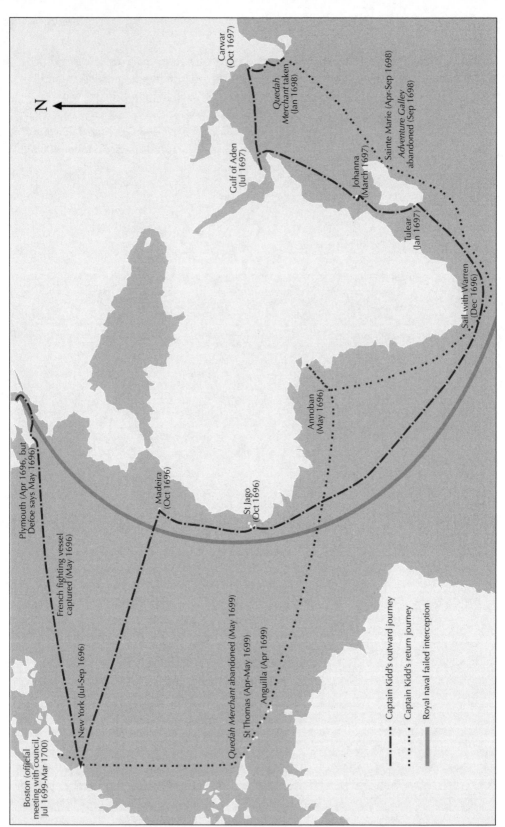

Captain Kidd's Voyages (from eighteenth-century maps)

Plymouth (Apr 1696, but Defoe says May 1696)

French fighting vessel captured (May 1696)

New York (Jul-Sep 1696)

Boston (official meeting with council, Jul 1699-Mar 1700)

Madeira (Oct 1696)

St Iago (Oct 1696)

Quedah Merchant abandoned (May 1699)

St Thomas (Apr-May 1699)

Anguilla (Apr 1699)

Annoban (May 1696)

Sail with Warren (Dec 1696)

Tulear (Jan 1697)

Johanna (March 1697)

Sainte Marie (Apr-Sep 1698)

Adventure Galley abandoned (Sep 1698)

Gulf of Aden (Jul 1697)

Quedah Merchant taken (Jan 1698)

Carwar (Oct 1697)

N

- Captain Kidd's outward journey
- Captain Kidd's return journey
- Royal naval failed interception

Introduction

In the Beginning

With every groan and creak of the ship, every roll and yaw the vessel made as it rode the waves on its trans-Atlantic voyage the man was tossed around as much as the chains binding him would allow. For what seemed an eternity he'd been kept below decks in a tiny cabin in steerage. Unwashed, his hair and beard flowing down his soiled clothes, illness wracking his body, he was a shadow of the man he used to be.

The prisoner was being taken back to England to stand trial for his life. As the days rolled by he must have wondered how on earth he had ended up where he was. For only three years earlier he'd been on top of the world, commanding one of the most impressive private warships ever built. His triumphant sail down the Thames towards open sea had quickly turned to disaster.

The ship yawed from side to side with every swell of the sea and the prisoner grew weaker. He ached for his young wife and family. To see them again would lift his spirits so much.

After weeks of being confined below decks he felt the ship heave to. Above him were the shouts of the crew as the sails were lowered. He could hear the tackle being pulled as men brought the sails down; he felt the ship slow in the water until it was simply rolling with the sea and not under way. The prisoner wondered what was happening. Then some men came and brought him roughly from his dark, stinking hole into the light and the wonderful sea air. It filled his lungs as they moved him across the deck and unceremoniously transferred him across to the ship that was tied up alongside. It was smaller than the one he'd left and seemed so familiar.

The ship they approached was the *Katherine*, the King's Yacht, and the prisoner, Captain William Kidd, must have had a profound sense of déjàvu.

The story of Captain William Kidd and his final voyage which ended so miserably has become the stuff of legend. In most of those legends he has been branded the most notorious pirate to ever sail the waters around America. Most historians still believe that Kidd was a pirate though he maintained to the last that he was a privateer doing the King's work. The first person to brand Kidd as a pirate was

Captain Charles Johnson who wrote a biography of Kidd in his book, *A General History Of The Most Notorious Pirates*, which was first published in 1724. There is some doubt as to who Johnson was: some believe he was the famous Daniel Defoe who wrote *Robinson Crusoe*, while others think he was a pirate because of his knowledge of the sea that comes through in his accounts of the pirates and their way of life.

For our purposes we will refer to him as Johnson. This is what he writes about Captain Kidd:

> We cannot account for this sudden change in his conduct, otherwise than by supposing that he first meant well, while he had hopes of making his fortune by taking of pirates, but now weary of ill success and fearing lest his owners out of humour at their great expense, should dismiss him, he resolved to do his business one way, since he could not do it another.[1]

The story of Kidd leads up to his final voyage where he sailed from England, across the Atlantic to New York, then to Africa into the Red Sea and India, and back to New York. His life culminates in this voyage for it is here that he is claimed to have turned pirate. We'll look at the facts of this voyage in much greater detail but first we need to look at the man and his earlier actions.

The fables and stories of Kidd say that he was a ruthless pirate, tremendously wealthy, and that he buried treasure up and down the eastern seaboard of America. Novels, plays, films and cartoons have helped to propagate the legend and myth of Captain Kidd. Famous writers like Edgar Allan Poe and Robert Louis Stevenson used the Kidd tales in their fiction, helping to propagate the piracy myth. 'Kidd leaped suddenly into piratical fame and never has lost ground.'[2]

More recent historians like Richard Zacks believe that Kidd was a victim of circumstance and that his unruly crew were the cause of his being branded a pirate. 'He was created by those forces of commercial and political exploitation that we recognise and in part deplore as typical of an expanding America.'[3]

However, in Kidd's case there are many grey areas and the facts can be interpreted in different ways. But the legend of Kidd that was built up during this voyage and after his trial and execution simply points to him as a pirate. 'Imagination was stirred in the tavern and down the backstairs as well as in the House of Commons and at the trial in the Old Bailey.'[4]

Let's see what the facts are.

1

Early Years

At the time of his last voyage Kidd was a respectable mariner who lived in New York at 119–21 Pearl Street. He was a substantial citizen of that great city and in 1691 he had married Sarah Bradley Cox Oort, a rich New York widow much younger than himself who had several properties of her own to which Kidd added. They owned property in Pearl, Pine, Wall and Water Streets and their fine brick house on Pearl Street had a good view of the harbour. It is said that Kidd had the first expensive Oriental rug, a Turkey carpet, owned in the New World.[1] Kidd also had a property in the country on what is now the edge of Harlem at the foot of 74th Street.

One pirate historian, David Cordingly, tells us that Kidd was born about 1645 at Greenock, a Scottish port situated on the Firth of Clyde. However, Richard Zacks states that Kidd was born in Dundee in Scotland on 22 January 1654 and that his father was a sea captain who died when Kidd was just 5 years old. Kidd went to sea after his mother remarried, drifting between ships and ports in the Caribbean for almost three decades.[2] He is known to have been commanding a privateer in the Caribbean around 1689.[3]

Little is known of his early days at sea and to speculate on what he may or may not have been doing during those years is a fruitless exercise. What we know is that he went to sea at a young age and some of the first references about him appear when he was serving aboard a French privateer ship. It is the years he spent in the Caribbean, working hard as a privateer, showing his courage and building a reputation as an honest, brave and respectable man that led to his last reckless ill-fated voyage. So it is necessary to concentrate on those years now. 'His reputation in the Colonies was so good, in fact, and his skill and achievements so notable, that the great and unfortunate exploit of his life could not have been undertaken except for them.'[4]

In 1689 at the age of 35 Kidd was in the Caribbean drifting from voyage to voyage. He had yet to make his mark that would propel him onto the international stage. He gravitated towards the French Island Isle á Vache, a small enclave off Hispaniola half way between English Jamaica and French Tortuga which at the time was growing as the main port for privateers. It was here that he met up with a young Englishman, Robert Culliford, who later would become his nemesis. But for now they became friends. Both men signed aboard an old French privateer ship, the *Sainte Rose* along with a handful of other Englishmen and the vast majority of French that made up the crew.

This was a rare period of peace for England but France was at war with Holland so Kidd and Culliford decided to join up with the French and take what they could from the Dutch – getting rich in the process if they could. With a commission from the French mayor of Isle á Vache, the *Sainte Rose* set sail to plunder Dutch ships wherever it could. The commission walked the tightrope between legality and illegality.

It wasn't long before the crew of the *Sainte Rose* found their first victim, a Dutch merchant ship that they stripped of her cargo, and sailed to New England to sell their plundered goods. Once they'd sold the goods and replenished they decided to sail for the South Seas in the Pacific because too many navies were cruising the Caribbean and the South Seas would be relatively safe. They sailed for Africa letting the winds take them.

They didn't get to the South Seas. Instead they made the Cape Verde Islands where they stumbled across a fleet of seven French privateers commanded by Admiral Jean DuCasse. He was a brave and respectable captain who would later become governor and command hundreds of privateers. His flagship, *Le Hasardeux*, had forty-four cannon.

The story of DuCasse's bravery had spread. He was the man who, outgunned by a giant Dutch man of war, boarded his enemy's ship with just twenty men, set fires in four corners of the huge vessel to keep the Dutch crew off balance and locked them below decks, taking the huge prize into La Rochelle. With Kidd serving aboard a French privateer it is quite likely that he had heard similar tales.

But now the Admiral's objective was to take Dutch Surinam (Dutch Guiana), one of the richest Dutch holdings in the area, a wealthy hub of sugar and slaves. Funded by wealthy French backers, including the King of France, DuCasse's mission seemed promising indeed. The crew of the *Sainte Rose* voted to join the fleet, bringing DuCasse's command up to eight vessels.

Within days of joining the fleet they ran across a Spanish merchant ship from Havana and gave chase. Cornered and outnumbered, the Spanish ship lay by awaiting her fate. But there was a problem. Spain and France were technically at peace so DuCasse couldn't legally capture the ship but the commission of the *Sainte Rose* was more ambiguous. The crew of the *Sainte Rose* boarded the Spanish ship took the cargo which was distributed amongst the fleet and locked up the crew.[5]

They took this great Spanish ship as their own and discarded the creaking, old *Sainte Rose*. The new ship was faster and had sixteen guns. What's interesting about this capture is that it borders on piracy and this is maybe where Culliford and Kidd had their first taste of it.

Surinam was a ripe target filled with sugar plantations and thousands of slaves.

For DuCasse it would be a huge feather in his cap. As they neared the coast they waited for night to fall and slowly moved to the mouth of the harbour at Paramaibo, darkness hiding the little fleet. It must have been an anxious night for Kidd and Culliford as they waited for action at the first light of dawn.

But when the sun came up the French discovered seven Dutch warships anchored in the harbour including a huge fifty-gun man of war. The Dutch crews were ready and pounded the French with musket and cannon fire. Harbour batteries poured accurate cannon fire onto the French who hastily beat a retreat and headed down the coast to attack another Dutch settlement at Berbiche. Again they were picked off by accurate fire from the Dutch and pounded by cannon situated in the settlement's fort.

DuCasse had no choice but to sail back the way he'd come. Heading for Barbados they heard the momentous news – England had declared war on France. King William, a staunch Protestant imported from Holland, was now on the English throne and had decided to continue his war against the French Catholics that was to spread across Europe and much of the globe. King William's War as it was known began in 1688 and raged until 1697.[6]

For DuCasse it was a godsend for now he had English targets he could add to his list. But Kidd and Culliford were in an uneasy position. The French believed that their English shipmates were true mercenaries, devoid of any national pride or patriotism. But they were wrong. While they stayed aboard with the French, the small band of English privateers kept up that façade.

Near Martinique DuCasse met up with other French ships, expecting to lead the operations against the English. Instead he was outranked by the Gouverneur-Generale of the French West Indies, the Comte de Blenac, and it was the Comte who decided to attack St Christopher's, a wealthy jointly owned possession of both the French and the English. This island was rich in sugar and tobacco plantations and had been divided into quarters. The English owned the north and south quarters while the French owned the east and west. The only way the French could reach their settlements was by either walking the English coastline or by sailing there.

It was an arrangement that was bound to break down and on 17 July 1689 a French fleet of twenty-two ships started that process. Kidd and Culliford were still aboard the Spanish prize which was sailing with this fleet. The English retreated to Fort Charles, a heavily reinforced fortress, as the French arrived. To make matters worse the Irish Catholics who were no better than slaves, being the white menials of the English Caribbean, revolted and joined the French in looting and destroying English houses. 'The Irish have revolted and under the protection of the French have destroyed property to the value of £150,000.'[7]

On 19 July the French began bombarding Fort Charles. From each of their ships cannon after cannon roared sending its deadly message towards the fort.

At the time the fort held more than 1,000 English men and women, along with several hundred fighting men. The French bombardment had little effect on the fort so the Comte decided to besiege it, digging deep trenches around the inland side of the fort to completely isolate it. After that, he had embankments built closer and closer to protect his cannon and to bring his guns to bear. From his ships cannon were brought onto the land and hauled up to the embankments. Over several days, the guns were brought closer, the range closer and the imminent destruction closer.

Finally, by the end of July the Comte was ready and he ordered his land attack which included the privateers from the *Sainte Rose* except for the English and a handful of French who had been left behind to guard the ship.

As the order went out across the fleet boats were lowered into the water, full of men, weapons, ammunition and all the paraphernalia they would need for the attack. From the Spanish prize, 110 men climbed into the boats and rowed towards land. Back on the ship were twenty men, some French and the English. The landing party reached the beach and joined up with the rest of the French forces marching towards the fort. From the ship the little group of English privateers watched helplessly.

In the sweltering tropical heat the men left on the ship could hear the guns firing and the shouting of men as the attack developed. There was nothing they could do to stop the attack on the fort but they might be able to do something on the ship so they kept a keen watch on the French crew, gauging, waiting, hoping for the right moment. It soon came.

Zacks tells us it was Kidd who orchestrated the attack on the unsuspecting French crew (he does not provide his source for this information however). The small English crew waited until the French were off guard and drew their daggers. If they were caught before they could attack and the French raised the alarm they would be killed.

The English privateers moved quickly in the baking heat and attacked the French, killing some outright while others were wounded. But they were all thrown over the side and Kidd ordered the anchors to be cut and the sails unfurled. Slowly, the Spanish prize left the harbour, heading for the nearby island of Nevis.

> On the 7th inst. I arrived here and found a French ship of sixteen guns that had been surprised and captured by the English. She was formerly a privateer manned by a hundred and thirty English and French, but mostly French. All but twenty of them made a descent on St. Christopher's, leaving the ship at anchor at Basseterre with twelve French and eight English on board. The last named set upon the French, soon overcame them without the loss of a man and brought the ship in here. She is now fitting for the King's service, her captain being William Kidd. This vessel with my two sloops is all our strength at sea, very inconsiderable in comparison with their fleet.[8]

Nevis, pronounced Neevis, is a sombrero-shaped island of twenty-six square miles lying near the top of the Lesser Antilles archipelago almost 200 miles south of Puerto Rico and just west of Antigua. The island itself is approximately seven miles long and five miles wide.

In Nevis, Kidd was given a hero's welcome and Governor of Nevis Christopher Codrington referred to him as Captain William Kidd, which fed his ego nicely. Codrington added four more cannon to their ship which was renamed the *Blessed William* in honour of the King but also possibly as a nod to Kidd's heroics. This brought the total number of guns up to twenty. As we have seen, the *Blessed William* and Codrington's two sloops were all the English had against the French.

St Christopher's fell to the French on 5 August and many of its inhabitants managed to make their way to Nevis, including English troops who hadn't been paid in six years and were, as Codrington wrote, 'almost naked'. They'd lost everything. When St Christopher's fell the French went on a rampage of pillaging and destruction, carrying off whatever loot they could find. Indeed, Comte de Blenac took such a haul from the island that he decided to return to the island of French Martinique so he could sell it all off and make a profit. DuCasse was furious: the English were weak so now was the time to seize the day and attack them en masse. But Blenac preferred his money and the English could wait.

Every day the English waited for reinforcements to arrive from England and each day they didn't come. The Irish rebelled on Montserrat and the French took Anguilla. Where was the Royal Navy?

In Nevis, Kidd continued to fit out the *Blessed William* and took on more crew, mostly ex-pirates and rogues, but they weren't enough. Codrington decided he couldn't wait for reinforcements from England so he hired Kidd to sail to Barbados, some 315 miles away, and pick up troops and ammunition. Barbados was away from the frontline and relatively safe. Kidd was also charged with picking up any intelligence he could about the French. He set sail on 26 September 1689.

Codrington owned some of the largest sugar plantations in Barbados and was one of the most influential and wealthiest men in the Caribbean. His family owned the entire island of Barbuda which had been given to them by the English monarch in 1685 in response to Codrington's plan to use it to breed slaves. Codrington had much to lose from the war with the French.

Kidd arrived back in Nevis more than a month after he'd sailed with three French prizes in tow. Sailing with him were much needed reinforcements in the person of Captain Heweston, an English privateer who commanded the *Lion*, a ship with forty guns and crewed by more than 150 men.[9]

Codrington hired Heweston and he now had two experienced captains at his disposal. But he desperately needed something to keep the French at bay, a victory that would rally the people of the English-held islands and possibly keep the Irish from joining the French. He settled on an attack on a small French island, Mariegalante off Guadeloupe, also French. In the Caribbean, Jamaica and

Barbados were the main English colonies while Martinique and Sainte Dominique were the main French ones, but there were scores of smaller islands spread over vast distances that were almost impossible to defend. Mariegalante was one such island of nothing but sugar plantations.

'Having some French Protestants here who knew Mariegalante well, we found on consulting them that an attack with six hundred men might be hopeful of success, and would serve the double purpose of discouraging the French and giving experience to our men', Codrington wrote in a letter to the Lords of Trade and Plantations that was received in London on 3 July 1690. In his account of the action he states that the risk was small 'for no fleet could well come here from Martinique unobserved by our ships at Mariegalante, and the latter Island is but twenty four hours distant from hence and less than half that time distant for the return voyage'.[10]

Codrington gave a commission to Heweston to command the expedition both by land and by sea and to take the troops ashore. 'So I gave him his own ship, our captured privateer of twenty guns under Captain Kidd, another ship of ten or twelve guns under Captain Perry, and my own two sloops, with five hundred and forty men of all kinds aboard.'

The fleet sailed on Saturday, 28 December 1689 and reached the island on the following Monday. The tension in the air must have been intense as they sailed towards their target. The men would have prepared their cutlasses, cleaned their muskets, checked their powder, sharpened their daggers and prepared for battle. Those who were religious likely prayed. That Monday as they anchored, the boats were lowered and Heweston ordered them to be rowed ashore. In all, 440 men were landed at Mariegalante.

Heweston ordered the rest of the men to stay on board the ships and sail to the main town 'in the Island, about ten miles distant', Codrington wrote. 'He then marched to the town, breaking up, though not without loss, several ambuscading parties on the way, engaged the main body of the enemy before the town and after a short dispute routed them.'

But two miles from the town the French rallied, digging themselves in, and began firing everything they had at the English in order to give the inhabitants of the town time to flee. They were overwhelmed by Heweston's forces: they 'were driven out and fled with precipitation', stated Codrington in his letter to the Lords of Trade and Plantations. 'Hewetson, judging it imprudent to follow them, then retired to the town for the night. Next day stragglers were taken, who gave intelligence that the Governor with most of the population had gained an entrenchment about twelve miles from the town, without artillery and with no provisions except a little cattle.'

Heweston called for a council of war, bringing Kidd and Perry ashore to decide what to do. After some deliberation they decided to demand that the Governor of Mariegalante surrender. The answer that came back that a reply would be made by noon of the following day.

Noon of 1 January came, but without an answer,

> but it was judged imprudent to attack the French so far from the ships and by dangerous paths, for it was rumoured that the French had sent for aid to Martinique. They therefore carried on board whatever plunder was near the shore and burned and destroyed the rest. This took four or five days, after which they returned hither after nine days' absence, bringing with them also two ships lately arrived from France. They burned fifty sugar-works and all the houses in the Island. The cane-fields were all fired, great quantities of sugar in cask were burned and about ten thousand horses and cattle killed. Thus though we have not ourselves reaped the benefit that might have been gained by a larger force, we have sufficiently mischiefed our enemies and avenged in some measure the injury done at St. Christopher's. In this action we had only three men killed and eighteen wounded most of who are since recovered. The enemy, as we learn from prisoners, had twenty killed and very many wounded.[11]

Kidd and Culliford, still sailing together, made the return voyage to Antigua loaded down with what they had taken from the houses on Mariegalante before they were destroyed, but Heweston took some of Kidd's crew and put them onto one of the prize French vessels. Nevertheless when they arrived in Antigua they celebrated their victory. But it was short lived.

A crisis loomed. 'At Nevis the Council and Assembly represented to me their want of provisions owing to the failure of their former supplies from Ireland', Codrington wrote. The council begged him to attack and plunder two islands, St Bartholomew and St Martin's, which were well stored with cattle

> so as at once to ease the Island for a time of the burden of their presence, and to furnish it with supplies by plunder. I consented, and on the 15th December Sir Timothy Thornhill sailed with instructions from me to attack St. Martins first, and if he thought the hazard would cost too dear or take too much time, to return to Nevis; though if he took St. Martins he might go on to St. Bartholomew, only sending a sloop to me for further orders. On the following day he came before St. Martins, but finding the inhabitants on the alert sailed to St. Bartholomew's and after some opposition mastered it.

After the French Governor of St Bartholomew surrendered Thornhill sent him, sixty prisoners and the black slaves back to Nevis. For three weeks Thornhill transported the cattle from St Bartholomew back to Nevis along with other plunder.

> When having burned all the houses but two or three he sailed again for St. Martins. He landed without opposition and after a few skirmishes drove all

the inhabitants into the woods. He marched through the Island in four or five days, but before he could do anything decisive against the enemy in the woods a French man-of-war of forty-four guns arrived with another ship at St. Martins, drove away our ships and landed a party to the assistance of the Islanders.

Pinned down, Thornhill sent letters to Codrington asking for help but Codrington in his letter to the Lords of Trade and Plantations he stated that he did not get those letters. 'Sir Timothy tells me that he sent several letters to Nevis, which were not forwarded to me, and that it was only on receiving no answer from me that he made so long stay. On receiving a letter from him asking for relief, I sent it off at once.'

Codrington ordered Heweston and Kidd to sail for St Martin's immediately to assist Thornhill. 'Hewetson was some days returned from Mariegalante when I received Sir Timothy Thornhill's message', Codrington wrote.

At the moment the better part of his seamen were on board one of the prizes taken at Mariegalante, which had fallen to leeward, and a number of men, making one hundred and forty in all, had gone in one of my sloops to bring her in. But there being no time for delay Hewetson sailed without waiting for them on the night of the 14th January with his own ship, the privateer [Kidd's the Blessed William] and one of my sloops, with a total force of about three hundred and eighty men.

According to Codrington's account Heweston and Kidd engaged the French on 16 January and the following day managed to bring off all the English including Thornhill. In an account written by one of the officers aboard Heweston's ship the *Lion*, we get the details of the St Martin's affair. 'We left on the night of the 14th January and on the following day lay about three hours to windward of Nevis, waiting for the sloop with the men from the prize, but went on without them.' This was one of the captured ships at St Bartholomew that Heweston had manned with almost half of Kidd's men. The account goes on to state that some hours before daylight they retook one of the sloops Thornhill had lost to the French. From the prisoners onboard they learned that DuCasse had been loading up provisions at Martinique when he'd received news of Thornhill's expedition.

He went at once first to St. Bartholomew's and then to St. Martin's where on the 11th he scattered all Sir Timothy's sloops, and took that which we have now retaken. They told us also that the inhabitants of St. Martin's together with the Irish refugees among them numbered about three hundred men, that DuCasse had landed half as many men and that now they were all united into one body, and that on the evening before five hundred men had arrived from St. Christopher's at St. Martin's and that two or three hundred more were on their way to land and attack Sir Timothy.[12]

Undaunted by this news Heweston's little fleet with Kidd in the *Blessed William* poured on the sail with the hope of surprising the French at anchor at daybreak. 'But on our coming within a league of them they slipped their cables and bore up to us, five ships to our three.' The three English ships had the wind and drew closer to the French. Watching his enemies come DuCasse ordered his gun crews to fire. The forty cannon roared before the English ships had a chance to return fire. 'When almost within musket shot we gave him ours; they then opened fire with small arms until they were out of reach, we returning the fire. Having passed him we received the broadsides of the other four ships successively, which we returned. We tacked about again, but lost the wind, their ships sailing better than ours and being better manned with sailors.'

Again the ships passed each other firing broadsides and small arms fire. Cannon balls ripped into the rigging and sails of each ship, shredding the canvas and splintering wood. One English sharpshooter was wounded. However, although damage was being done, nothing was being achieved. Heweston who was ill decided to call a council of the captains to decide what to do. Because he was ill, more responsibility fell onto Kidd's shoulders, Kidd knew that the English were undermanned and lacked the firepower to achieve a decisive sea victory. He decided to try to board the French. It was a bold move.

It was then agreed at a council of war that we could gain little advantage, except by boarding, since then Captain Perry and your sloop would be of good service whereas at a distance it could do little, its guns being too small to do the enemy much harm. Having taken this decision we made a big stretch in hopes of regaining the wind, but failed, as we only passed each other as before.

For a fourth time the English tacked away trying to gain the wind and this time they did. As they drew closer to the French they readied themselves for boarding. Grappling hooks were brought up on deck, pistols made ready as the men waited and watched the French ships getting closer. 'Observing our intention they did not tack but bore away with all sail for St. Christopher. We then made towards the shore and sent a message to Sir Timothy to prepare to embark, which he did; and the sloops were making for the shore as fast as they could to receive him.'

But suddenly on the horizon they spotted the French ships, this time with one more coming directly for them. DuCasse was coming back with reinforcements. The English ships turned to face the French and bore up to them, 'and seeing that DuCasse designed to board us we lay by till Perry, who sailed very badly, came up with us and prepared to receive them with a broadside and a volley of shot, but there was no boarding at all'.

Again they passed each other firing broadsides and musket fire. The French managed to bring themselves close into the shore, forcing Thornhill to retreat under volleys of cannon shot.

> It was now near sunset, and a council of war was held, when it was resolved that we should stand away till after midnight, and then tack so that in the morning we might be sure of the wind in order to board the enemy if necessary. We did so accordingly and between one and two in the morning tacked and crowded all sail to try and come up with the French before daylight and surprise them at anchor, but failed.

When the dawn peered over the horizon the English found the French at anchor opposite Thornhill's camp and headed straight for them. But the French weighed anchor and sailed away to Anguilla. Instead of going after them, Kidd decided to use the opportunity to take Thornhill's force off the island as quickly as possible. 'A message was sent to Sir Timothy, who returned about noon with the reply that Sir Timothy was just then engaged with a party of the enemy but would get ready to embark as soon as it was over.'[13]

According to the same account, another English sloop arrived which was ordered to cover the retreat of Thornhill who by this time had managed to get to the beach, having routed the French forces he'd been engaged with. 'Before the last of his men were shipped a great party of the French was in view, but our men embarked under cover of our guns without loss of a man. About four in the afternoon of the 17th Sir Timothy came aboard, and on the Sunday following we all arrived safely at Nevis.'

The account of the St Martin's debacle also includes the mention of a flag of truce from

> Mons Guiteau, Governor of St. Christopher's, about an exchange of prisoners. Those of ours who came with the flag tell us that all the French at St. Christopher's except three hundred went to the relief of St. Martins. They said also that DuCasse thought we had gone quite away on Thursday night and wanted to fight us on Friday morning, but was forbidden by Guiteau, who had no fancy for a fight, not doubting that he would land his men in time to cut off Sir Timothy's retreat. Both Guiteau and DuCasse were much vexed at missing the prize they made so sure of.

Once again, DuCasse had been thwarted by a high-ranking official. In his grasp he'd had all of Thornhill's troops and the three English ships and yet he'd been unable to capture any of them. According to DuCasse's account he was stopped at the last moment when bearing down on the English who were embarking Thornhill's troops by 'a flock of fifty miserable citizens' who were too afraid to take such a risk. So DuCasse had to tack away losing his opportunity.[14]

What of the damage? 'DuCasse's ship was much damaged by our shot and many men wounded. All of our ships were hit though not a man was killed and but one wounded.'[15]

Codrington also wrote about the flag of truce. Thornhill had sent two agents, Major Crispe and Mr Garnet, to St Christopher's to negotiate the exchange of prisoners. He wrote to Codrington about the information the two men received.

> They learned that there was certain news of thirty sail of merchantmen and other ships at Martinique, most of them lately arrived from France, and that four ships of war were lately arrived from Canada or France with soldiers; that the ships had all been laden but were unloading, and that one small frigate and two merchantmen were to be fitted with all speed; that another man of war was only lately come with a Guineaman of ours taken, containing two hundred odd negroes; that Count de Blenac was coming in person to St. Christopher's with all the regular troops that he had, and after gathering more men was about to attack Nevis.

If this information was correct then the English were still in great danger. Codrington still hoped that reinforcements would arrive from England in the form of the Royal Navy. 'I at once applied to the Governor of Barbados for help, and for the encouragement of such supplies as might be sent from Barbados giving the gentleman who bore it £500 in addition for the purchase of arms and ammunition.' When the agents Codrington had sent to Barbados to ask for help returned his hopes were dashed.

> It is very strange that out of a magazine of twelve hundred spare arms they could lend us only a hundred old matchlocks, far from being in good order, and out of fourteen hundred barrels of powder could only lend twenty; but it is still more surprising that out of a hundred sail and thirty ships of good countenance they could not spare us one. We had hoped indeed that our friends in Barbados would have given us a seasonable loan of money in our great strait, not that they would not only deny us but hinder us from reaping the fruits of our own credit. Had they been in real danger themselves, they could not be blamed, but surely four or five ships out of thirty is no great weakening. Besides even if they had not a ship in the harbour they could have no rational fear of all the power of France in the West Indies. For, apart from the fact that the French fleet is engaged nearer home, the Island is fortified all round, not only with breastworks but with platforms and guns, and they can raise eight thousand white men and as

great a number of intelligent blacks. I own an estate there myself as considerable as most, so was not likely to endanger it, but I am afraid that worse motives than fear have denied us this assistance.[16]

Codrington could not understand why his request had been denied. 'If this disappointment proves our ruin it will be some advantage to Barbados but a great loss to the Crown', he wrote. To gain more intelligence Codrington sent a sloop to cruise the area. 'He returned with some prisoners from whom we learn that there are twenty sail at Martinique, and six or seven of them fitting out; but they do not confirm the news of soldiers arriving from Canada and France. Still their account is sufficient to fill us with apprehension.'

It was in this atmosphere that the citizens of Antigua and of Nevis toasted Kidd and Heweston for rescuing Thornhill's troops from under the noses of the French with minimal loss of life. Each of the captains received some rewards for their exploits, most of it in silver, but the crews of the ships received nothing. Thornhill's rescue had proven to be empty. They'd laid their lives on the line and though Thornhill had personally thanked the crews they had not been given any cash.

Kidd's crew especially were restless wanting to use the *Blessed William* to go off plundering French and Spanish vessels and they asked Kidd to leave patriotic actions and turn to piracy. He refused.

Codrington wrote in his letter to the Lords of Trade and Plantations that

on the 2nd February the privateer-ship ran away from us, being well stocked with arms and manned by eighty or ninety men. They took their opportunity when Captain Kidd (who has behaved himself well) was ashore and have carried off goods of his to the value of £2,000. Most of the crew were formerly pirates and I presume liked their old trade better than any that they were likely to have here. I sent after them, but without success, to the Virgin Islands and to St. Thomas's, where it was most likely that they would have gone to water.

Robert Culliford, along with William Mason and Samuel Burgess led the mutiny that saw the *Blessed William* taken while Kidd was ashore in Antigua. Culliford and Kidd had chosen different paths, one piracy, the other respectability, but it wouldn't be the last time their paths would cross. Indeed, in only a few short years Kidd would find himself in a very similar situation, eerily reflecting the loss of the *Blessed William*. But for now he was stranded on Antigua.

2

In New York

Kidd was now stranded without a ship in Antigua. Not only had Culliford and the others taken the *Blessed William* out from under him, they had also taken £2,000 that Kidd had stowed safely aboard her. However, Kidd was not long without a ship. 'Governor Codrington who had been impressed with his services against the French rewarded him with a recently captured French vessel, renamed the *Antigua*'.[1]

Robert C Ritchie states in his book, *Captain Kidd and the War against the Pirates* that Kidd's career 'became the search for the patronage of influential men who could further his quest for wealth and prestige'. It is this search for patronage that gives us an insight into Kidd's motivation. 'The political system thrived on patronage', Ritchie writes, 'Every position – menial or great – was in someone's control, and all the associated salaries, fees and privileges could be used to further the career of relatives, friends and protégés. Patronage was the heart and soul of politics, and Kidd reaped the benefits.'[2] However, he would soon find that there was a downside to patronage.

With the gift of a new ship from Codrington, Kidd set about putting together a new crew, one that hopefully would be more loyal than the last. According to Ritchie, Codrington gave Kidd permission to go after his old ship and hunt down Culliford. This was Kidd's first attempt at pirate hunting.

Because of the war more powerful naval ships were operating in the Caribbean to protect the colonies of different powers such as the French, Spanish and English from attack by their enemies but also from pirates. Indeed many of the fleets building up in the area were there to hunt down pirates. In this atmosphere many pirates and buccaneers were forced to flee the Caribbean to ensure they didn't get pressed into fighting or being hunted down themselves. With easy targets rapidly dwindling as the war escalated between European nations, they looked for more rewarding and safer hunting grounds. Africa and the Indian Ocean were the most appealing as few naval ships rarely sailed in these waters. It was highly unlikely that Culliford would have stayed in the Caribbean, especially since Codrington had written to all the other governors to be on the look out for the pirates.[3]

The *Blessed William*, now commanded by William Mason,[4] attacked and looted two Spanish ships as they headed northeast and then decided to attack the Spanish island of Banquilla about sixty leagues from Barbados.

Just south of the harbour the anchor splashed into the water and hit the bottom, quickly holding the *Blessed William* in position as she rode the Caribbean swell. On deck, orders were shouted, muskets were primed and loaded, cutlasses shined and readied. The ship's boats were lowered into the water, filled with armed men, and quickly, quietly they rowed towards the shore. The three main pirates in charge, Robert Culliford, William Mason and Samuel Burgess, surprised the Spanish in the town, rounding up men, women and children, and demanded money for their hostages. Hours of negotiations dragged on. Culliford and the rest, tired of the wait, started to burn houses to speed things up.

It was enough, the frightened Spaniards handed over goods, mostly cacao nuts and sweets worth 2,000 pieces of eight.[5] Back onboard the *Blessed William* the victorious pirates weighed anchor unfurled their sails and headed out to sea. But they didn't go for Africa or the Indian Ocean. They needed a place where they could sell their loot and feel free to do so. That place was New York.

In 1664 New York became an English colony when an English expedition captured the colony then run by the Dutch West India Company and was brought under the direct control of the Duke of York, who would later become King James II. A governor was set up by the Duke to run the settlement and rule with a hand-picked council. But there was no Assembly so the government of New York resembled that of a court dominated by the local merchant community. The council needed the support from the merchants in order to maintain the expensive garrison and with their support the city was able to acquire new territories, mostly local metropolitan areas such as Long Island and Albany. Over time, the colony became more and more English, and the key institutions became English rather than Dutch. Tension mounted between the English administration and the Dutch majority and was made worse in 1685 when the French started aggressive actions on the northern frontier of the city.

When Protestant William became King and Catholic James II fled to France a section of the people of New York rose up against their own government. These insurgents were mostly disenfranchised Dutch who felt as if they had been trampled underfoot by the arrogant English government. The captain of the militia and a leading merchant, Jacob Leisler, emerged as the new leader. He dissolved the council, sending some members to jail, others into exile while the rest retired into the country. As Leisler tried to make himself governor, the ex–council members who had gone into the country began a letter campaign to the authorities in England. They denounced Leisler at every turn. Leisler did himself no favours as he set up an administration which wasn't much better than the one he replaced.

Into this atmosphere came the *Blessed William* sometime in May 1690. They arrived in the harbour in the middle of the insurrection. The arrival of such a powerful ship was a godsend for Leisler. The crew sold their cargo and their slaves, and spent the money refitting the ship. Leisler gave them a commission to attack

French shipping in the St Lawrence River, which they did with great skill capturing six French vessels. In September they returned triumphantly to New York and sold the *Blessed William*. Culliford and Mason transferred their command to one of the French prizes they'd captured in their actions in the St Lawrence River – this they renamed the *Jacob*. The other prizes they'd captured they sold and then sailed the *Jacob* for Rhode Island and then for the Indian Ocean at the end of December 1690.

Kidd arrived in New York sometime in February 1691 missing Culliford and Mason by two months. Once in the city he heard stories about Culliford and the rest of the pirates squandering his £2,000 on whores and drink which must have infuriated him. He also heard that Leisler had welcomed Culliford and the others with open arms and given them commissions to attack French shipping.

Leisler's administration was alienating many of the people who had previously sided with him. The English throne was now firmly in the hands of William and Mary and the English government sided with the old council of New York that Leisler had deposed.

On 25 September 1689 a new governor, Colonel Henry Sloughter, had been appointed. He was given enough military force, under the command of Colonel Richard Ingoldsby, to deal with the Leisler insurgence. However, severe delays and poor navigation meant that Sloughter did not arrive in New York until 18 March 1691,[6] while Ingoldsby had arrived two months earlier. He had immediately demanded Leisler's surrender but the stubborn Leisler refused and fled to Fort James[7] where he locked himself in with many of his followers. Instead of attacking, Ingoldsby placed his troops carefully into position, at the same time opening negotiations with the members of the old council who now came out of hiding.

Tension grew as both sides dug in, each demanding the other's surrender. Some sources play down Kidd's part in restoring the rightful government to the city and say that Kidd just decided on his own to support the incoming government while others suggest that it was a group of wealthy merchants in New York who approached Kidd for help in overthrowing Leisler.

Finally, on 15 March, the tension erupted and, as Ingoldsby's men circled the fort, Leisler's men fired from the blockhouse, killing one old soldier and wounding several others, while each side claimed to be representing the English government and taunted the other like playground bullies.

The most powerfully armed vessel in the harbour at that time was Kidd's *Antigua* and he made the most of it. The rich merchants – the government that Leisler had overthrown – wanted him to bombard the blockhouse with his cannon. He moved his ship into position, his cannon trained on the blockhouse. Poor weather, however, prevented him from firing but the presence of this well-armed ship sitting in the harbour, its guns ready to fire, was a clear danger to Leisler.

Three times Sloughter demanded that Leisler surrender and three times Leisler sent messengers with his reply. The new governor ordered each messenger to be arrested. He'd had enough. He ordered Kidd to sail around the tip of Manhattan Island and position himself so his cannon could bombard the back of the fort. As Kidd hove into view behind him Leisler realized he had no choice but to surrender.

Now Sloughter could get on with governing the colony. The first thing he did was to set up a trial that saw Leisler and his son-in-law and second in command Jacob Milborne hanged and beheaded. Their supporters were either jailed or exiled. Leisler's influence was finished. A new provincial assembly was set up and on the governor's orders they paid Kidd £150 reward for his help in dealing with the uprising.

Kidd profited a second time from the new administration. The six French prizes that Culliford and crew had captured had been made legal (condemned) under Leisler's Admiralty Court and sold to his supporters. Sloughter set up a new Admiralty Court to investigate the activities of the privateers that Leisler had commissioned. 'Kidd presented a libel against the *Pierre*,' Robert Ritchie states in his book, 'One of the captured French ships, stating that Leisler's administration had no authority to appoint an Admiralty Court and that this French vessel had to be properly condemned as a prize before it could be sold.'[8]

Kidd won his case and the ship was sold to a wealthy merchant for £500, of which Kidd received £250.[9] At last he was able to profit from his old crew and though it didn't repay the £2,000 he'd lost it probably helped in some way to satisfy his thirst for revenge for he decided to stay in New York.

War in Europe affected the colonies as well. In 1686 New York felt the effects of war when the French attacked in the north. Another French attack in 1690 saw Schenectady destroyed. The only defences the English had in North America were in New York and Albany but because it was undermanned they could not guard the north and the colony as well. To fight the French they had to recruit locally which meant raising taxes that many New Yorkers resented. This resulted in many leaving and others such as migrant workers not wanting to come into the colony.

At the same time, England's economy was spiralling down into depression as the French had declared a war on trade. Their settlements in Lower Canada along the St Lawrence and in the eastern part of the region meant they were well placed to attack the English and Dutch ships plying the North Atlantic. French privateers that did most of the interdicting were so effective that the English government had to borrow in order to stay afloat.

The North Atlantic trade routes were lifelines for the colonies like New York so when the English economy slumped so did New York's. At the time, New York had two growth areas in its economy, the first of which was the reliance on pirates coming into the city to refit and resupply. The merchants bought their ill-gotten loot with no questions asked and sold them their provisions. The second growth area was Madagascar. Most of the pirates coming into New York used Madagascar as a base. Most of the merchants in the city knew Madagascar because they went there to buy slaves so it made sense for them to supply the pirates there with guns, liquor, gunpowder, clothing and anything else they had to sell. In exchange the merchants could get textiles, drugs, spices, jewels, and gold from the pirates who would have obtained them from pillaging and looting. Although Madagascar was far away, it benefited from the lack of competition and was far from the scrutiny of official eyes.

Though the voyages were long and the risks were great it was still profitable and, in this way, when the rest of the economy was suffering those merchants who had the ability to get involved with this illegal trade did so. Governor Sloughter who had dealt with Leisler died within a year of his arrival and the man who took over, Benjamin Fletcher, set up a council full of merchants who traded with the pirates. According to Ritchie, Fletcher was a morally bankrupt man whose love of money ensured that illegal trade flourished under his administration.

While all of this was taking place, Kidd became respectable. He married Sarah Bradley Cox Oort and they settled down to married bliss in a fine house on Pearl Street.

From his association with Codrington Kidd had learned about the benefits of patronage. While he busied himself in New York as a respectable man and looked after his wife and child he made it his mission to cultivate friendships and acquaintances with local politicians and influential men. Two of these were Robert Livingston and James Graham. Graham was the provincial attorney general and Livingston was an influential and rising star of the merchant world in New York. The two men met when Livingston bought the Kidds' property on Dock Street. Both Graham and Livingston were fellow Scots and all three struck up a friendship.

It must be remembered that most of the wealth that Kidd had came from his marriage to Sarah, as Robert Ritchie writes in his book, 'the new Mrs Kidd bought a sizeable estate to the marriage', most of which had been left to her by her first husband, William Cox, a very wealthy flour merchant who married her when she was 15. The couple had no children but Cox had several properties – a house in Pearl Street, one in Wall Street, more than 38 acres of land on Saw Mill Creek or what is now 73rd–74th Streets and the East River. Not only Sarah benefited from this but also her brother Samuel, her younger brother Henry Bradley and even her father.[10]

However, Cox's money was tied up under the administrative bureaucracy created by Leisler's administration. While he was in power the Cox family were allowed to live in and keep their various properties but when old man Cox died, the rest of the family had to fight with the Leisler government to get access to the money. Sarah married John Oort and when he died suddenly Sarah was only 21. Then on the scene came Captain Kidd, a larger than life war hero who had helped to bring Leisler down. Leisler's downfall was celebrated all over town and it was at one of these celebrations that Kidd met Sarah.

They were married on the day of Leisler's execution. What made Kidd attractive to Sarah was that he was accepted into society. He owned his own ship, the *Antigua*; he'd received £150 for his efforts during the uprising and made money from the sale of one of the French prizes Culliford had taken so by all accounts he was a good catch.

Indeed, five days after they were married Governor Sloughter hired Kidd to protect the waters around Long Island, for a French privateer had attacked a settlement at the island's tip. In the company of the frigate *Horne* commanded by Captain Walkington he managed to drive away the French privateer and when they arrived in Boston the governor there wanted to hire them both to go after French ships that had lately kidnapped some wealthy merchants.

Kidd already had a commission from Sloughter so he didn't need another one. But what he did need was a crew. Leisler for all his faults had been a popular leader with the people and so, according to Zacks, as Kidd had played a big part in his downfall, he had difficulty getting a crew in New York. The Governor of Massachusetts Bay, Governor Bradstreet, situated in Boston, said that Kidd could take forty citizens for his crew provided that he had the consent of parents if he took boys or consent of masters if he took slaves, that he was to cruise for fifteen days and return all the people he'd brought on board to shore. He was to give the list of the crew to the governor who offered him £20.

Kidd's counter-offer was £100, with £30 to be paid up front; for the wounded to be taken off the ship and the county to take care of them; and that he was to keep the prizes they took, with the proceeds from the sales being divided up amongst the crew. He said he would only cruise for ten days and then return to Boston and let any man leave the ship who wanted to. Bradstreet refused and Kidd went on his way.

It's at this juncture that we start to hear false stories about Kidd. This incident 'tarred Kidd in the eyes of many New Englanders. When reports came in a month later that a New York privateer had sacked Great Island off Cape Cod, Captain Kidd was the first name mentioned and repeated across New England.'[11] In fact Kidd had been in Canada when this took place and had captured a French ship, the *Saint Jean* which he brought back to New York in the late summer of 1691. Kidd made a tidy profit on the sale of this prize.

In New York Kidd was a wealthy man, mingling with the high society of the city where he was respected and admired. Had he not been in this position he would not have been able to strike up an association with Livingston, who was involved in the illegal trading that was rife throughout the city. Livingston went one step further than most other merchants who traded with pirates: he traded with the hated French. He sent his own ship, the *Orange*, on a voyage to Hispaniola to trade with the French but according to the ship's captain, Cornelius Jacobs, the *Orange* ran into a storm and was blown into a French port miles away from his destination. The French took the cargo, paying Jacobs only a quarter of what it was worth. When Livingston heard this he immediately claimed for the rest but the customs officer in New York noted that the return cargo Jacobs brought back was worth more than the £500 of the original cargo Livingston claimed the French had taken from him. The customs officer took the case to the grand jury. The charge was trading with the enemy. However, the jury ruled that there was insufficient evidence for a prosecution and the case was thrown out. The foreman of that grand jury was none other than Captain William Kidd. Livingston didn't forget what Kidd had done for him and only a few years later he was able to return the gesture – ultimately bringing Kidd to the gallows.

But in the years preceding 1695 there must have been something slowly building inside Kidd, something he couldn't shake. He had everything a man could want: property, a beautiful wife, a wonderful family, wealth and respectability. Yet all of this he would risk on a possibility, on a venture that would destroy him.

On the streets of New York the pirates walked freely and as Kidd went about his business he must have seen these rough men and possibly seen something of himself in them. Indeed, some of his old shipmates, Samuel Burgess and John Browne, were there.[12] They had served under Kidd's command onboard the *Blessed William* and had joined with Culliford in leaving Kidd stranded. Whether Kidd ever met these men again is unclear but the point is that everywhere he looked the old life of adventure and freedom beckoned him.

The hankering for adventure must have finally caught up with him for in 1695 he received a cargo bound for London. He left his family in New York and sailed towards England, towards adventure and the freedom of the open sea.

3

An Idea Blossoms

If I had kept Mr. Secretary Vernon's orders for seizing and securing Kidd and his associates with all their effects with less secrecy, I had never got him to come in, for his countrymen, Mr. Graham and Livingston would have been sure to caution him to shift for himself, and would have been well paid for their pains. (Lord Bellomont to the Lords of Trade and Plantations[1])

Kidd set sail for London and with him he had a letter of introduction from his friend James Graham who was a protégé of the Secretary of War, Sir William Blathwayt. The letter outlined Kidd's experience, his bravery and the service he'd performed on behalf of His Majesty's Government as well as praising his skill. According to Robert Ritchie, Kidd wanted to enter the world of imperial patronage and secure a privateering commission from the King. If he couldn't get a privateering commission he wanted to be the captain of a ship in the Royal Navy. Of course this was an impossibility, as the rise to captain in the Royal Navy was a long and arduous one even for titled aristocrats with money. Kidd had no chance. But a privateering commission might have been another matter all together.

But we will really never know his motivation for leaving New York for England where he would risk everything. Why would a man who had everything want to leave all of that behind to become a privateer? Was it patriotism, the need to make more money for self-esteem or to go back to his old life of sailing the seas?

Kidd arrived at the mouth of the Thames and sailed the *Antigua* down the twenty-five-mile stretch of the river into London. He was arriving in a city filled with ships and people from every corner of the world. The noise was incredible, with peddlers shouting their wares, boys banging drums outside alehouses, horses and carts running over rutted and cobbled streets. Both sides of the river were crowded with ships tied up at docks unloading goods from all over the world. The city was divided, with a large part of the population just scraping by on a pittance while the wealthy merchant class and aristocrats enjoyed all the pleasures the city had to offer for those with money and title. This was especially true when Parliament was in session as it attracted all the wealthiest people from all over the country to the capital.

As Kidd arrived he found himself in a long line of ships waiting to dock. Ahead of him were the masts of hundreds of ships. Realizing that it would be hours if not days before he could unload his cargo of bales of cloth he left the task of docking and unloading to one of his crew and went ashore with his young brother-in-law, Samuel Bradley. The two men lodged with a distant cousin of the Bradleys, Mrs Sarah Hawkins, in the maritime community of Wapping.

Once settled in, Kidd's first task was to find Secretary Blathwayt and give him the introductory letter from Graham. However, when he arrived he discovered the Secretary was in Amsterdam with King William. Even worse was the crowd in the Secretary's waiting room all hoping for an audience with the important man. Kidd's prospects of even getting to Blathwayt were slim. He, like everyone else, would have to wait.

In the close heat of August Kidd waited. If he was to realize any part of his ambition he was going to need help. That help came from Robert Livingston who had arrived in London on 25 July 1695 after a long, horrendous voyage across the Atlantic.[2]

Livingston and his son John had set sail in the *Charity* under the command of Captain Lancaster Syms in December 1694. Only a day out of New York a savage storm ripped into them. High winds and lashing rain tore at the ship for three long weeks, shredding the sails. Frantically the crew tried to repair the damage and during a period of calm most of the sails had been repaired, but on 3 January 1695 the worst storm hit. It was so vicious it ripped the rudder right away and tore a hole in the bow. Crew and passengers filled the gap with anything they could lay their hands on but the sea simply tore away whatever they put in place, forcing the crew to man the ship's two pumps twenty-four hours a day.

As it drifted rudderless, the roaring wind ripped through the ship's rigging. The topmast cracked, splintered and fell to the deck, leaving the *Charity* utterly without power, no sail, no rudder, and for days, weeks, the ship drifted further south away from the shipping lanes, away from rescue. Food was running low too and after fourteen weeks fresh water was even scarcer. Finally, land was sighted and they landed in Portugal. From there the journey to London was uneventful.[3]

Livingston had come to London to restore his fortune. He claimed the government owed him £4,000 from the money he'd spent on providing supplies to troops fighting the French in Albany and northern New York. The Lords of Trade and Plantations could, with their decision on his claim, make or break him. It was on Livingston's journey from Falmouth to London that he met William Carter who promised to introduce him to Lord Bellomont, the newly appointed governor of New England and a man who would be instrumental in the downfall of Captain Kidd.

England was allied to the Dutch as King William's War or the Nine Years War was still raging at this time. In Parliament there were two factions: the Whigs and the Tories. The Whigs believed in a controlled executive and a vigorous Parliament while the Tories believed in a strong monarchy, controlled of course by the Tories.

At the beginning of the war the King was content to allow the two parties to run the war themselves and didn't ally himself with one faction or the other. But as the war progressed and was going badly for England the King realized he would need money to continue. As the costs rose, the Tories gradually stopped supporting the monarchy's policies. They believed the English Army should be recalled from Europe and made ready to fight in England behind a much stronger Royal Navy. The Whigs wanted the troops fighting in the Low Countries to be fully supported as they were fighting for England far better there than they would in the fields of the southeast.[4]

The King allied himself with the Whigs who managed to raise an astonishing one million pound loan, the first ever, in order to pay for the war and they followed this a year later with another million pound loan plus a charter for the Bank of England. With this money pouring in, the tide of the war began to change away from the French in favour of the Allies. In 1694 King William showered the Whigs with a string of offices and titles for their support and help in the conduct of the war. The Whigs revelled in their new rewards and rapidly replaced as many Tory officeholders as they could. Many Whigs were nominated for Parliament and their support for the war brought them to power in 1693. Anyone now looking for patronage had to go to the Whigs.[5]

Another significant fact that Ritchie states in his book is that Livingston hated the Whigs but he was enough of an astute businessman to understand that the Whigs were the only game in town so he changed his plans. 'If he had to be a friend of the Whigs to get his money, he would be a friend of the Whigs.' So Livingston took up Carter's offer to be introduced to Richard Coote, Lord Bellomont, who was a zealous Whig.

On 14 June 1695 King William had agreed to the nomination of Lord Bellomont as governor of the Massachusetts Bay colony. But Bellomont's fortunes were very low and the salary for this position would not be enough to regain his wealth so he pressed for help from his great friend Lord Shrewsbury. Bellomont had been one of the early supporters who went to Holland to enter the service of then Prince William and Princess Mary in 1687. William gave Bellomont, who was an Irish peer, command of a regiment of English troops and later made him a steward of the household of Princess Mary.

When William was brought over from Holland to be King of England Bellomont came to the attention of the Whig leadership and was given a seat in the House of Commons. However, as the Whigs gained more and more power and attacked the Tories in the House, Bellomont joined in but made the mistake of attacking Lord Coningsby about his financial dealings in Ireland. This could be because Bellomont had his Irish holdings taken away from him because of his support for William but Coningsby was a favourite of the King and so Bellomont suddenly found himself out of Mary's household and out of royal favour. So he needed help and Shrewsbury came to his aide.[6]

By the time Livingston met with Bellomont the Lord was still waiting to hear if he was to become governor of New York in addition to his nomination as governor of Massachusetts Bay. Their first meeting took place on 10 August 1695 'at the lord's Dover Street mansion'.[7] The following day, a Sunday, Livingston met with Kidd, a New York City merchant Phillip French, another New Yorker Captain Giles Shelley commanding the *Nassau* out of New York along with William Carter who had been the man instrumental in bringing Livingston and Bellomont together. They all met in the park suburb of Chelsea, drinking, talking, walking and dining away the hot August afternoon.

In the meeting Bellomont had told Livingston that 'the King had a passion to wipe out the pirates operating out of the American colonies', Richard Zacks states in his book, *Pirate Hunter*. On the walk the following day the talk must have covered various topics including pirates. Indeed, Zacks suggests that Kidd boasted about his knowledge of pirates of their secret harbours which he had either heard of or picked up first hand. According to Zacks Livingston went back to Bellomont with an idea for 'fitting out Captain Kidd in a Royal Navy ship to attack pirates'. He praised Kidd's skill, reputation and experiences to Bellomont who was interested.[8]

Bellomont had the ear of the King despite his gaffe over Lord Conningsby. He was an influential and important man. Livingston's credentials were that he could trace his ancestry as far back as 1124 to the earls of Linlithgow in Scotland. Without this Bellomont wouldn't even have seen him and Kidd had no chance of getting into see Bellomont without Livingston's help.

Although we have one source saying that it was Livingston who hatched the plan to fit out Kidd in a ship to attack pirates, other historians say the origins of this idea are muddied and unclear. When the whole thing went wrong everyone blamed everyone else. Indeed, Ritchie states that Kidd claimed that Livingston told Bellomont about the pirates in New York and that it was Livingston and Bellomont who approached Kidd to take command of a vessel to attack pirates. Kidd apparently refused but Bellomont threatened to take away his ship *Antigua* so Kidd relented. However, Bellomont's version puts the blame entirely onto Kidd who convinced Livingston that his (Kidd's) plan to attack pirates in a specially built vessel and steal their loot and sell it would work.[9]

Whoever came up with the idea it was Livingston who took that plan to Bellomont and the Lord duly mentioned it to the King through his secretary who ignored it. Livingston went back to Kidd and they revised the plan, agreeing to put up one-fifth of the costs. Bellomont took this revised scheme to the King who approved it and agreed that private individuals could have full possession of the goods they recovered. The King refused however to put up any government money for the scheme so Bellomont began looking for other backers.

One other unlikely version of the events is that the East India Company proposed the plan to the government and that the King agreed to use up to £3,000 of his own money. Kidd was put up to lead the expedition because of his knowledge of pirates.

What is clear is that the three main players, Kidd, Livingston and Bellomont, put the plan together. Indeed, Livingston wrote in his journal that he had spent a great deal of time in October working on the plan. Once the plan was finalized it was down to Bellomont to approach the necessary backers as only he had the influence.

Who were these men? They were extremely powerful influential Whig Lords: Lord Somers, Admiral Russell, the Earl of Romney and Charles Talbot. Lord John Somers was educated at Trinity College in Oxford and entered the legal profession rising to Solicitor-General and was also a trusted adviser to the King. He then became Attorney-General, a speaker of the House of Lords, was knighted, and became a member of the Privy Council – formally known as His Majesty's Most Honourable Privy Council – which directly advised the Monarch on matters of state, often bypassing Parliament. He became Lord Justice and then Lord Chancellor. After funding Kidd, Somers was to become President of the Royal Society, which had been formed in 1660 and where the name John Somers joined a distinguished list of other notable and famous names, including Sir Christopher Wren, Samuel Pepys and Sir Isaac Newton. In 1695 he worked with Sir Isaac Newton on the problem of coin clipping when Newton was Master of the Mint. He was also the Lord Keeper of the Great Seal that was begun and used by Edward the Confessor and subsequently used by each monarch as an alternative to signing documents. It carried an image of the monarch and, in the case of William III, the words 'William III, by the Grace of God of Great Britain, France and Ireland, King, Defender of the Faith'.[10]

Admiral Edward Russell was the younger son of the Duke of Bedford; he provided Bellomont with a share of the financial backing he needed. The Admiral had risen rapidly through the ranks but left the Royal Navy when he began to work on helping Prince William gain the crown. He even accompanied the new Dutch King on his triumphant march through England in 1688. Once William was in power, the Admiral was rewarded with the position of treasurer of the Navy, then Admiral of the Blue Squadron and, when Kidd was in London, Russell was First Lord of the Admiralty. More often than not this post was held by a monarch or peers and it was a post that Russell was to hold twice more during his lifetime.[11]

The Earl of Romney, Henry Sidney, was another of the secret four backers behind Bellomont. A soldier and a politician, he was the first to hold the title of Earl of Romney and most sources claim he had a talent for intrigue in the bedrooms of some of the nation's most aristocratic women! When William was in Amsterdam, Sidney personally delivered several secret documents to him and was rewarded with 50,000 acres of confiscated estates in Ireland worth £17,000 per year. Sidney never married but is said to have fathered many children.

Charles Talbot, the twelfth Earl of Shrewsbury and first Duke of Shrewsbury, was the fourth of the backers. He was one of seven noblemen who in June 1688 signed a letter inviting William of Orange to England. In August of that year he travelled to Holland along with Edward Russell and mortgaged his estate to raise £12,000, which he placed in a Dutch bank for the prince's use. This financial assistance to William certainly helped to oil the rise to power of both himself and his new monarch. Talbot was the godson of Charles II and he, along with John Somers, had become one of the Lord Justices who ruled the kingdom while the King was away in the Netherlands for a brief period. He was also Secretary of State for the Southern Department, responsible for all affairs of state throughout Southern England, Wales, Ireland and the American Colonies.[12]

Most histories of Kidd mention these highly influential men but there was one more: Sir Edmund Harrison, one of the wealthiest merchants in London.[13] 'Edmund Harrison, a prosperous City merchant, was a director of the New East India Company, and as such, would of course have a personal interest in the suppression of piracy in Eastern waters. Harrison was undoubtedly a shrewd man, supervising the selection of the crew by Kidd, and rejecting all Scotsmen and colonists on the grounds that their sympathies would probably be with smugglers and pirates.'[14]

Some accounts have omitted him completely. Evidence of the importance to the mission of this extra person is provided in the actual wording of the sailing orders that Bellomont would eventually issue to Kidd, stating that he was to provide updates of the mission to Edmund Harrison.[15]

The first agreement was signed on 10 October 1695 by the three main partners, Kidd, Livingston and Bellomont. Essentially it stated that Kidd was to capture pirates who had left the colonies and headed for areas such as the Red Sea. Bellomont was to get the commission from the King through the Lords of the Admiralty as well as secure a grant from the government that everyone was free to keep their prizes without being sued. Bellomont also agreed to raise four-fifths of the cost which was to be divided into five parts. All three men agreed that by 6 November 1695 they would raise a total of £2,000. Kidd was to raise a crew of more than 100 men and pay them only on the value of what they'd captured, which meant no salary. If they didn't capture a ship they would get nothing. Any prizes that Kidd took were to be brought intact to Boston where Bellomont, who would be in office by that time, was to have the cargo and ships declared as prizes in the local courts, enabling him to distribute the profits to the backers and bypass the English courts altogether.

Let's take a look now at this first agreement. It reads as follows:

Articles of Agreement Made This 10th Day of October in the Year of Our Lord 1695 between The Right Honourable Earl of Bellomont on the One Part and Robert Livingston Esq. and Capt William Kidd on the Other Part.
Whereas the said Capt William Kidd is desirous of obtaining a

commission as Captain of a Private Man of War in order to take prizes from the King's enemies, and other ways to annoy them, and whereas certain persons did sometimes since depart from New England, Rhode Island, New York, and other parts in America and elsewhere with an intention to become Pyrates, and to commit spoils and depredations, against the laws of the nations, in the Red Sea or elsewhere and to return with such goods and riches as they should get to certain places by them agreed upon; and in desirous to fight with and subdue the said Pyrates, as also all other Pyrates with whom the said Capt Kidd shall meet at sea in case he be empowered so to do. And whereas it is agreed between the said parties that for the purpose of the aforesaid a good and sufficient Ship to the liking of the said Capt Kidd shall be forthwith bought, whereof the said Capt Kidd is to have the command. Now these present do witness and it is agreed between the said parties;

That the Earl of Bellomont doth covenant and agree at his proper charge to procure from the King's Majesty or from the Lords Commissioners of the Admiralty as the case shall require, one or more commissions, empowering the said Capt Kidd to act against the King's enemies, and to take prizes from them, as a private man of war in the usual manner; and also to fight with, conquer, and subdue pyrates and to take them and their goods, with other large and beneficial powers and clauses in such commissions as may be most proper and effectual in such cases.

The said Earl of Bellomont doth covenant and agree, That within three months after the said Capt Kidd's departure from England, for the purposes in these presents mentioned, he will procure at his proper charge a Grant from the King, to be made to some indifferent and trust person, of all such merchandises goods, treasure and other Pyrates whatsoever, by the said Capt Kidd or by the said ship or any other ship or ships under his command.

The said Earl doth agree to pay four fifths parts, the whole in five parts to be divided, of all moneys which shall be laid out for the buying such good and sufficient ship for the purposes aforesaid, together with rigging and other apparel and Furniture thereof, and providing the same with competent victualling, the said ship to be approved by the said parties; and the said other one fifth part of the charges of the said ship to be paid for by said Robert Livingston and William Kidd.

The said Earl doth agree, That in order to the speedy buying the said ship, in part of the said four parts of five of the said charges, he will pay down the sum of sixteen hundred pounds by way of advance on or before the sixth day of November next ensuing.

The said Robert Livingston and William Kidd do jointly and severally covenant and agree that on or before the sixth day of November when the Earl of Bellomont is to pay the said sum of sixteen hundred pounds as aforesaid, they will advance and pay down four hundred pounds in part of the share and proportion which they are to have in the said ship.

The said Earl doth agree to pay such further sums of money as shall complete and make up the said four parts of five of the charges of the said ship's apparel, furniture, and victualling, unto the said Robert Livingston and William Kidd within seven weeks after the date of these Presents; and in like manner the said Robert Livingston and Capt Kidd do agree to pay such further sums as shall amount to a fifth part of the whole charge of the said ship within seven weeks after the date of these Presents.

The said Capt Kidd doth covenant and agree to procure and take with him onboard of the said ship one hundred mariners or seamen, or thereabouts, to make what reasonable and convenient speed he can to set out to sea with the said ship, and to sail to such parts or places where he may meet with the said Pyrates, and to use his utmost endeavours to meet with subdue and conquer the said Pyrates or any other Pyrates, and to take what prizes he can from the King's enemies, and forthwith to make the best of his way to Boston in New England, and that without touching at any other port or harbour whatsoever, or without breaking bulk or diminishing any part of what he shall so take or obtain, on any pretext whatsoever, of which he shall make Oath, in case the same be desired by the said Earl of Bellomont, and there to deliver the same into the hands and possession of the said Earl.

The said Capt Kidd doth agree that the contract and bargain which he will make with his said Ship's Crew shall be No Purchase No Pay, and not otherwise; and that the share and proportion which his said Ship's Crew shall by such contract have of such Prizes, goods, merchandises, and Treasures as he shall take as prize or from Pyrates, shall not at the most exceed a fourth part of the same, and shall be less than a fourth in case the same may reasonably and conveniently be agreed upon.

The said Robert Livingston and Capt Kidd do jointly and severally agree with the said Earl of Bellomont, that in case the said Capt Kidd do not meet with the said Pyrates, which went from New England, Rhode island, New York and elsewhere as aforesaid, or do not take from any other Pyrates or from the King's enemies, such goods merchandises or other things of value as, being divided as hereinafter is mentioned, shall full recompense the said Earl for the moneys by him expended in buying the said four fifth parts of the said ship and premises, that they then shall refund and pay to the said Earl of Bellomont the whole money by him to be advanced in Sterling money or money equivalent thereunto, on or before the five and twentieth day of March which shall be in the year of our Lord

1697. (The Danger of the Seas, and of the King's enemies, and Mortality of the said Capt Kidd always accepted.) Upon payment whereof the said Robert Livingston and William Kidd are to have the sole Property in the said ship and furniture and this Indenture to be delivered up to them, with all other covenants and obligations thereunto belonging.

It is agreed between the said parties that as well as the goods, merchandise, treasure and other things which shall be taken from the said Pyrates, or any Pirates, by the said William Kidd, as also such prizes as shall be by him taken from any of the King's enemies, shall be divided in manner following, that is to say, such part as shall be for that purpose agreed upon by the said Capt Kidd (so far as the same do not in the whole exceed a fourth part) shall be paid or delivered to the Ship's Crew for their use, and the other three parts to be divided into five equal parts, whereof the said earl is to have his own use four full parts and the other fifth is to be equally divided between the said Robert Livingston and William Kidd and is to be delivered them by the said Earl of Bellomont without Deduction or Abatement on any pretence whatsoever; But it is always to be understood that such Prizes as shall be taken from the King's Enemies are to be lawfully adjudged Prize in the usual manner before any Division or otherwise intermeddling therewith than according to the intent of the said commission to be granted in that behalf.

Lastly it is covenanted and agreed between the said Parties to these presents, that in case the said Capt Kidd do bring to Boston aforesaid, and there deliver to the Earl of Bellomont, goods, merchandises, Treasure or prizes to the value of one hundred thousand pounds or upwards, which he shall have taken from the said Pyrates, or from other Pyrates, or from the King's Enemies, that then the ship, which is now speedily to be bought by the said parties, shall be and remain to the sole use and behalf of him the said Capt William Kidd, as a Reward and Gratification for his Good Service therein.

Memorandum

Before the Sealing and Delivery of these Presents it was covenanted and agreed by the said Earl of Bellomont with the said Robert Livingston and Capt Kidd that the Person to who the Grant above-mentioned in these Articles shall be made by his Majesty shall within eight days at the most after such grant has been passed by the Great Seal of England, assign and transfer to each of them the said Robert Livingston Esq. and Capt William Kidd respectively, their Heirs and Assigns, one full tenth part (the Ship's Crew's share proportion being first deducted) of all such goods, Treasure or other things as shall be taken by the said Capt Kidd by virtue of such commissions as aforesaid; and the said Grantee shall make such assignment as aforesaid in such manner as by the said Robert Livingston Esq. and Capt William Kidd or their Council Learned in the Law shall be reasonably advised and required.

Obviously, there were no guarantees that Kidd would even sight a pirate ship let alone capture one. If he didn't he would have to pay back the costs of buying the ship in the first place and pay back Bellomont's costs as well. In addition to this, there was the risk of mutiny from the crew as if no ship was captured they wouldn't get paid. Kidd had already lost one ship to a crew who had risked their lives for nothing – was he setting himself up now for a repeat performance?

However, the articles of this agreement state that a ship was to be bought to Kidd's liking and that if he brought in more than £100,000 in treasure then the ship would be his completely. 'The investors knew that if Kidd captured just two rich pirate ships, they were looking at a tenfold return on their investment.'[16] This was a real gamble for Kidd and to make matters worse 'as security for the due performance of his obligations he was required to enter into a bond of twenty thousand pounds and Colonel Livingston was required to enter into another bond of ten thousand pounds as guarantor of Kidd's integrity'.[17]

This was a staggering amount of money for the latter part of the seventeenth century. Even today raising that kind of money is difficult for most people and would have been difficult for Kidd. If the venture failed where would Kidd get this money from? The stakes were very high indeed. The investors wanted a way to be able to claim the pirate goods captured by Kidd and divide it up before the crew were paid and, if that is clear as it seems, that means that unrest with the crew was an almost certainty.

What is so relevant about this agreement is that it forms the basis of Kidd's eventual downfall. This agreement shows two things: Kidd's supreme confidence in himself and his arrogance that, no matter what, he could get this done. At no point in his past had he taken such a massive gamble. Certainly in dealing with Leisler he'd chosen the right side, which was a risk, but then the stakes weren't as high and it was fairly obvious Leisler wouldn't win while he was holed up in a fort. Kidd had already had the experience of a mutinous crew when they took away the *Blessed William* from him because he would not turn pirate and, at that time, the crew who had helped to rescue Thornhill hadn't received much in the way of reward for risking their lives.

After the agreement was signed Bellomont realized he could not pay his share and he borrowed from Sir Edmund Harrison who also paid Orford and Shrewsbury's shares. As we have seen, Harrison took an active interest in the expedition not least because he was one of the directors of the East India Company according to Ritchie.

The next part of the agreement was to get a commission from the Admiralty which was granted on 11 December 1695 as a privateering commission to attack enemy shipping and capture any loot from enemy merchant ships. The Admiralty were reluctant to grant a commission for hunting down pirates so the partners obtained a patent under the same office that gave the Lords of the Admiralty their powers – the office of the Great Seal.[18]

Here is the full text of the Royal Commission, issued under the Great Seal of the Crown of England, officially making Captain Kidd a privateer:[19]

William The Third, by the Grace of God, King of England, Scotland, France and Ireland, Defender of the Faith.

To our Trusty and well-beloved Captain William Kidd, Commander of the Ship Adventure Galley, or to the Commander of the said Ship for the time being; Greeting. Whereas we are informed, That Captain Thomas Too, John Ireland, Captain Thomas Wake, Captain William Maze or Mace, And other of our Subjects, Natives or Inhabitants of New England, New York, and elsewhere in our plantations in America, have associated themselves with divers other wicked and ill-disposed persons; and do against the Laws of Nations, daily commit many great Piracies, Robberies, and Depredations, upon the Seas in the Parts of America and in other Parts, to the great Hindrance and Discouragement of Trade and Navigation, and to the Danger and Hurt of our loving Subjects, our Allies, and all others, navigating the Seas, upon their lawful Occasions; Now know ye, That we, being desirous to prevent the aforesaid Mischiefs, and, as far as in us lies, to bring the said Pyrates, Free-booters, and Sea Rovers, to Justice, have thought fit, and do hereby give and grant unto you, the said William Kidd to whom our Commissioners for executing the Office of our Lord High Admiral have granted a Commission as a private Man of War, bearing date the Eleventh Day of December, 1695; and unto the Officers, Mariners and others, which shall be under your Command, full power and Authority to apprehend seize and take into your custody as well the said Captain Too, John Ireland, Captain Thomas Wake, William Maze alias Mace, as such Pyrates, Free-booters, and Sea Rovers, being either our own Subjects or of other Nations associated with them, which you shall meet upon the said Coasts or Seas of America, or in any other Seas or Parts, with their Ships and Vessels; And also such Merchandizes, Money, Goods, and Wares, as shall be found on board, or with them, in case they shall willingly yield themselves, but if they will not submit without fighting, then you are by Force to compel them to yield: And we do also require you to bring, or cause to be brought, such Pyrates, Free-booters and Sea Rovers, as you shall seize, to a legal Tryal, to the end they may be proceeded against according to the law in such cases: And we do hereby charge and command all our Offices, Ministers, and other our loving Subjects whatsoever, to be aiding and assisting to you in the Premises; And we do hereby enjoin you to keep an exact journal of your proceedings in the execution of the Premises; and therein to set down the Names of such Pyrates, and of their Officers and Company, and the Names of such Ships and Vessels, as you shall, by virtue of these Presents, seize and take; and the Quantities of Arms, Ammunition, Provision, and Loading of such Ships, and the true value of the same, as near as you can judge: And we do hereby jointly charge and Command you, as you will answer the same at your utmost Peril, That you do not, in any manner, offend or molest any of our Friends and Allies, their Ships or Subjects, by Colour or Pretence of these Presents, or the Authority hereby granted. In witness thereof, we have caused our Great Seal of England to be affixed to the Presents. Given at our Court at Kensington, the 26th Day of January, 1696, in the Seventh Year of Our Reign.

This agreement made Kidd a legal privateer enabling him to hunt down Thomas Tew, John Ireland, Thomas Wade, William Mayes and other New England and New York pirates operating on the Atlantic coast of America and any that had gone into the Red Sea to disrupt the shipping lanes there as well. On 26 January 1696 the patent was issued by the Lord Keeper of the Great Seal, none other than Lord John Somers, a partner in Kidd's expedition to capture pirates.

To sum up, the agreement states that a ship was to be bought to Kidd's specifications; he, Livingston and Bellomont were to raise £2,000 up front for victualling and supply costs; more money was to be raised by Bellomont. Bellomont was to raise four-fifths of the cost of buying a ship to meet the requirements of the expedition while Kidd and Livingston were to put up the remaining fifth of all the costs. Kidd was required to post a performance bond of £20,000 while Livingston was required to post a bond as guarantor to Kidd's performance of £10,000. With this agreement, if things went wrong then Kidd would have to pay the performance bond and the costs of buying the ship, which would mean he would be penniless and most likely end up in debtor's prison along with his family, while Livingston would be financially crippled.

For these three men to sign this deal the prize must have been huge indeed. Livingston was gambling everything and when events turned sour for him he would do his best to wriggle out of the contract.[20] Bellomont later wrote to the Lords of Trade and Plantations that 'Livingston demanded up his bond and the articles which he sealed to me upon Kidd's expedition, and told me that Kidd swore all the oaths in the world that unless I did immediately indemnify Mr. Livingston by giving up his securities he would never bring in that great ship and cargo, but that he would take care to satisfy Mr Livingston himself out of that cargo.'[21]

The Admiralty Warrant differs from the Royal Commission, in as much as it details the nature of the ships that Kidd was allowed to attack. While the Royal

Commission concentrates on piracy, the Admiralty Warrant delves deeper into the validity of attacking ships of the King's enemies, principally France:

> Whereas by Commission under the Great Seal of England bearing Date the 26th Day of June 1689, or any Three or more of us, are required and authorised to grant Commissions unto such Persons as we deem fitly qualified in that Vessels and Goods belonging to the French King and His Subjects and Inhabitants within the Dominions of the said French King; and such other Ships, Vessels and goods as are or shall be liable for confiscation; with other Powers in the said Commission expressed. These are therefore to will and require you forthwith to cause a Commission or Letter of Marque or Reprisal to be issued out of the High Court of Admiralty of England unto Captain William Kidd, Commander of the Adventure Galley, Burden 287 Tons, 34 Guns and 70 men, to set forth in warlike Manner the said ship called the Adventure Galley, whereof the said Captain William Kidd is Commander, and to apprehend seize and take the Ships, Vessels and Goods belonging to the French King or his Subjects or inhabitants, within the Dominions of the said French King; and such other Ships, Vessels and Goods as are or shall be liable for confiscation; according to the said Commission granted unto us for that Purpose, and certain Articles and Instructions under her late Majesty's Signet and Sign Manual dated the 2nd of May 1693, a Copy whereof remains with you; and according to the Course of the Court of Admiralty and Laws of Nation; And you are therein to insert a Clause, enjoining the said Captain William Kidd to keep an extract journal of his Proceedings; and therein particularly to take notice of all Prizes which shall be taken by him, the Nature of such Prizes, the Time and Place of their being taken, and the Value of them, as near as he can judge; as also the Station, Motion, and Strength of the Enemy, as well as he can discover by the best Intelligence he can get; Of which he is, from time to time, as he shall have an Opportunity, to transmit an Account for us to our Secretary, and to keep a Correspondence with him by all Opportunities that shall present; Provided always, That, before you issue such Commission, Security be given thereupon, according as directed in her late Majesty's Instructions afore-mentioned; as also, That a Recognisance, or sufficient security, not exceeding 500 l. be entered into, obliging him not to carry in the said Ship more than one half of her Complement of Seamen but that all the rest of her Company be Landsmen; and that he do, at the end of the Voyage, give in to the Secretary of the Admiralty a perfect List, in Columns, of his Ship's Company, expressing their Names, Qualities, Age, Place of Abode, and whether married or single Men; and also, That he do give security strictly to conform himself to the Regulations contained in their Majesties'

Proclamation of the 12th of July, 1694, concerning Colours to be worn onboard Ships. This to continue in force till further Order; for which this shall be your Warrant.

Given under our Hands and the Seal of the Office of Admiralty, this Tenth Day of December, 1695.

Kidd was now tied into these three documents. He had until 25 March 1697 to sail into Boston with any captured pirate or French ships, along with the loot from those ships and any he had taken elsewhere. If he didn't the consequences were too much to think about. Even in today's world of satellite navigation, radar, sonar, computer-guidance systems and everything else used to find ships at sea, there are no guarantees that Royal Navy ships will find pirates or drug runners. They do using these aids but for every one captured how many get through? So how in the vast expanse of oceans was Kidd to find pirates?

Now with the agreements signed and the backers in place, it was time for everything to move up a notch. Kidd sold his own ship to help pay for the costs of fitting out his new vessel, which was the *Adventure Galley* and it was launched at Castle's Yard, Deptford, around 4 December 1695.[22]

4

A New Ship

This grand idea that was becoming a reality needed a grand ship and the *Adventure Galley* fitted the bill perfectly. Official documents held at the National Archives in Kew state that the new ship was 125 feet long and weighed in at 287 tons,[1] and had an impressive armament of 34 cannon. Only naval ships and the largest of merchant men could boast this kind of firepower. To all intents and purposes, the *Adventure Galley* was a ship of war and any potential victim that dared to fight it would be smashed to pieces. The hope was that most victims would surrender when faced with such firepower.[2]

Not only did she have the firepower but the *Adventure Galley* was a huge vessel with three main masts. A square-rigged vessel where the tops of the main sails ran perpendicular to the masts rather than being tilted at an angle, the size of her sails when fully extended[3] provided her with speed in all but the lowest wind, enabling her to catch fleeing prey or to escape herself from ships more powerful than her. In addition she had the ability to approach vessels stranded in calm seas.

Most ships of the day relied solely on the wind in their sails to keep them moving over the sea but when the wind dropped and the waves died away, these ships were left floundering. The *Adventure Galley* had a feature that would circumvent this problem: twenty-three pairs of oars. 'It may have been modelled after the galley frigates developed as patrol craft by the Royal Navy in the latter half of the seventeenth century', Robert Ritchie wrote. The *Adventure Galley* was perfectly suited for the job of hunting pirates. The oars gave the ship that extra edge in mobility and speed and on one future occasion they would help Kidd escape the clutches of the Royal Navy.[4]

Sources differ on whether the ship was built to Kidd's specifications or whether it was already built and registered when it was bought by Kidd and his partners. Ritchie simply says that the ship the partners settled on was the *Adventure Galley*. Richard Zacks states that the ship was built for the expedition in just five weeks.[5] Historian Peter Earle suggests that 'Kidd fitted out a suitable vessel, the *Adventure Galley*, which had been purchased by the syndicate (Kidd's backers and partners).'[6] Sadly, Zacks does not indicate his source for the information that Kidd had the ship built to his design.

While Kidd was fitting out his new ship and signing on the crew some ominous rumours began to spread through the taverns, coffee houses and the docks. If they were true then Kidd could well be delayed. French privateers had attacked and captured three English East India merchantmen. Alarm was spreading. The threat of invasion was imminent.

During this time 36 barrels of gunpowder, over 100 pistols and muskets, more than 1,000 cannon balls were loaded onboard, along with all the other stores needed for the voyage.

The ship was designed to carry a crew of 150; but historians such as Daniel Defoe wrote that Kidd sailed out of Plymouth with a crew of 80. His privateering commission only allowed him to raise a crew of 100 men, half of whom should be experienced sailors. The reason for this is that the Royal Navy was desperate for experienced men, as were the merchants who demanded their convoys be escorted to protect them from enemy privateers and pirates. 'The navy needed unprecedented numbers of men at the same time that the merchants insisted on the share of able bodied mariners.' There were never enough experienced men to meet the demand and often the Lords of the Admiralty, working with the merchants, assigned experienced mariners to the merchant fleets on a ship–by–ship basis. Commissions for privateering work would take men away from the much needed merchant fleets and the desperate navy so the Admiralty rarely issued such commissions. 'A privateering berth attracted sailors because it held out the promise of quick money and anything was better than the discipline of the Royal Navy.'[7]

As Kidd signed up his crew Bellomont worked to get the money promised by the backers in order for the bills to be paid so Kidd could sail. At the same time the rumours of French invasion increased. Imagine the tension that Kidd must have felt. If the French did come would his beautiful ship be pressed into fighting in the war and if so would he be liable for not living up to the agreements? Could he be excused because of the war? He needed to get out of London and out to sea as soon as possible. To pay the bills and get some quick capital Kidd sold his ship, the *Antigua*, while both he and Livingston sold a third of their 10 per cent shares of the profit.

According to Admiralty papers, reports received on 19 February suggested the French were massing near the ports of Dunkirk and Calais in preparation for their invasion of England. This was terrible news for Kidd. They were still waiting for the Lords to deliver their investment. Remember one of those was Admiral Russell and he was now urgently involved in readying the fleet before England was attacked. It was 20 February when Russell left London. Three days later the Admiralty put an embargo on all merchant ships leaving the city and demanded they give up one-third of their crews to the Royal Navy. Kidd had to get going. For the moment privateers were exempt from this embargo so the faster he set sail the safer he would be.

With the alarm building the Lords finally delivered their investment. Bellomont had no money and borrowed his share from Harrison, who also paid for part of

Shrewsbury's share too.[8] Kidd immediately gathered his crew in preparation for sailing. He'd spent considerable time picking the crew under the watchful eyes of Edmund Harrison. We know from the Calendar of State Papers held in the National Archives at Kew some of the names of Kidd's crew. For example, James Mead was the second-in-command (some sources refer to him as Henry Mead), George Bullen was the master or first mate, Alexander Milbourne was the ship's boatswain (the ship's officer in charge of sails), Walter Dorman was the gunner, John Peake the ship's carpenter, John Oate the ship's cook and Arnont Fielde as the ship's doctor.[9]

However, after all of his efforts in getting together a crew that he could rely on, half of whom were experienced, they would never sail with him. Instead he would end up with some inexperienced rotten apples. One in particular was the man who would end up in the position of chief gunner: William Moore. He would blight the voyage and be one of the main reasons for Kidd's downfall.

The crew entered into a standard contract where, once loot had been captured, its total value declared and the expenses of the voyage deducted, it would then be divided up amongst the participants which included the backers. The King would get 10 per cent, Bellomont would get 60 per cent to be distributed to the rest of the backers, 15 per cent would go to Livingston and the final 15 per cent to the crew.

Daniel Defoe wrote that 'Lord Bellomont and some others, who knew what great Captures had been made by the Pyrates, and what a prodigious Wealth must be in their Possession, were tempted to fit out a Ship at their own private Charge and to give Command of it to Captain Kidd.' Some sources break the distribution of spoils down even further. Kidd would get thirty-five shares of any loot captured, his officers would get more than one share, while experienced sailors would get full shares and those who were not experienced would get half a share.

There were other stipulations. The plunder had to be handed over and kept in one place and if anyone was caught stealing they would lose their share of it. Before the shares could be divided any crew member that was wounded would be compensated.[10] Other measures within the contract ensured that men did their duty when engaging enemy ships. For example, cowardice meant loss of shares as did any crew member being found drunk. At the same time discipline was generally decided by the captain and the majority of the crew. Completely at odds with the discipline within the Royal Navy, where the captains could mete out punishment as they deemed necessary, privateers stuck to this old tradition where the captain consulted with his more experienced crew members over discipline and handling of the ship.

As Kidd prepared to sail we can only speculate on what must have been going through his mind. Did the prospect of sailing on the open sea again fill him with excitement? Did he truly feel that he could capture enough pirate and French vessels to make his backers happy and make himself a rich man? If he had doubts did he push them to the back of his mind or did they remain at the forefront of his thinking, driving him on?

Finally, on 25 February 1696 Kidd received his sailing orders from Bellomont:

Captain William Kidd

You being now ready to sail, I do hereby desire and direct you that you and your Men do serve God in the best Manner you can: That you keep good Order, and good Government in your Ship: That you make the best of your Way to the Place and Station where you are to put the Powers you have in Execution, and, having effected the same, You are, according to Agreement, to sail directly to Boston in New England, there to deliver unto me the whole of what Prizes, Treasure, Merchandizes and other Things, you shall have taken by virtue of the Powers and Authorities granted you: But if, after the Success of your Design, you shall fall in with any English Fleet bound for England, having good convoy, you are, in such case to keep company with them and to bring all your Prizes to London, notwithstanding any Covenant to the contrary in our Articles of Agreement. Pray fail not to give Advice, by all Opportunities, how the Galley proves; how your Men stand, what Progress you make: and, in general, of all remarkable Passages in your Voyage, to the time of your Writing. Direct your letters to Mr Edmund Harrison. I pray God grant you good Success and send us a good Meeting again.

Two days later, the *Adventure Galley* began its epic voyage.[11]

Kidd alone was responsible for the success of the voyage. If he couldn't get his ship out to sea before events took a turn for the worse then the expedition would have failed, he would be ruined, disgraced and end up in debtor's prison. But his mission would almost be ended before it began because of his arrogance.[12]

The description of what follows comes from Admiralty papers held at the National Archives in Kew, and from other sources such as Ritchie and Zacks. The night before leaving, Kidd went ashore and spent the night drinking in the taverns along the docks with Royal Navy captains. He boasted about how his commission came directly from the King and that it meant he didn't have to dip his flag to anyone and could sail with impunity. 'Kidd earned a reputation for extravagant and arrogant boasts. Around the docks he lorded it over his peers and bragged about his commission and his sponsors', Robert Ritchie wrote.

At Greenwich the King's yacht, the *Katherine*, was moored and at the time it was law for every ship that passed it to dip their flag in deference and respect. Hearing of Kidd's boasts about his influential backers and that he had a commission direct from the King the captain of the *Katherine* told his crew to ensure that Kidd did in fact show the proper respect when the *Adventure Galley* sailed past.[13]

In the morning Kidd ordered the sails to be raised, the anchor heaved out of the water and the mooring let go. Gradually, the ship slowly moved away from her berth, tiptoeing amongst the hundreds of other anchored ships heading slowly down the river towards open sea. A few hours later they reached Greenwich and, true to his bragging the night before, the *Adventure Galley* sailed past the *Katherine* without the customary dipping of the flag in recognition. Naval traditions and regulations were very strict in the seventeenth century and Kidd had managed to cross the extremely powerful Royal Navy before he had barely left the docks.

Did Kidd realize what he was doing? If he did, what made him ignore this tradition, one which he must have known about as an experienced mariner? Perhaps he felt as if he was more important than anyone else or that the clauses of the agreements he was now tied to overwhelmed everything else so that dipping his flag seemed a trifle compared to the task ahead. Whatever his reasons, he didn't dip his flag. After all he had a commission from the King, he hadn't lost any men when everyone else had and he was on the King's business so why did he have to dip his flag to a tiny yacht? He was financially backed by earls and admirals (indeed the First Lord of the Admiralty) and was in command of one of the most impressive and powerful warships afloat.

Greenwich, where the *Katherine* was moored, was an important home of the fleet, which meant that there were many Royal Navy ships anchored in that area. The response to Kidd's misconduct was instant. The *Katherine* fired a shot across Kidd's bow, demanding Kidd's flag be dipped; but Kidd ignored it and continued sailing downstream. His confidence and exuberance must have been infectious because some of the crew in the topsails turned their backs to the royal yacht and in a rude mariner's salute 'clapped their backsides' in derision.[14]

When Kidd sailed past the *Katherine* we don't know if not dipping his flag was intentional or unintentional. However, after the *Katherine* fired a warning shot and Kidd still didn't dip his flag that was intentional. He had previously fought under Governor Codrington and he had a reputation as a strong reliable forthright captain. So he couldn't have been ignorant of the rules of the sea. The disrespect of the crew towards the *Katherine* and the lack of deference to the King's flag showed that the captain, who at all times is responsible for his ship and his crew, had not only forgotten the custom but had also deliberately chosen to insult it.

As the *Adventure Galley* sailed towards the Nore, the naval staging post located at the mouth of the Thames, Kidd passed naval vessel after naval vessel and again did not lower his flag. 'When Kidd repeated the insult shortly afterward to another royal ship at the mouth of the River Medway, the Admiralty ordered Captain Have Munden to board the *Adventure Galley*, remove all its sailors then anchor the offending vessel at Sheerness', Robert Ritchie wrote.[15]

His men were transferred to HMS *Duchess*, commanded by Captain Stewart, where they languished. Now, had the *Duchess* been the only naval ship there, Kidd could easily have blasted it out of the water. But all around him were naval ships of different shapes and sizes as the fleet prepared to attack the French.

More than thirty experienced sailors were taken away, leaving Kidd with only five experienced men; the rest were landsmen. His royal commission had been ignored. The fact that one of his backers was the First Lord of the Admiralty made no difference. Kidd lost his men.[16]

This grand new voyage that Kidd had embarked on lasted all of three days. With the rumours of imminent attack by the French and Admiral Russell at the Downs assembling the fleet, Kidd must have prayed for the French to stay in their harbour. However, if Kidd had dipped his flag as they passed the *Katherine*, more than likely he would have been in open sea by then and he might have ended up as just a footnote in history.

Kidd lowered his anchor at Nore and waited. He spent most of his time trying to find his backer, Admiral Russell, in order to get his crew back. Discovering that the Admiral's headquarters were at Sittingbourne, Kent, Kidd hurried down there but then had to wait in outer offices to get access to the Admiral. His notes went unanswered.[17] Through navy dispatches and reports of the day it wouldn't have taken long for Admiral Russell to know what Kidd had done. Kidd had abused his position and an important backer like Russell couldn't compromise his own position to help him.

Time was ticking by. After several weeks Russell finally ordered Captain Stewart to return Kidd's men. But Stewart did not return the men he took from Kidd. Instead he lumbered Kidd with his own inexperienced landsmen, rotten eggs and troublemakers. These included Joseph Palmer of West Chester; another was William Moore, the chief gunner.[18]

The embargo restricting shipping around the southern coast of England was also hampering Kidd in his efforts to get away. He now had seventy crew members but he couldn't leave until the embargo had been lifted. On 1 April 1696 Admiral Cloudiseley Shovell attacked Calais and set it on fire. After that merchant shipping was allowed to leave port again.

Finally, on 10 April 1696, Kidd sailed passed the Downs and continued onto Plymouth where he collected some more crew members, including the young William Jenkins.[19] In his own account of the voyage Kidd stated that they left Plymouth and sailed across the Atlantic for New York.[20]

According to crew member Abel Owens's deposition taken in Boston in July 1699, sometime in May 1696 the *Adventure Galley* sighted a ship on the horizon. Kidd ordered more sail to increase their speed. As the sail on the horizon came closer and closer they could see that it was a small French fishing vessel 'which they took and carried into New York and the same was condemned there as a lawful prize'.

The vessel was bound for Newfoundland. Kidd's commission legally gave him permission to attack this vessel as it was an enemy ship but no attack was necessary. Compared to the *Adventure Galley*, this little French fishing vessel with a crew of four men and a cargo of slate and fishing tackle was puny and virtually unarmed.

Facing the massive size and firepower of the *Adventure Galley*, the crew of the fishing vessel surrendered almost immediately.[21]

On arrival in New York, the unfortunate crew of the fishing vessel were despatched by court order to Boston as a fair exchange for English prisoners held by the French in Canada. Their ship was deemed to be worth around £350, a reasonable sum for a fishing vessel in the seventeenth century. Kidd purchased supplies and provisions for the *Adventure Galley* with his share of the prize money.

As we have already seen, New York was a den of mercenaries, prostitutes, pirates and corrupt merchants but it was also Kidd's home. Imagine the homecoming he must have had with his wife Sarah. He soon set about searching for a quality crew to replace the one he'd lost, and bring the total number up to 150. Kidd needed a crew who preferred life on the open sea and wouldn't desert the moment they saw land. Above all he needed a crew he could mould into a well-oiled fighting machine. But his initial efforts bore little fruit indeed. People wanted cash and all Kidd could offer was a share of the profits of his expedition. He was offering promises not money.

Kidd had to be a good salesman if he wanted a crew based on no payment unless ships loaded with loot were captured. There were no guarantees that this would happen. This concept of payment based solely on the percentage of the takings was called 'no prey, no pay'. The crew did all the work and took all the risks while the backers were in their plush offices making money off their hard work.

To most, becoming a pirate would be more financially viable than being a privateer hunting pirates. Crews of pirate ships had no allegiances to any nation, had no hangers-on sitting behind desks and counting profits that should have gone to the crew. Pirates shared 100 per cent of the takings amongst themselves and in many respects took similar risks as were being proposed onboard the *Adventure Galley*. Given these choices we can see how hard it was for Kidd to recruit his crew.

He devised a plan which enabled him to recruit the fresh crew members he needed but also managed to alienate his backers in London. He allocated the bulk of the takings to himself and his crew, leaving the backers with the scraps that remained. One can see why this move would have angered his backers. If Kidd did bring in captured loot and plunder they would get very little in the way of a return on their investment. Yet, if Kidd could not get a crew then there would be no return at all.

The plan worked. With the promise of higher personal rewards for their hard work, Kidd finally had his crew, mostly made up of ex-pirates and other undesirables. If they were ex-pirates then they knew the sea and they knew how to handle a ship.[22]

While all of this was going on what of his insult to the Royal Navy and his refusal to dip his flag in deference to the King's yacht? Would that have been forgotten? It is highly likely that through dispatches and signals most Royal Navy captains had heard of Kidd's insult and that it had been sensationalized in the retelling. Because of the agreements he was tied into he couldn't afford to fail yet he had managed to upset the Royal Navy. They would not easily forget or forgive.

Hunting Pirates

Rear Admiral Benbow tells me that Kidd was so wicked as to murder all the Moors he took in the ships he made prize of, in cold blood; and that he murdered several English and Dutch among 'em; only there were 10 or 12 young Moorish boys he saved, intending to make slaves of 'em, and one of 'em has some way or other got to Jamaica, who has discovered this villainy of Kidd's. The Lieutenant Governor of New York has sent me a parcel of papers belonging to Capt. Kidd, which were delivered him by Capt. Clark of New York, whom I formerly mentioned as having been on board Kidd's sloop at his coming to Long Island, and received a good quantity of East India goods and treasure from Kidd and Company. (Governor the Earl of Bellomont to the Council of Trade and Plantations, 23 April 1700[1])

This quotation from Bellomont shows the malice that had built up against Kidd in only a few short years. This malice was coming from the Royal Navy and from the East India Company, as we shall see.

It was now mid-1696 and Kidd was in New York readying the *Adventure Galley* to leave for the Red Sea. As we have seen he had to change his plans in order to attract men to sign on for his long voyage. 'When an additional 90 crew members had signed, the recruiting stopped as the *Adventure Galley* could only hold about 150 men.'[2]

New York was still in the grips of depression. King William's War was continuing and the French were attacking the British colonies along the northern frontier. Governor Benjamin Fletcher was forced to send his militia north up the Hudson River to engage the enemy in Albany and many of them died due to the harsh winters, lack of adequate clothing, disease and poor food. Fletcher scoured the rest of the colony for men he could send into battle but many left, heading for the surrounding colonies. The loss of men was so great that Fletcher issued a proclamation to try to halt the flow. When Kidd arrived with his commission he offered men another way out and once he had changed the payment plan to the crew getting the bulk of the takings his proposition became much more attractive. Governor Fletcher wrote a letter to the Council of the Board of Trade and Plantations (created in 1696 from the Lords of Trade and Plantations) complaining about Kidd. 'One Captain Kidd lately arrived and produced a commission under the Great Seal of England for the suppression of piracy. When he was here many flocked to him from all parts, men of desperate fortune and necessities, in expectation of getting vast treasure.'[3]

So what kind of men signed up for life at sea and in particular for a long voyage to the Red Sea without a salary? Samuel Johnson stated that men in jail had better company, better food and even more room than those men who risked danger everyday when they went to sea. And jails in the late seventeenth century were terrible places to be.

Kidd recorded the names of all the crew members he recruited, according to Robert Ritchie. They all came from different backgrounds. Patrick Dremer, Michijah Evans and Samuel Kennels, for example, were labourers from Philadelphia who came to New York to sign on. Baker Isaac Deenes left New Jersey to join up while a respectable New York vintner put one of his servants, Saunders Douglas, aboard so he could collect half of his share. Carpenter Edward Grayham left his job to come aboard the *Adventure Galley* and sail away, as did John Burton and William Wakeman who were both shoemakers.

Three young apprentices signed on as well: Robert Lamley, William Jenkins and Richard Barlycorne.[4] Twelve-year-old Lamley served his apprenticeship with the ship's cook, Abel Owens, while Jenkins, who was 14, served his apprenticeship with the chief mate, George Bullen. Barlycorne served his with Captain Kidd. Kidd's young brother-in-law Samuel Bradley, who had journeyed with him to London, also continued to sail with him on the *Adventure Galley*. Out of the full crew complement by far the majority were English, with some twenty-five Dutchmen and a handful of men from different nations including seven Scots.

Such a disparate group of men had to be moulded together to form a fighting team if they were to capture prizes. But many had no background in fighting at all. Darby Mullins was an Irishman born around 1661 near Londonderry. A hearty young man, he'd been taken to be a servant in the colonies and after working for four years in Jamaica he became an odd-jobber in Port Royale. When the earthquake of 1692 destroyed the city he set sail for New York where he worked around the docks. When his wife died he signed aboard the *Adventure Galley*.

Another individual, Edward Buckmaster, started out as a sailor but had switched to keeping a tavern in the docks area of New York by 1689. He took part in opposing the Leisler regime and his tavern was a den for anti-Leisler conspirators. Buckmaster was jailed by Leislerites. Upon his release he continued his agitation against the regime and was arrested again. However, when Governor Sloughter arrived and the royal government was restored Buckmaster became a free man. He resurfaced again when he joined Kidd's crew.

Perhaps, the most unusual member of the crew was Benjamin Franks. He was 46, which made him older than most of the crew. The Franks were an influential mercantile Jewish family who traded to North America, India and the West Indies.

But Benjamin, a jeweller by trade, was not as successful as the rest of his family. He'd set up a business in Port Royale which was wiped out by the 1692 earthquake. He headed for New York and by 1696 was signing onto the *Adventure Galley* because he planned on setting up a business in India which was, at that time, the leading supplier of jewels, particularly diamonds, in the world. The Franks family centred their trade in Bombay and Surat so Franks wanted to be dropped off in Surat when the *Adventure Galley* got there.[5]

Finally, on 6 September 1696 Kidd kissed his wife goodbye. The anchor of the *Adventure Galley* was raised and the ship pulled slowly away from the dock. Its sails unfurled, it moved slowly into the great harbour. Accompanied by HMS *Richmond* and a brigantine, the three ships sailed towards Staten Island and then to Sandy Hook where the *Richmond* parted company and the two remaining ships headed out into the rough seas of the Atlantic.

> He sailed from here with 150 men, as I am informed, a great part of them from this province. It is generally believed here that they will get money per fas aut nefas, and that if he misses the design named in his commission he will not be able to govern such a herd of men under no pay.[6]

Kidd would have been on his way to the Red Sea at the end of February 1696 if it were not for the insult he'd paid to the captain of the *Katherine*. He was now eight months behind schedule. The articles of the agreement stated that he was to return with his prizes to Boston by 25 March 1697. That left him only seven months to capture pirate ships or French ships loaded with loot. Could he do it?

Their first port of call was the islands of Madeira and on the way Kidd put the crew through their paces, teaching them how to handle the ship. Kidd organized his crew and his officers as best he could. They had exercises in gunnery where the chief gunner, William Moore, taught the landsmen how to handle the cannon on a heaving deck.

All of this was interrupted when a sail was spotted on the horizon. The ship put up as much sail as it could to get away from the *Adventure Galley*. Kidd ordered more sail and the chase was on. Now he could put his men to the test. They gained on the ship until it gave up and hove to as Kidd brought the *Adventure Galley* alongside, his gun ports open and cannon ready. However, the ship turned out to be a Portuguese merchantman on its way to Madeira and, as England and Portugal were at peace, this was not a legitimate prize so Kidd let her go.

They arrived at Madeira and stayed only a day, long enough to take on fresh water, food and wine. His route from there was to take him down the west coast of Africa around Cape of Good Hope at the tip of South Africa to the island of Madagascar. Kidd then sailed south away from Madeira, heading for the Cape Verde Islands – the last European outpost before ships continued on into the South Atlantic. They stopped at Boa Vista and spent four days loading supplies, especially salt to keep the food preserved. They then moved on to Santiago Island where they spent another eight days taking on fresh water and more supplies. They needed to be sure their supplies would last on the long voyage around the Cape into the Indian Ocean.

Finally, they were ready to sail and once again they headed south. As they reached the equator, the wind died away as they were now in the area known as the doldrums, a pocket between two wind systems. They took advantage of every squall or breeze that sprang up; otherwise they simply drifted. The heat was oppressive, humid and every man aboard the ship took up whatever shade they could find during the day. At night the men remained on deck to escape the terrible heat below decks.

There was nothing they could do except wait for the wind. The mainstay of their diet was salt beef or salted pork with peas and hardtack. This would be washed down with water for those crew members who didn't have money enough to buy strong beer which flowed freely; 'the water that increasingly acquired a life of its own in this tropical zone had to be strained through teeth', Ritchie wrote.[7]

In the heat, tempers would often flare amongst the crew and Kidd's officers had to be quick to stop any conflict before it endangered the entire ship. Such heat could also turn the crew against the officers. Why go for targets in India when West Africa lay at their doorstep? But Kidd, who was a large and aggressive man, was able to keep any rumblings of this sort at bay.

Two months out of the Cape Verde Islands the ship had not touched land and it was drifting in heavy fog. It was early December 1696. The fog cleared on the morning of the 12th and the lookout high above the deck in the crow's-nest shouted 'Sail!' Kidd threw up his telescope and stared. Sure enough there was a ship behind them and it was putting on more sail, heading directly towards him.

Moments later, the lookout again cried out and three more ships appeared over the horizon heading directly for the *Adventure Galley*. Kidd must have wondered what on earth was going on. He would soon discover that in all the expanse of the South Atlantic he'd run across a Royal Navy squadron commanded by Commodore Thomas Warren.

Kidd wrote in his own account of the voyage that there were four ships in the squadron: the *Windsor*, *Advice*, *Tiger* and *Vulture*.[8] It must be stated here that life aboard a Royal Navy ship in the late seventeenth century bore no resemblance to life aboard a Royal Navy ship today. England was still building its trade routes and it had competition from the Dutch, the French, the Portuguese and the Spanish, all imperial powers themselves. At that time the Royal Navy could simply take men from wherever they found them – in the fields, off the streets, from villages and towns – and could press gang them into service. A man who may have been a farmer, for example, and was press ganged into service with no choice at all would find life very hard indeed. The pay was always very late and in some cases the Royal Navy issued tickets to their crew that could only be redeemed in certain places. On top of the lack of pay there was the very high chance of an early death from disease or from battle. During times of war the Royal Navy could also take men from other ships whenever they wanted and Kidd was painfully aware of this. Now, he found himself with the Royal Navy almost on top of him.

Not wanting to lose any more men he ordered more sail. But it was to no avail as HMS *Tiger* commanded by Captain John Richmond caught up with them and forced them to wait for the rest of the squadron to arrive. Several hours later they did arrive, in company with an East India merchantman ship commanded by Captain John Clarke. Kidd was ordered to come aboard HMS *Windsor* to meet Warren.[9]

For the crew serving on HMS *Windsor* life was harder than on most other Royal Navy ships for Commodore Warren was a strict disciplinarian and cared nothing for the men under his command. Aboard his ship he was God. Some sources, for example, indicate that Warren had brought his barber's wife on board to act as his personal washerwoman so he would be immaculate at all times, directing precious fresh water away from the crew to suit his own ego. Warren and his officers feasted on the finest food and wine, while the crew starved on meagre rations.

Kidd was accompanied on board the *Windsor* by Benjamin Franks, who wrote 'I was onboard the Commodore's ship when he told me that Kidd's commission was firm and good and that he would not molest or hinder his proceedings for his putting his hands to his ears.' As Kidd was invited to feast with Warren and his officers he must have wondered how long it would take for Warren to ask or demand men from him. In his sworn deposition Franks wrote that 'Kidd promised to spare the Commodore twenty or thirty men and a day or two after he went on board one of the men-of-war, and returning much disguised in drink left the squadron without furnishing the men.'

On the *Adventure Galley*, the crew waited for the blow to come for them to taken off their ship for service into the navy. Commodore Warren was short of men because he'd lost so many to disease. His squadron had left England on 19 May 1696 in company with five East India Company merchantmen all bound for the West Indies, along with a host of other ships. By June the frigates and Company ships were still ploughing southward and the navy was making very slow time due to frequent dinners between the Company ships and Warren's ships. Warren's experienced sailing master died, leaving him without a guide, and then the first cases of scurvy appeared.

The captains of the Company ships were to stay with the navy for as long as they could and they had been ordered not to stop at the Dutch colony on the Cape of Good Hope. But with the spread of scurvy and the rising death toll they had to do something. The Company captains, disgusted at the navy's snail pace, realized they had no choice but to head for the Cape. On 14 July the *Charles* and the *Dorrill* East India Company merchantmen left the safety of the navy and tacked away to the east. The rest of the fleet plodded on until 12 August when Company ships the *Sceptre*, the *Sampson* and the *Chambers* left the fleet and headed for the Cape of Good Hope.

Warren's orders were to sail to the island of St Helena to wait for the return fleet of East India Company ships and escort them back to England. But with his experienced master dead and his own navigation so poor he couldn't find the island. For weeks the fleet sailed on blundering first north, then west and then south. Finally, Warren gave up trying to find St Helena and headed for Rio de Janeiro. By this time he'd lost sixty-eight men and the rest of his crew were sick with scurvy.

In August Warren finally reached Rio with a ship full of sick and dying men. Now, Warren had to wait for his men to recover until he could blunder out to sea again to try to intercept the East India Company fleet. He waited for as long as he could and set sail in mid-November, heading southeast. By December he'd not run across the Company ships but on the 12th his squadron ran into Kidd.[10]

Kidd found himself surrounded by Royal Navy ships, along with an East India Company merchantman that had joined the squadron in Rio. The time limit for his mission was running out. He was supposed to have his captured prizes in Boston by March of 1697, only a few months away, and here he was stuck with the navy and Warren seemed to be in no hurry to let him go.

For a week Kidd sailed with the naval squadron, invited by Warren to one meal after another where the wine and brandy would flow copiously. Commodore Warren needed men and it was his right to take the men he needed from wherever he found them, in this case from the *Adventure Galley*. Eventually Warren made it clear he was seeking replacements for the men he'd lost to disease. On the night of 18 December 1696 Kidd hurried back to the *Adventure Galley*, drunk from the wine and liquor served at Warren's table, and barked out an order. There was no wind so he ordered the oars to be manned and quietly they made ready to leave. Under the cover of darkness, and as quiet as they could be, the men of the *Adventure Galley* bent their backs to the oars and rowed away from the Royal Navy. 'That night he rowed away in a calm and next morning was almost out of sight. He talked very big while on board, which made many suspect the honesty of his design.'[11]

Warren was furious, for this upstart privateer had fled from him and worse had not given him the men he'd requested. To make the insult worse, Kidd had been the recipient of Warren's generous hospitality. The Commodore was determined to make an example of this Scots privateer who was a criminal of the high seas, a pirate no less. 'Kidd apparently confessed to them, perhaps during a drinking bout, that he did not care what ships he captured; and from his behaviour they believed him to be a pirate.'[12]

Warren wasted no time in spreading his opinion of Kidd when he arrived at the Dutch colony at the Cape of Good Hope, where he enthusiastically told the Dutch officials and the captains of the five East India Company merchantmen anchored there of his encounter with Kidd whom he now branded a criminal and a pirate. Meanwhile, Kidd headed for Madagascar.

Bad Luck and Trouble

Madagascar should have been the place where Kidd's fortunes changed. They arrived in Tulear, the island's capital on the southern tip of the island facing the African coast, in the nick of time. The crew were riddled with disease and they were running out of food and water. After escaping the clutches of the Royal Navy they'd sailed around the Cape hoping to find a harbour on the African coast to put in for much needed supplies. But instead they found nothing and sailed on until they finally made Tulear on 27 January 1697.

Once they dropped anchor Kidd sent the sick men ashore where they were able to recover over a period of days. Other members of the crew joined their sick crewmates ashore to get away from the cramped conditions on board. Their water barrels were filled with fresh water and fresh food and vegetables were brought aboard as well. In those days everything was handled by either manpower or rope and tackle so it took time to fill one water barrel and roll it to the shore, into the boat then out to the ship.

While they were there, another ship came into St Augustine Bay nearby and Kidd sent several men round to see where the ship was from. She was the *Loyal Russell*, a sloop from Barbados that had come to buy slaves in Madagascar. This encounter is remarkable for two reasons. Kidd wrote in his own account of the voyage that 'a sloop belonging to Barbados, loaded with Rum, Sugar, Powder, and Shot, one French Master and Mr Hatton and Mr John Batt, Merchants; and the said Hatton came to board the said Galley and was suddenly taken ill and died in the Cabin'.[1] By this Kidd means that Hatton came aboard the *Adventure Galley*, was taken ill and died in his (Kidd's) cabin.

That in itself is remarkable but according to Ritchie, the *Loyal Russell* had visited the colony at Cape of Good Hope where Warren's squadron was anchored. Warren 'suspected it of being in consortship with Kidd', Ritchie wrote in his book. 'There is no evidence of such a partnership, but their meeting was fortunate for Kidd because he could acquire information about the ships at the cape and also learn that Warren was spreading the word that he was a pirate.'[2]

The island of Madagascar in the late seventeenth and early eighteenth century was teeming with native tribes, each with their own territories and often at war with their neighbours. Here's what Johnson says about the natives on Madagascar.[3] 'The natives of Madagascar are a kind of Negroes, they differ from those of Guinea in their hair, which is long and their complexion which is not so good a jet.' Any prisoners the tribal princes had, Johnson states, were their slaves 'and they either sell them or put them to death, as they please'. When pirates first came to Madagascar the princes of each of the tribes eagerly aligned themselves with the pirates to gain an advantage over the other tribes; 'they were sure to be victorious,' wrote Johnson, 'for the Negroes here had no firearms, nor did they understand their use: so at length these pirates became so terrible to the Negroes, that if two or three of them were only seen on one side, when they were going to engage, the opposite side would fly without striking a blow'.

As more and more pirates came to the island they took control, marrying as many of the most beautiful native women as they chose 'so every one of them had as great a Seraglio as the Grand Seignior at Constantinople', Johnson wrote. The pirates also had slaves, presumably captured natives and prisoners taken during conflicts, civil war and any other skirmishes. Gradually, the pirates themselves became princes. 'Now they begin to divide from one another, each living with his own wives, slaves and dependants, like a separate prince; and as power and plenty naturally beget contention, they sometimes quarrelled with one another, and attacked each other at the head of their several armies.' So according to Johnson these pirates acted in almost the same way as the natives were doing when they first arrived. These pirates had children by their many wives and the number of dependants grew, forcing the pirates to find bigger living space for their entourage.

'It must be observed', Johnson wrote, 'that these sudden great men, had used their power like tyrants for they grew wanton in cruelty and nothing was more common than upon the slightest displeasure to cause one of their dependants to be tied to a tree and shot through the heart let the crime be what it would.' The cruelty of the pirates was so barbarous that the natives of the island conspired to attack and kill the pirates, freeing themselves from tyranny. They gathered their weapons and crept towards the settlements where the pirates lived. However, Johnson states that the wife of one of the pirates ran some twenty miles to warn that the natives were on the march. The pirate princes joined together and met the native army who then retreated.

To avoid being attacked again by the natives, the pirates began to sow discontent, pitting one tribe against another. Those that survived these wars ran to the pirates for protection, bringing with them their families. Over the years, the pirates, now princes or kings themselves, settled in more open spaces, setting up their own colonies and fortifying their houses against attack from other pirate kings and from the natives.[4]

So Madagascar was a pirate haven. But when Kidd sailed into it he didn't find a single pirate ship. In his own account Madagascar is only a few lines where the only remarkable incident is the death of Hatton in Kidd's quarters. Kidd was in Madagascar for almost a month taking on supplies, waiting for his crew to recover and perhaps even lying low to avoid Warren's squadron. Gabriel Loff, a crew member on the *Adventure Galley*, provided a brief description of Kidd's movements during this time in his deposition. 'I sailed on the *Adventure Galley* from New York to Madeira, Bonavista, St. Jago, Madagascar, Johanna, Mohilla and back to Johanna and thence into the Red Sea to cruise for pirates.'

By the end of February Kidd left Madagascar. He was now less than a month away from his deadline with nothing to show his backers and he had to do something so he headed for Johanna (now Anjouan) in the Comoros (Comoro) chain of islands. It was a clear area where he could attack pirates. The islands were strung across the northern end of the Mozambique Channel on the edge of the Arabian Sea and they made an excellent stop for ships heading towards India, which was Kidd's ultimate destination.

Sailing in consort with the *Loyal Russell*, the *Adventure Galley* headed north. But Kidd's luck was again bad and on the way the two ships were hammered by heavy seas and high wind. As the waves washed across the ship and the decks heaved underfoot, Kidd ordered everything to be tied down. Men had to cling to rigging or be washed overboard. During this horrendous storm Kidd's great ship began to leak. For more than a week the *Adventure Galley* rose and fell in the rough seas, pounded by water tearing across her decks, the wind whipping through her rigging until finally, by the end of March, he was half a day's sail from Johanna and shelter.

At the time, Johanna was rich in citrus fruits, a tropical island paradise. Rather than entering the harbours of the island where the natives were, pirates preferred to remain just beyond the open waters, waiting for any merchant ship that had lain over to replenish supplies and attack them as they came out to resume their journeys.[5]

As they headed for Johanna the lookout spied two sails on the horizon. Could this be the break he'd been longing for? Could he capture these two ships and head for Boston with his prizes and loot intact? But as he stared at the rapidly approaching sails Kidd could see that they were no prizes: one was a heavily armed East India Company merchantman, the *Sydney*, and the other the *Scarborough* was 'an interloper in the India trade'.[6] Both ships were a match for the *Adventure Galley* and Kidd could not afford to be arrogant. The three ships entered the harbour at Johanna.

In his own account Kidd states that he arrived in Johanna where there were four East India ships already. Captain John Clarke commanding the *East India Merchant* wrote in his letter to the Board of Trade that

> two of the ships, East Indiamen, entering Johanna harbour found Kidd then at anchor. Kidd hoisted English colours and the King's jack and pendant, fired at the *Sydney*, East Indiaman, and ordered her to strike her colours, with threats. Just then two more East Indiamen came into the

harbour, and we sent Kidd word that unless he behaved civilly we would call him to account. He gave us all an invitation on board his ship, and gave out that he was bound for Port St. Mary's on the east side of St. Lawrence to hunt for pirates, but for all his pretences his men confessed that they expected to find no ship in Johanna but a single East India ship, which they knew was bound for Surat.

Captain Gifford commanding the *Sydney* was the senior captain of the Indies fleet and as such was entitled to fly a commodore's flag. Some sources indicate that Kidd tried to assert himself over Gifford by flying the King's jack and pendant, as Clarke (Clark) wrote in his letter. Kidd maintained that his commission from the King gave him ascendancy over any ship of the East India Company. Of course Kidd had to back down when confronted by four East India merchantmen.

But he would not be bullied out of the harbour. Kidd maintained cool relations with the four captains from the East India Company. For their part they suspected him but did nothing to apprehend him at this time. Warren's poison was beginning to work as these captains, according to Clarke were already considering him as an undesirable element. Though Kidd told the company captains he intended to sail to the island of Sainte Marie, his men, who mingled on shore with the crews of the company ships, said that Kidd was waiting to catch one of the merchantmen alone so he could take sails, stores and anything else he needed. Kidd's crew were behaving already as if they were pirates rather than privateers, though they had yet to commit an act of piracy.

In addition to this Kidd had no money and on Johanna cash was the only currency. Indeed, merchants there refused his bill of exchange drawn on King William. After taking on water and wood Kidd raised his anchor, unfurled his sails and moved slowly out of the harbour towards Mohilla.[7]

Throughout all of this the *Loyal Russell* had remained in consort with Kidd. But the *Adventure Galley* was in a bad way. It needed to be careened (cleaned) and repaired as soon as possible. 'We then went from thence to Mohilla: where the Galley was laid onshore, and cleaned', Jenkins said in his deposition.

The island of Mohilla was far less civilized and populated than Johanna. It was also further out of the shipping lanes so unlikely to attract prying eyes of pirates, East India Company ships or the Royal Navy. Kidd used this time to repair his ship. 'Sailed March 22 for Mohilla, 10 leagues from Johanna and careened the Galley', Kidd wrote in his account. Careening – pulling the ship onto one side then the other while the hull was scraped, cleaned and repaired – was a time when the ship was vulnerable to attack and it had to be done on a relatively flat stretch of shore in as remote a place a possible. Mohilla was as good as Kidd could get.

Everything had to be taken off the *Adventure Galley* including the guns and ammunition. Fortunately, he still had the *Loyal Russell* in tow and that sloop was used to take the guns from the *Adventure Galley*. 'Usually the gravest danger during careening was the threat of attack while the ship was immobile and defenceless. Kidd lessened that risk by mounting cannon on the *Loyal Russell*, his guard ship and he probably also took some other cannon and mounted them in strategic spots along the shore.[8] Everything else that had been taken off the ship remained on the shore. 'Barrels upon barrels of salt meat and water would be hoisted out of the hold,' Richard Zacks writes in his book. 'Cannonballs, gunpowder, and ballast were lugged ashore.' Up until this point Kidd had barely fired his cannon. He'd loaded around 36 barrels of gunpowder, over 1,000 cannonballs and 100 pistols and muskets in London so most of that had to be removed before the ship could be cleaned.

Once the ship was on its side then Kidd could see just how bad the damage to the hull was. It was severe.[9] The hull was shot through with worm holes and would take several days of repair work; while the seams between the beams and planks had opened up, causing leaks. Throughout the rest of the voyage the ship would leak and the pumps below decks would have to be manned continuously in the stifling heat to keep her afloat. Kidd's men got to work pounding scraping irons on the 2.5 inch thick planks to scrape off the encrustations, while others packed in oakum fibres reinforced by tar to seal the joints between the beams.[10]

Kidd wrote in his account that within ten days of arriving at the island his crew began to die of a mysterious illness. 'He states that some fifty of his crew died with a week, probably of cholera.'[11] It could have been malaria, cholera, typhoid or any other tropical disease to which the crew from the distant lands of America and England would not have any tolerance and immunity. So in a matter of days Kidd had lost a third of his crew and was down to approximately 100 men, which was not enough to man the guns completely. He was once again in need of crew members to fulfil his mission.[12]

That one mistake of not lowering his flag in deference to the King's yacht in Greenwich cost him most of his crew and six months. He could have arrived in the waters around Madagascar so much earlier, possibly when the place was teeming with pirates. But when Kidd arrived at Madagascar there were no pirates to be seen. Johnson provides a possible explanation for this. 'It happened that at this time the pirate ships were most of them out in search of prey; so that according to the best intelligence Captain Kidd could get, there was not one of them at that time about the island.'[13]

With the repairs completed, the ship rolled back into the water and everything back on board, Kidd was ready to sail. But before he could go pirate hunting again he had two pressing needs: for supplies and for more experienced crew members. So after five weeks careening the ship, Kidd ordered the anchor to be raised and set sail for Johanna.

The most likely reason for his return to Johanna was to recruit new sailors. Indeed, Hugh Parrot joined the *Adventure Galley* there as he stated in his deposition; 'at the Island of Johanna I left the Vessel I then belonged to, and entered myself on board the *Adventure Galley*'.

Finally, Kidd had a bit of good luck in that he recruited five men who had taken the pinnace belonging to the *East India Merchant* commanded by Captain Clarke. According to Johnson, when Kidd was at Johanna for the second time, 'he found means of borrowing a sum of money from some French men who had lost their ship, but saved their effects, and with this he purchased materials for putting his ship in good repair'. Robert Ritchie mentions the same incident, suggesting that these French (and English according to Ritchie) not only loaned him money but also signed on with him. They must have done as he left Johanna at the end of April 1697 heading for the Red Sea, still hunting pirates.

He'd been at sea for more than nine months, the deadline had passed and he had not seen or captured a single pirate ship or even a French ship for that matter. If, instead of sailing for the Red Sea, he had headed back to Madagascar he would have run across Captain John Hoare, a pirate who had brought in a 300 ton prize. He was still there in July so if Kidd had gone back to Madagascar he could have captured Hoare and his men and their prizes. But he didn't.[14]

Local intelligence was crucial to Kidd and the French men he'd picked up at Johanna told him that the best place to hunt for pirates was the Red Sea. Some of the richest ships in the world sailed the sea lanes between India and Arabia and this time of year would see the ships returning from Arabia to India full of wealthy Muslims returning from their pilgrimage to Mecca. Indian merchants bringing back their treasures and profits from selling to the pilgrims also had passage aboard these ships which carried silver, gold and jewels. Any European pirate looking for a quick way to get rich would very likely head for the Red Sea.

But Kidd's luck had still not improved. He sailed north passed Zanzibar, Mombassa, Melindi and Lamu then around the Horn of Africa and turned west towards the Gulf of Aden. All this time no pirate ship was spotted. At its western end the Gulf of Aden dramatically narrows into the strait of Babs-al-Mandab, known to most sailors and pirates as the Babs. The Arabian Peninsula thrusts out into the strait on the northwest side, with Perim Island as part of that headland. On the African shores near Sijan are shoals and large sandbars, so shipping had to sail close to Perim Island to avoid these hazards. This made Perim Island an ideal place for intercepting shipping passing through the Babs.

The *Adventure Galley* arrived in the harbour at the south side of Perim Island. Kidd barked orders. The anchor lowered with a mighty splash into the water, dragging along the bottom until it brought the ship to a standstill. Eyeing the lie of the land Kidd ordered men to climb Signal Hill on the western side of the harbour and to take flags with them to signal for any shipping in the strait.

He knew that fifty miles to the north was the harbour at Mocha (modern-day Yemen) and his intelligence told him the fleet of Muslim ships would, at some point, be at this harbour. He ordered his quartermaster, John Walker, to make a reconnaissance voyage to that harbour to find out what the Muslim fleet were doing. The pinnace was lowered from the *Adventure Galley* and splashed into the water. Kidd watched Walker and a few men row away from the ship and disappear over the horizon. All he could do now was wait.

What Kidd didn't know was that the English East India Company had sent three heavily armed ships to protect the Muslim fleet. 'The East India Company having communicated some information they had received from their Factors in the East Indies of piracies committed by Captain Kidd, circular letters were thereupon sent to all the American Plantations by the Secretary of State commanding the Governors there to make search and seize him if he came within their reach.'[15]

Two years earlier the pirate Captain Henry Avery had attacked the Muslim fleet and captured one of the Great Mogul's own ships, the *Ganj-i-Sawai* or the *Gunsway*. The story goes that Avery's men carried out atrocities on the ship as well as plundering it of everything of value.

Furious, the Great Mogul ordered the Dutch, French and English East India Companies to protect Indian shipping, especially the Muslim fleet, or they would be expelled from India. The stakes were high indeed. As a result of Avery's attack the Great Mogul had suspended English trade because the pirates had been English. No matter how much they protested, the officials of the East India Company in Bombay could not convince the Great Mogul that the pirates didn't work for the Company. If another English pirate struck hard at the pilgrim fleet the English East India Company would no longer be able to trade in India.

This was the situation when the *Sceptre*, under the command of Captain Phinney, was anchored in Bombay in early April 1697. At this time Kidd was still in Johanna. But on 13 April 1697 the *Sceptre* set sail from Bombay, while the *Adventure Galley* left Johanna on 10 May, both ships heading for the Red Sea.

The first mate of the *Sceptre*, Edward Barlow was an experienced mariner. He kept a sea journal that he even illustrated with some of his own watercolours. He had gone to sea as a boy and worked his way up the chain to become the first mate and when Phinney died of disease while they were in India Barlow was made captain. When he arrived at Mocha in command of the *Sceptre* he traded his own cargo of sugar, pepper, knives, scissors, lead and iron for Mocha's famous coffee, its chief commodity. But rumours were spreading that a ship was waiting in the Babs for the fleet. The last thing Barlow needed was for a replay of Avery's attack. The Muslim fleet was preparing to sail and Barlow was there to protect it, with two Dutch ships that had been assigned to help him.

On 10 August 1697 Barlow watched the lifeboats of the two Dutch captains approach the *Sceptre*. He heard the shouts from his own men as they threw the guide ropes down to the men waiting in the boats. Moments later the two Dutch captains came on deck and were ushered into Barlow's cabin. They began their preparations.

As they did, the situation for Kidd was getting worse.

Walker had returned from his reconnaissance mission and told Kidd there were seventeen pilgrim ships in the harbour at Mocha making ready to sail. The rumours that Barlow heard were based on the fact that Walker had been seen during his reconnaissance voyage as well as on reports that had come in that a pirate had stopped at a town called Motta to take on water and when the inhabitants of that island had refused to help them forty men from the ship went ashore and took what they wanted, while on another raid for food the sailors killed some of the natives who resisted.[16] That pirate, according to the reports, was Captain Kidd.

Johnson mentions another incident in his account of Kidd. 'The first outrage or depredation I find he committed upon mankind was after his repairing his ship, and leaving Johanna; he touched at a place called Mabbee, upon the Red Sea, where he took some Guinea corn from the natives by force.'

Kidd also had another problem: he had an unhappy crew. Rumblings and discussions about turning to piracy were growing. He was running out of fresh water. Johnson states 'near Mohilla and Johanna both, he met with several Indian ships richly laden, to which he did not offer the least violence, though he was strong enough to have done what he pleased with them'. Tension onboard the *Adventure Galley* was running high. For weeks they'd waited for the lookouts on Signal Hill to wave their flags to let them know when the fleet was coming. The oppressive heat forced the men from below decks but the ship was leaking so some had to stay below constantly manning the pumps. After everything Kidd and his crew had been through – the storms, the risk of being press ganged into the Royal Navy – they had nothing to show for their efforts 'It is therefore not surprising that the ship's company had reached a state of rampant discontent, and that from those who had been recruited in New York came open suggestions of piracy as the only means of improving their unhappy lot.'[17]

So the whispers grew louder and the crew of the *Adventure Galley* became more unruly. 'Doubtless Kidd found his crew already beyond his control.'[18] Fifty miles south of Mocha, Kidd and his crew waited. Days went by. In Mocha, Barlow had been trying to convince the suspicious authorities that he was not an English pirate but an English East India Company man and that there was a difference. He even rented a house while he waited for the authorities to verify his papers. Time drifted by as the crew of the *Adventure Galley* continued to consume the depleted supplies of fresh water in the baking heat.

Finally, on 11 August 1697, the Muslim fleet left Mocha and a short time later, the lookouts on Signal Hill shouted and waved their flags. The fleet had been spotted. Once again the *Adventure Galley* bristled with activity as the crew hoisted the anchor, the sails were unfurled, the decks cleared and the ship set sail heading for the fleet looking for any pirate vessels that might be following nearby.

Under cover of darkness on 14 August the fleet steered south slipping past the Babs and by the time the sun peered over the horizon Barlow looking through his spyglass saw something that shouldn't have been there. He spotted an extra ship in the convoy. It was the *Adventure Galley*. He looked around for his two Dutch consorts but they were far behind him. He was on his own.

One of the Muslim vessels in the convoy was a large ship with 700 passengers, no doubt filled with riches. Crew member William Jenkins said in his deposition that 'the said *Galley* did not endeavour to come up or speak with any of them, apprehending they were too strong'.

The *Adventure Galley* was moving fast on a slight wind, only her topsail unfurled, with a pennant flying from the masthead that had a long narrow strip of red on it that would be used by a commodore in a Royal Navy vessel (or by the lead ship in a convoy of merchant men). But the wind was disappearing and Barlow needed to make a decision. The more he studied the other ship the more he believed he was facing a pirate. He must have cursed the waning wind as his sails flapped in what was left of the breeze. He waited for the other ship to come closer.

Gradually, the *Adventure Galley* came in closer and as it passed the *Sceptre*, Barlow raised the East India Company flags and fired his guns. Kidd must have been stunned to find that the convoy was escorted. Walker, his quartermaster, had only seen seventeen ships in the harbour. Now, through his spyglass, Kidd could not only see the *Sceptre* but the two Dutch ships as well. Cannonballs splashed into the water around him as Barlow fired. Without wind Barlow launched two of his long boats, ordering them to tow the *Sceptre* towards Kidd. It is at this point where historians differ as to who was the aggressor.

Kidd, being pursued and fired upon by Barlow, headed for a fat Moorish ship which by now had been alerted to his presence. Most historians who believe that Kidd turned pirate here base their theories on Johnson's account: 'Kidd fired at a Moorish ship which was next him; but the men of war taking the alarm, bore down upon Kidd, and firing upon him obliged him to sheer off, he not being strong enough to contend with them.'

The Moorish ship opened fire at the *Adventure Galley*, sending cannonballs smashing into the rigging. Splinters flew everywhere and Kidd, having had enough, ordered his gun captains to open fire. Five cannon from the *Adventure Galley* roared their cannonballs, ripping into the sails and hull of the Moorish ship.

All the while Barlow was still in pursuit. He'd ordered some of his men to climb the rigging and shout and curse at the *Adventure Galley* as they got closer. In his journal Barlow wrote that Kidd never fired upon him, though he fired on Kidd: 'We fired at him as long as he was anything near and judged did hit him with some of our shot'. Kidd, having the faster ship, pulled away as a breeze sprang up and stayed out of range but still close to the fleet. The pattern continued as Barlow gave chase and 'twice more pulled toward him in a direct challenge, with cannon firing and men yelling'.[19]

Each time Kidd edged away. The *Sceptre* with its 36 guns matched the *Adventure Galley* and although Kidd had the edge in speed he could not be sure that one lucky shot from Barlow would not disable his ship, leaving him helpless. Finally, the game of cat and mouse ended when Kidd sailed away from the fleet for good.

Barlow wrote in his journal that the Muslim ships were carrying large quantities of money and riches and that the ships in the lead in the convoy could have been easily plundered by the pirate if he'd attacked them. Kidd could have captured a ship, plundered it and then sailed away, with the *Sceptre* or any other ship unable to do anything to stop him. Instead, Kidd brought his ship to the end of the convoy where he was closer to the *Sceptre* and the two Dutch escorts.

The ship that Kidd had fired at could have been a great prize and might have saved him had he decided to take it then and there. Some say that was his intention and it was only Barlow in the *Sceptre* who managed to keep him away. Even so, would he have had the time to capture the ship, board it and take it out of the convoy, with the *Sceptre* not far away and the two Dutch ships also coming up? We'll never know because Kidd decided that the risk wasn't worth it or he stuck to his guns that his was a legal mission and there was no justification for him to attack this ship.

In his account Johnson states that Kidd brought the men on deck before they set sail for the Mocha fleet and said: 'We have been unsuccessful hitherto, but courage, my boys, we'll make our fortunes out of this fleet.' This statement supports the historians who believe that Kidd fully intended to turn pirate at this time.

Now away from the fleet, in the middle of August and its intense baking heat, Kidd ordered the men on deck and laid before them two choices: linger near the Muslim fleet with their fresh water supply at a critical stage or put on all sail and head for the highlands of Saint John (now Daman) on the northwest coast of India. Saint John was used by ships as a convenient landfall before they turned north for Surat. Indeed, Avery had captured his biggest prize the *Gunsway* off Saint John and most mariners knew the story, so it was a good place to go for local shipping. The men chose Saint John. Kidd ordered the sails to be fully raised and the *Adventure Galley* headed for India.

A few days later, Kidd again brought the crew on deck and placed before them another decision. Their water supplies were running low. The crew had been grumbling about it and Kidd now wanted to know if they should stop along the way for water or remain on their present course and get water when they arrived at Saint John. The crew chose to stay on their present course.

Many of the men were disillusioned. Those who had still believed they were on a privateering mission now realized they were on a pirate ship. This is supported by Johnson's claim that Kidd's crew had committed acts of piracy at Mabbee. Some crew members were sick with disease and others wanted to get off the ship at the first opportunity. In addition, the *Adventure Galley* was leaking worse than ever. Pumps were manned by tired, hot and thirsty men day and night. So they sailed on with supplies running low, lack of water and an unhappy crew, Kidd must have wondered what his chances of success really were.

We know that by now he was already hearing rumours that he was the most infamous pirate on the high seas. Indeed, Captain John Clarke had left Johanna and gone directly to Bombay, arriving there in June, and he wasted no time in providing the East India Company officials there with a report about Kidd's interactions with Warren and his actions in Johanna. This report is on file in the National Archives and was sent to all the Company factories so that by the time Kidd arrived at Saint John he was already a suspected pirate.

Was he a privateer or pirate by this time? Johnson tells us he had already committed acts of piracy, or that his men had. Other historians such as Ritchie also follow that claim. But soon there would be absolutely no doubt.

Pirate or privateer, Kidd needed success and he needed it fast. He knew the consequences if he returned empty-handed: he'd have to pay the investors out of his own pocket and pay the performance bond which he couldn't do. So he was facing debtor's prison and ruin. He was well past the March 1697 deadline. Something had to be done.[20]

7

India

Some reports suggest that Kidd committed acts of piracy at Motta, which meant he had crossed the line there. Benjamin Franks, the jeweller, made this statement in his deposition at Bombay. 'Thence we sailed for India and touched at a place called Motta, where the natives refused us water, whereupon the Captain sent two armed boats ashore, which brought off provisions and six natives, for two of whom he demanded and obtained two cows and two sheep ransom. The other four escaped.'[1]

This sounds a bit like kidnapping doesn't it? That would mean that Kidd had indeed crossed the line in Motta. However, any doubt about his crew turning to piracy was removed before they reached the coast of Saint John.

Far south of the highlands of Saint John, their intended destination, a sail was spotted by the lookouts in the crow's-nest. Kidd ordered more sail to be raised and the *Adventure Galley* surged forward slicing rapidly through the waves giving chase. Gun crews manned their cannon, waiting for the orders to fire. Their target was a small local trader out of Bombay. But it was no pirate: it was flying English colours. There are many different accounts of what took place but this is a crucial incident in Kidd's career because it really is the moment when he or his crew turns to piracy.

To stop the trader, the *Adventure Galley* fired a shot across its bow and the ship hove to. The boat from this vessel was lowered into the water with the captain and rowed over to the *Adventure Galley*. Captain Thomas Parker came aboard and was taken into Kidd's cabin by Walker, the quartermaster.[2] There the three men talked. Meanwhile, some of Kidd's crew, having sailed so long with nothing to show for it and having lost the opportunity of attacking one of the rich Muslim ships, could stand it no more and went aboard Parker's ship. They were led by William Moore, the gunner and chief troublemaker.

They grabbed some of the crew and hoisted them up on ropes, their shoulders straining, their muscles slowly tearing. Then, the same men were beaten with naked cutlasses to force them to tell where the wealth was hidden. All that was found was 100 pieces of eight, a paltry sum for which these men had been tortured. Nicholas Alderson, a crewmate aboard the *Adventure Galley*, said in his deposition that they 'chased and plundered a ship under English colours. The people were tortured to make them confess where the money was, and the master was carried off to act as pilot.'³ Moore and his boarding party plundered the stores, taking several coffee bales, plumb lines, instruments for navigation, a large sack of pepper and Arabian gold.

This ship was probably the *Mary* and had a crew of a dozen 'Moors' or dark-skinned Indian natives. It was heading for Bombay out of Aden and some historians state that there were passengers aboard: five Portuguese monks along with a Portuguese interpreter. Its owner was a local broker for the East India Company based in Bombay.⁴

In his account of the incident with the *Mary*, Johnson wrote: 'The master was an English man, his name was Parker. Kidd forced him and a Portuguese that was called Don Antonio, which were all the Europeans on board, to take on with them; the first he designed as a pilot, and the last an interpreter.'

The details of this incident are sketchy indeed. We have Alderson's deposition as well as the testimonies of the five monks, which were taken sometime later and are now filed under the India Office papers at the British Library (IOR #6444). While the details are in some cases contradictory there is one exception. All of the sources that mention this incident are unanimous in one thing – that the men of Parker's ship were tortured for money. Whether Kidd was in his cabin all the time with Parker and knew nothing of what happened or whether he ordered it to take place is irrelevant. His crew carried it out and the captain was responsible for his crew and his ship. Without a doubt Kidd had crossed the line. He forced Parker to stay on board because he knew the waters very well and the Portuguese interpreter stayed on board as well. From Parker's ship he transferred food and water and then let it go.

Franks, who didn't see what was going on because he lay sick in his bunk, said he heard 'a great noise' which may have been Moore and the others torturing the Moors. According to the monks' testimony, when Kidd found out what his crew had done he ordered them to return everything. 'Two Compasses, six Musquets & Four Bales of Coffee they returned again.' But it was too late, the acts of piracy had been committed and now there was no turning back.⁵

David Cordingly in his book *Under the Black Flag* suggests that this was Kidd's turning point. 'While Kidd was interviewing Captain Parker, some of Kidd's crew tortured Parker's men to find out where they had hidden their valuables. Several seamen were hoisted up on ropes and beaten with cutlasses. Kidd then seized provisions form Parker's vessel and forced him to stay on board and act as a pilot.'

So now Kidd the privateer and pirate hunter, two legal roles he had monumentally failed in, was faced with a reality he probably didn't want to admit – that he was a pirate. That's why this incident is so important in the final voyage of Captain Kidd because from this moment on he was considered a pirate and wherever he would put into port his reputation as a pirate preceded him.

After letting the *Mary* go, Kidd continued heading for India. His supplies were so low that he had no choice but to find a port as soon as possible. The crew were hungry, thirsty and dressed in rags and to make matters worse the ship itself was in a bad way. Turning south they sailed past Bombay and into the harbour at Carwar (Karwar), dropping anchor on 3 September. Carwar was owned by the East India Company and the agents here were in regular touch by letter with the Company HQ in Bombay. Reports and letters sent from the Bombay HQ to England relating to acts of piracy in the area stated that Kidd was 'a pirate who has done much mischief in those parts'.

Wherever he landed in this area he would either be setting foot on land owned by the East India Company or he would meet their agents. This was the case in Carwar. Remember Captain Clarke and Commodore Warren? Both men when they had gone ashore had ensured that officials of the Company heard their tales of Captain Kidd the notorious pirate. So his reputation as a pirate was building. Time was now running out for him and he personally hadn't done anything wrong yet.[6]

One of the most powerful organizations at the time in the world, the East India Company, started life during the Tudor years when it was granted a Royal Charter by Queen Elizabeth I in 1600 (three years before she died). Though its headquarters were in London the Company stretched its tentacles far and wide across the globe and was at the forefront of British colonial expansion. As this expansion increased the East India Company was transformed from an influential organization based on commerce to a force of political and economic control. It virtually ruled India and would be the most significant player in the formation of the British Raj. However, when Kidd sailed into Carwar, the Company was based on a combination of military and government influence controlling extraordinary levels of wealth and trade.

Kidd was now desperate for wood and water. As his men came ashore the two East India Company agents, Thomas Pattel and John Harvey, could not stop them from filling their water casks and buying wood. But they viewed Kidd with great suspicion, the reports and rumours of his acts of piracy having already reached them. 'They did attempt to find out everything they could about the ship and Kidd's plans,' Ritchie wrote.

Apparently Kidd held nothing back from the two agents, who immediately sent a letter off to their headquarters in Bombay stating that Kidd had told them he was a legally commissioned pirate hunter and though he'd been to Johanna, Madagascar, Mohilla and Mocha he'd yet to encounter any pirates or any French vessels. They ended their hasty note to their headquarters by saying that; 'He is now wooding and watering . . . we do not think it is prudent to molest him for fear it should aggravate him to mischief.'

The jeweller, Benjamin Franks, was anxious to go ashore at Carwar, as he wanted to set up business in India and try to re-establish the family fortune. He repeatedly asked Kidd to let him go ashore. Finally Kidd relented. 'He afterwards put into Karwar, where I gave him a beaver hat to let me go ashore, Most of his men seemed dissatisfied and anxious to escape,' Franks said in his deposition dated 10 October 1697.

Nine men crowded into the pinnace that rowed away from the *Adventure Galley* with Franks also aboard. Kidd must have watched the little boat row into the harbour and tie up at the dock. Once in the harbour these men and Franks immediately deserted, 'and from them the company acquired a detailed picture of conditions on board the *Adventure Galley*'. The ship was leaking and much of the wooden hull was rotten with sea worm. Supplies were dwindling fast and they were down to one month of provisions. Worse still was morale. Some historians suggest that Kidd regularly ordered troublemakers to be whipped in order to keep discipline but under the privateer articles corporal punishment had to be agreed by a majority of the crew. So all he could do was impose his will on them.[7]

Two men came aboard the *Adventure Galley* while it was still anchored in Carwar: Captain Perrin and William Mason. Mason had served under Kidd as part of the crew of the *Blessed William* and had been in command of the *Jacob* when it left New York with most of Kidd's crew from the *Blessed William*. Mason had sailed the *Jacob* to India and while they were cruising along the coast a dispute had split the crew and Mason had left the ship at Mangalore along with other crew members. With no other prospects he'd offered his services to the East India Company who decided to use him to negotiate with pirates.[8]

When Mason stepped on board the *Adventure Galley* we can only wonder at how he was greeted by Kidd – as an old friend or suspiciously as he had been one of the men involved in taking the *Blessed William*. But there is no mention of how the two men met. However, Kidd freely told Mason that he was a pirate hunter and had a commission to capture pirate ships and French ships. He told Mason the various places they'd been to but he said nothing about the capture of the *Mary* or that Parker was onboard the *Adventure Galley* confined below decks.

While he was aboard, Mason observed the mood of the crew and the conditions they were living in. On his return to shore, Mason related what he'd seen to the company agents who wrote a report including some of Mason's observations:

> His commission having heretofore procured respect and awe, and this being added to by his own strength, being a very lusty man, fighting with his men on any little occasion, often calling for his pistols and threatening any one that durst speak of anything contrary to his mind to knock out their brains, causing them to dread him, and are very desirous to put off their yoke.[9]

The two East India Company agents at Carwar sent another letter to their Bombay headquarters dated 9 August 1697.

> Two of Captain Kidd's men have come to the factory, who tell us that they

have taken an English vessel at Bombay and have the commander a prisoner on board. They took out of her about £100 of gold and other goods. Their going to Mocha was with full intent to take the Surratt ships, had not the convoys prevented them. They were on the watch for a rich native ship. They intend to take into their own use the first good ship they meet with, as their own is rotten and leaky. We believe he intends to lie off here, so if you send a force against him, it is ten to one that you find him hereabout.[10]

While Kidd remained in Carwar harbour three of his crew quietly slipped over the side and swam ashore. Here, they discovered there was a ship leaving for Goa, a Portuguese colony, and so they climbed aboard and once in Goa offered their services to the Portuguese as well as telling them that the infamous pirate, Captain Kidd, and his ship the *Adventure Galley* was still sitting in Carwar harbour wooding and watering.

At the time, Catholic Portugal was a fading empire, many of her holdings and colonies had been taken from her by France, Spain and Protestant England, the new upstart. The three deserters had handed the Portuguese in India a chance to have a go at the English: even if they weren't the Royal Navy they were still English and should therefore be taught a lesson. They hurriedly sent two ships to Carwar in the hope of catching Kidd in the harbour where they could blockade him and pound him to bits. From the letters the two agents sent to East India Company Headquarters in Bombay we've seen how alarmed they were at Kidd's presence yet Kidd paints a different picture in his own account. 'The gentlemen of the English Factory informed me that the Portuguese were fitting out two men-of-war to take me and advised we should get out to sea.'[11]

In the early hours of 12 September, Kidd ordered the anchor raised and brought Thomas Parker out of confinement back up on deck to act as pilot. As the crew moved quietly over the deck raising the sails, the *Adventure Galley* slipped out of the harbour at Carwar and headed for open sea.

For a few hours all was well until the lookout high up in the crow's-nest spotted two sets of sails heading directly for them. It was the two Portuguese warships and they were closing. As the sun rose on the horizon Kidd could see through his spyglass that the largest warship had 44 guns and the much smaller sister ship had 22 cannon. The gun ports were open ready to fire and they were almost within range. The wind was light and Kidd could have ordered his men to the oars so they could row the ship to safety but, instead, he chose to stay where he was and wait for the two men of war to arrive.

In his account, he wrote 'the said Two Men of War standing for the said Galley; and spoke with him and asked him, Whence he was?' Kidd waited for some time then shouted his reply. 'We are from London.' He then asked them the same question. 'We are from Goa,' came the reply.[12] There was a practice among pirates, privateers and even navies of the day to carry flags of other nations and fly them when it was necessary in order to conceal their real nationality from their enemies or intended targets. So, before the Portuguese could start blasting away at this ship they had to know if this was the notorious Captain Kidd from London.

No guns were fired after this brief exchange. It seemed as if the tension had been dissipated. 'And so we parted,' Kidd wrote in his account. 'Making still along the coast, the Commodore of the said Men of War kept dogging the said Galley all the Night waiting for an Opportunity to board her.' By morning the two warships were within range and to Kidd's surprise the largest one fired six of the great guns at the *Adventure Galley*. Cannonballs ripped into his ship. Shards and splinters of wood whistled through the air, tearing into the exposed skin of Kidd's half-naked crew. Four men were wounded.[13]

Warfare at sea during this time was not a matter of standing off some miles and pounding the other ships with huge naval guns. For the Portuguese warship to have been able to attack Kidd and wound some of his men she would have been running almost parallel to the *Adventure Galley*.

On the *Adventure Galley* the crew moved quickly to their battle stations while the powder monkeys carried gunpowder and cannonballs to the gun crews. More shots were fired by the Portuguese warship. Splinters flew below decks as cannonballs smashed into the wooden hull and men screamed in pain.

Kidd was down another four men wounded and out of the battle. All the while Kidd had been returning fire but realizing he was outgunned he decided to run. 'But finding her too strong to be taken, he quitted her, for he was able to run away from her when he would.'[14] Even though the wind was light Kidd ordered as much sail as possible and used the speed of the *Adventure Galley* to rapidly pull away from the big 44-gun warship, leaving it far behind. However, the smaller, lighter armed sister warship kept pace with Kidd.

With the big brother far behind, the advantage had changed in Kidd's favour. He suddenly changed direction off the Malabar Coast, hoping to catch what little wind there was. If it caught his sails then he would be in a position to control the fight but if his sails remained limp then the Portuguese ship, even with her smaller number of cannon, could stand off and pound Kidd. For a few anxious moments Kidd waited, then suddenly the wind filled his sails and Kidd was now bearing down on the enemy warship.

The gun crews were ready. As they came up on the smaller ship Kidd shouted for his guns to open fire and they raked the enemy vessel with their side cannon. His cannonballs smashed the rigging and masts of the enemy ship, bringing the mast down. More balls plastered into the side, smashing wood, sending shards of it into the decks where the men were. 'The fight continued all the day', Kidd wrote.

By now the wind had died away, leaving the sea calm and smooth. 'The other Portuguese lay some distance off and could not come up with the Galley, being calm', Kidd wrote in his account. But Kidd did not come away from the fight unscathed. Eleven of his men were wounded. 'The fight was sharp and the

Portuguese left with such satisfaction that no Portuguese will ever attack the King's colours again in that part of the world especially', Kidd wrote.

The *Adventure Galley* was now in a bad way and although Kidd was victorious in the fight his ship was battle-damaged, sea-ravaged and leaking. Something had to be done but up and down the Indian Coast word was spreading about this infamous pirate Captain Kidd, making it difficult for him to put into harbour for supplies, water and wood and to repair his leaky ship. Reports from the East India Company were branding him as a notorious pirate and murderer. For example, in his journal, Barlow wrote that at the Maldives island chain Kidd took the boats of the natives and broke them into pieces to use as firewood, and that he forced the people to work for him for nothing. Barlow also claimed that Kidd's men ravished the native women and as a result the islanders killed Kidd's carpenter by slitting his throat. Kidd's men went on a rampage, according to Barlow, and killed several of the natives and took whatever they wanted.

This incident that Barlow describes as taking place in the Maldives Ritchie places in the Laccadive Islands. 'They used the local boats for firewood and raped a number of the native women,' Ritchie wrote. 'In revenge the ship's cooper had his throat slit, an act that elicited a savage response from the crew, who attacked a village, killing and maiming the inhabitants before retreating to the ship.' In his own account, Kidd doesn't mention this stop, just as he doesn't mention the incident with the *Mary*. But this incident was put on record, Ritchie states, 'when the islanders went to the mainland to complain about the behaviour of the pirates'.[15]

How accurate the details are for this incident we don't know but like every myth or story or legend it is embellished in the retelling. With reports like this coming into Bombay any doubt that the East India Company officials may have had about Kidd being a pirate were gone. So what was being done about apprehending Kidd? If he showed up at any of the English colonies on the Atlantic Coast of America the Secretary of State had commanded the governors of those colonies to 'search and seize him if he came within their reach'.

In Kidd's day communications of any sort was a slow process. Any requests to send warships to India from Britain would take as long to send as the ship that carried the request. Travelling overland was just as difficult and dangerous, so this time-consuming snail pace of communications worked in Kidd's favour as well as against him because he couldn't plead his case without heading for home: another long and difficult journey. But if he returned triumphantly with a French prize or a captured pirate prize then that might soften things up a bit for him.

So he continued sailing along the Malabar Coast heading southwards, tracing the coastline, waiting for pirates to appear. With the ship in such poor shape he couldn't get involved in another major battle.

He stopped at Calicut, a major depot for pepper and owned by the East India Company. Kidd sailed in boldly firing off his cannon to announce his presence. Such an action made the head of the factory and representative of the Company very suspicious. Thomas Penning (Pennynge according to Ritchie) had already received reports about Kidd from Bombay headquarters and from ships that had come into the harbour. To discover what this strange ship wanted, Penning sent a boat out to investigate 'but Walker cut it off and returned to shore with it, not allowing anyone to get too close to the *Adventure Galley*', Ritchie wrote. The note that Walker brought from Kidd stated 'I cant but admire the People is so fearful to come near us, for I have used all possible means to let them understand that I am an English man and a friend, not offering to molest any of their Canoes, so thought it convenient to write this, that you may understand whom I am, which I hope may end all suspicion.' The note went on to say that he was from England and had the King's commission to hunt pirates and that all he was interested in doing was to wood and water. In addition he promised that he and his crew would pay for anything they took or used.[16]

There was nothing Penning could do so Kidd began his wooding and watering. But this didn't last long as another East India Company merchantman was spotted on the horizon heading for the port. Kidd had to leave: on 7 October he weighed anchor and headed out to sea. Penning immediately sent his report to Bombay Company headquarters and that report is now on file with the British Library.

Shortly out of Calicut a sail was sighted on the horizon and Kidd gave orders to pile on as much sail as they could muster. He was flying French colours but the other ship the *Thankful* commanded by Captain Charles Perrin continued to fly his English colours. 'Kidd, dropping his French flags at the last moment, ran up the king's jack and pendant and ordered Perrin on board.' Once aboard the *Adventure Galley*, Kidd questioned Perrin extensively about his knowledge of the area and where the Moor ships were but Perrin knew nothing and was freed by Kidd.[17]

A few days later, the lookout in the crow's-nest of the *Adventure Galley* spotted a sail on the horizon and the men hurried to their posts, the decks a heaving hive of activity as sails were raised to their fullest. With the wind filling his canvas Kidd ordered his helmsman to give chase to the ship and the *Adventure Galley* sliced through the waves heading for its prey.

But his luck was as bad as ever and this ship turned out to be yet another East India Company ship. This ship was the *Loyal Captain* under the command of Captain Howe and as it came alongside the *Adventure Galley*, Kidd ordered Howe aboard. The ship was on its way to Surat. According to some sources Howe already knew about Kidd, having met with Captain Gifford of the *Sydney* a few months previously, as well as hearing various reports from Company agents about Kidd. The last thing he wanted was for his ship to be taken so he came aboard quickly and willingly so that Kidd could examine his pass. Despite the events that had already taken place Kidd was still behaving as if he was a legally commissioned privateer.[18]

On board the *Adventure Galley*, Howe was respectful, civil and smiling to Kidd when the Scot showed him his commission from the King. But it was an act and all he wanted to do was get away. While the two captains were talking Kidd's crew mingled with the sailors who had come over with Howe. 'But having two Dutchmen on board, they said that they had Greek and Armenians on board, who had precious Stones and other rich Goods on board.'[19]

When his crew heard that there were riches on the other ship the temptation was too much to bear. They'd existed for so long on a percentage share of nothing and finally the riches they signed on for were within their grasp. The crew were tired, hungry, frustrated and disillusioned. They wanted something for all their work and effort and hard times they'd been through. Plundering the *Loyal Captain* was the best option.

So piracy it was as Kidd's chief gunner, William Moore, goaded many of the men to take up arms and board the *Loyal Captain*. 'They swore they would take the Ship; and two-thirds of his men voted for the same', Kidd wrote in his account. By now the *Loyal Captain* was tied up alongside the *Adventure Galley* as Moore ensured some of the key mutineers got guns and the rest of the men prepared to board the other vessel. But the mutinous crew were thwarted when Kidd and Howe came on deck and Kidd imposed his will again, demanding the guns be returned. 'Kidd refused to give them arms and raged at them not to leave the ship. Captain Howe helped him by swearing he carried nothing but sugar.'[20]

Standing firm, the men demanded that the English ship be taken. Emotions were running high as Kidd shouted over the noise of the men. 'I shall not take her. I have not come to take any Englishman or lawful Traders. If you desert my ship you shall never come aboard again. I will force you into Bombay and I will carry you before some of the council there,' Kidd wrote in his account.

It must be remembered at this juncture that Kidd wrote his account when he was in prison in Boston so he had to put himself in the best possible light in order to redeem himself. 'I could scarce restrain them,' Kidd wrote. 'But I at last prevailed and with much ado got clear. All of which Captain Howe will attest.'

The stand-off continued for a few minutes then the men backed down. Once again, Kidd had imposed his will on them but it was only a matter of time before that would no longer be effective. When Howe managed to leave the *Adventure Galley* he sailed away as fast as the wind would allow him, not wanting to be caught up in the unhappiness aboard Kidd's ship.

If Kidd was going to satisfy his crew in any way he needed a prize full of treasure and he needed it fast. So he continued to cruise off the Malabar Coast for the next ten days searching for pirates. Fresh water was now at a premium aboard the *Adventure Galley* as was edible food. Dissent and mutiny however lay just below the surface, chiefly stoked by Moore . . .

After ten days of cruising and finding nothing a sail was sighted in the distance. But again Kidd's luck was bad as this turned out to be a Dutch ship. 'I was coming up within a league of the Dutchman and some of my men were making a mutiny about taking her.'[21] Because the English and the Dutch were allies Kidd refused to plunder this Dutch vessel according to his later testimony. Moore was sitting on deck sharpening a chisel or as the cook Abel Owens said, 'The gunner was grinding a chisel on the grindstone.'

According to Kidd he overheard Moore say to the crew nearby him that 'I can put the captain in the way to take the Dutch ship and be safe.' Kidd turned to him. 'How will you do that?' 'We will get the captain and men aboard?' 'And what then?'

'We will go aboard the ship, and plunder her, and we will have it under their hands that we did not take her', Moore replied. Kidd refused, saying 'This is Judas-like I dare not do such a thing.' Now the exchange was getting heated as Moore retorted. 'You may do it, we are beggars already.' Pacing the deck in a fury Kidd shouted at the gunner. 'May we take this ship because we are poor?'

Kidd in his defence said he was so furious about this exchange that he just picked up the closest thing, which was a bucket, and threw it at Moore. Witnesses such as Joseph Palmer and Abel Owens said the exchange continued with Moore shouting 'You have brought us to ruin and we are desolate.' 'I have brought you to ruin,' Kidd retorted. 'I have not brought you to ruin. I have not done an ill thing to ruin you: you are a saucy fellow to give me these words.'[22]

Kidd was furious, bellowing out these last words. Inside him something must have snapped as he grabbed the bucket which had iron hoops and swung it at Moore hitting him a full blow on the side of the head.[23] Moore fell to the deck, dropping the chisel. As he was taken down to the gun room Moore was heard saying, 'Captain Kidd has given me my last blow.' The following day the gunner died. Indeed, at Kidd's trial Robert Bradinham, the ship's surgeon stated that 'the wound was small, but the skull was fractured. I believe he died of the wound.'

Was this premeditated murder? From witnesses like Abel Owens and William Jenkins it seems as if rage overcame Kidd and he simply lashed out at the gunner with the closest thing he could find. 'This dispute was the occasion of an accident, upon which an indictment was afterwards grounded against Kidd.'[24]

But Joseph Palmer who deserted Kidd and was later questioned by Bellomont in Boston had a different story to tell. He said that when Kidd asked Moore how he could take the Dutch ship and be clear, Moore replied that he never said such a thing upon which Kidd called him a 'lousy dog'. Palmer then testified that Moore said that Kidd had made him a 'lousy dog' and had ruined him (Moore) and everyone else. It's at this point that Palmer's testimony becomes damning for he stated under oath that 'Moore was not struck immediately after he had answered Captain Kidd, but after the latter had paced up and down the deck once or twice.'

So it is Palmer's testimony given formally under oath that sets the stage for the indictment of murder against Kidd.[25] The ship's surgeon added an extra nail into Kidd's coffin by testifying that two months after Moore's death Kidd said 'I do not care so much for the death of my gunner, as for the passages of my voyage: for I have good friends in England that will bring me off for that.'[26]

Though some testified that the act of violence was an accident Palmer's testimony shows that Kidd when he paced the deck must have thought about attacking Moore. The fact that he hesitated before picking up the bucket is what damns him. Although it is interesting to note that Palmer is the only one who testifies that Kidd paced the deck before he picked up the bucket and struck Moore with it. The rest of the testimonies all say that he simply picked up the bucket and hit the gunner. No one stated that Kidd threw the bucket at Moore.

Shocked by his violence the crew were cowed but mutiny and dissent lingered under the surface. Kidd's exploits as a pirate were being circulated by the East India Company agents and officials up and down the Malabar Coast so any port he put into he would likely find a reception committee. It must have seemed to him that everyone on land was against him and just about every ship he encountered was against him, as were most of his crew.[27]

Indeed this is shown in Captain Johnson's account of Kidd and the incident with the *Mary* where Captain Thomas Parker was forced to come aboard the *Adventure Galley* to act as master and kept below decks as a prisoner when he wasn't needed. Johnson states that 'news of what he (Kidd) had done to the Moorish Ship had reach'd them; for some of the English Merchants there received an Account of it from the Owners; wherefore, as soon as Kidd came in, he was suspected to be the Person who committed this Piracy'.

On 3 November 1697 he sailed into Tellicherry for food, wood and water. Owned by the East India Company Tellicherry was a well fortified pepper factory with a harbour on the Malabar Coast and had a battery of cannon on its high walls. The *Sceptre*, still under the command of Edward Barlow, had got there first and Barlow wasted no time telling the Company agents there about his encounters with Kidd and his piratical ways. Armed with these reports the factory prepared for Kidd's arrival. When the *Adventure Galley* did sail into the harbour Kidd must have been shocked to find cannonballs raining down in the water all around him. He immediately raised his sails and left the harbour, raising French colours in place of the English ones he was flying when he entered it.[28]

Continuing his voyage, Kidd headed south and finally his luck changed. Around the 18 or 19 November Kidd wrote that the *Adventure Galley* crossed paths with a 'Moors' ship of about 200 tons that was sailing out of Surat. Calling for more sail, Kidd shouted for the helmsman to change course and give chase to the unknown ship. According to Robert Ritchie this ship was the *Rupparell* and Kidd approached it still flying French colours.

Now a game of cat and mouse began which, according to apprentice William Jenkins, lasted about nine hours until the *Adventure Galley* finally came alongside the *Rupparell*. 'Then Captain Kidd ordered that two shots be fired at the same, to bring her to; whereupon she accordingly brought to, and the Master, being a Dutchman came onboard.' Crewman Hugh Parrot confirmed this in his testimony but interestingly he and Jenkins give a different name for the Dutch skipper. Parrot said in his testimony that the Dutch master's name was Mich Dicker and Jenkins that he was 'Skipper John'.[29]

The Dutch captain, according to Ritchie, was Michael Dickers and he was ordered aboard the *Adventure Galley* to show his pass. One of the French pirates who had joined Kidd at Johanna acted as the captain of the *Adventure Galley* when Dickers came on board. Kidd was still flying French colours so Dickers thought he was facing a French ship and showed his French pass. At that point Kidd said: 'My God have I catched you? You are a free prize!'

Under his commission, Kidd was legally entitled to take French ships and here was a French pass so finally his luck had turned and he had something to show for all the hardship and hard work he and his crew had endured. It was a Dutch-owned vessel but as Dickers had shown the French pass it gave Kidd the legality he needed.

Carrying an unusual cargo of horses, sugar and cotton, the ship was destined for trade in Malabar. Various testimonies put the number of crew between twenty and fifty, mostly Moors with three Dutch officers. Jenkins testified that there were between twenty and thirty Moors onboard while Hugh Parrot thought there were about fifty in total. Several of these, including the pilot, were soon to join the crew of the *Adventure Galley*.[30]

This is confirmed by the testimony of Hugh Parrot who stated that Dickers 'declared, that his ship and lading was lawful Prize: and accordingly was made Prize of by the said Kidd and Company: the Dutch Master remained in the Galley with the other Two Dutchmen and took up arms to serve under Captain Kidd'.[31]

Finally they had something to show for their hard work. The crew originally renamed the *Rupparell* the *Maiden* as it was their first prize but a short time later they voted to change the name to the *November* after the month in which it was captured, according to Ritchie. Aside from the horses, sugar and cotton there were two chests of opium and some quilts. In order for Kidd to keep the crew happy he needed to sell the cargo fast and divide up the shares amongst his men so they sailed for the port of Caliquilon, a little north of Anjengo. Here, Kidd sold the cargo to a renegade East India Company employee, which only helped to fuel the fears of local merchants that Kidd was in fact in league with the Company.[32]

All the money from the sale of the goods was divided up amongst the crew and it was enough to keep the men in line for a little while.[33] In addition to the three Dutchmen who came across to the *Adventure Galley* some of the Moor crew from the *November* also joined Kidd and were put to use manning the pumps in his leaky ship. The rest of the *November* crew took the lifeboats and rowed into Calicut where, of course, they told the story of Kidd taking their ship.

With the *November* attached to the *Adventure Galley* by a towline and a handful of trusted men placed on board Kidd continued his voyage down the Malabar Coast for almost two months. Around about December 1697 Kidd captured a small ketch carrying sugar and coffee, which eased his supply problems somewhat. Two weeks after that they robbed a Portuguese ship that was carrying a cargo of rice, iron, butter and cloth. Kidd doesn't mention these in his own depositions and accounts but some of the crew including Bradinham testified during their trials that these incidents did take place. If true then these were definite acts of piracy and Kidd had nothing he could hide behind in terms of legality of his actions. He and his crew robbed these ships pure and simple, if the testimonies are to be believed. However, the East India Company who made extensive documents about Kidd's activities do not mention these incidents and as Kidd would not be able to use Caliquilon as an infrequent base where he could trade with the locals if he was attacking and robbing them.[34]

While the *Adventure Galley* and the *November* continued their hunt for bigger prizes Muslim merchant ships sailed up and down the same busy coastline without ever encountering the pirate until 30 January 1698. High in the crow's-nest the lookout spied the white sails of a large ship on the horizon. Staring at it through the spyglass Kidd could see it was a large ship but what was it? Was it another East India Company vessel or a Royal Navy warship? He needed to get closer so he ordered more sail and gave chase. 'Having chased her about Four hours came up with the same, the said Galley having aboard French Colours, and the other Ship Armenian: which Ship was of the Burden of about 400 Tons.'[35]

Luckily for Kidd this vessel wasn't East India Company or Royal Navy it was a huge merchant ship, the *Quedagh Merchant*. In his own account Kidd wrote 'Upon the same coast, we cruised under French colours with a design to decoy and met with a Bengal merchantman belonging to Surat, 4 or 500 tons, 10 guns.'

In his account Kidd states that the captain was a Frenchman. 'The Commander, a Frenchman from the French factory at Surat, and the gunner came on board as Master. Then I caused the English colours to be hoisted. The Master was surprised and said, "Here is a good prize," and delivered him the French pass.'

However, this Frenchman was in fact the gunner sent over by the real commander, Captain Wright, who was English, 'and he had on board Two Dutchmen, who were mates of the said Ship; and a Frenchman, who was a gunner; six or eight Armenians; and the rest of the Company Moors being about Ninety in Number: all of which Captain Kidd sent ashore in the Boats that came off the said Ship'. So stated William Jenkins in his deposition. However, interestingly, Captain Johnson in his account of Captain Kidd states that Kidd told Wright he was a prisoner.[36]

So the big prize had finally crossed Kidd's path and it carried a cargo of muslin, calico, opium, silk, sugar, saltpetre (potassium nitrate used in gunpowder), anchors, guns and iron, along with a variety of other goods. This cargo, valued by some historians at around £50,000, would have more than doubled the investment of the men who backed the *Adventure Galley*.[37]

Kidd and his crew must have thought they'd finally struck it rich with this prize. The French pass that the French gunner had given to Kidd enabled the *Quedah Merchant* to freely trade in all the ports up and down the coast was a legal pass, so taking this prize was a legitimate action for Kidd.

Johnson argues that Wright was the master of the ship because 'the Indians often make use of English or Dutch men to command their ships, their own mariners not being so good artists in navigation'. This explains why Wright was commanding a ship that had a crew of different nationalities and showed that he had no allegiance to the cargo or the owners. Indeed, Johnson states that the Armenians were part owners of the cargo.

The Armenians were desperate to get the ship back and offered Kidd 20,000 rupees, 'not quite three thousand pounds sterling; but Kidd judged this would be making a bad bargain, wherefore he rejected it', Johnson wrote in his account of Kidd. The reason the Armenians were desperate to get the ship was, according to some historians, because there was more cargo aboard than Kidd originally thought. This additional cargo forms the basis of the legend of Kidd's buried treasure. Lord Bellomont wrote to the Council of Trade and Plantations on 31 August 1699 that Kidd was trying to sell 'threescore pound weight of gold in dust and ingots, about a hundred weight in silver and several other things'. He goes on to say that Kidd 'sent jewels by Campbell to my wife'.

Some sources say that Kidd found this treasure locked away in a chest in the captain's cabin of the *Quedah Merchant*.[38] He certainly did find some form of treasure on that ship over and above the cargo she was carrying because Bellomont issued an order to seize Kidd's goods which is dated 7 July 1699. In Kidd's personal box they found several bags of silver bars, an enamelled silver box 'in which are Four Diamonds set in Gold Lockets. One Diamond loose, one large Diamond set in a Gold Ring.' In Kidd's chest they found 'Two Silver Basins, Two Silver Candlesticks, One Silver Porringer, and some things of Silver Quantity.' Also sixty-seven small and large rubies were found along with two green stones and one large lodestone. These items were only a small portion of Kidd's treasure. For example, Bellomont's inventory shows that John Gardner, whom we will look at later, received several bags of gold dust, gold coins, bars and jewels, along with other precious stones and goods such as bags of sugar. So the haul from the *Quedah Merchant* for Kidd would have made him a wealthy man had things gone better for him.

According to William Jenkins's deposition, a few days after the *Quedah Merchant* was captured Kidd assembled all the men on deck to put a proposal to them. 'He proposed to them to return the said Ship to those from whom they had taken her, or sell her to them.' In this instance Kidd said he would agree to whatever the men wanted to do but he cautioned them that the taking of this huge ship would 'make a great Noise in England'.

The crew voted in favour of keeping the ship as a prize rather than selling it back to the owners: 'But the Company of the Galley agreed not to the said Captain Kidd's proposal.' We don't know if this was before or after the Armenians offered Kidd 20,000 rupees for the ship.

Instead, the crew voted to sail for Sainte Marie off Madagascar. It is interesting at this point in the voyage that Kidd decides to go with the desire of the crew – one of the few times we see him doing this. Most of the time he'd imposed his will but this time he was content to get away from the Malabar Coast and head for pirate haven on Sainte Marie. The *Adventure Galley* now was so leaky that the pumps needed to be manned night and day; perhaps he thought he could get it into a safe harbour where it could be completely repaired before he headed home? We will never know. But he now had two French passes, one he'd taken from the *Rupparell* and one from the *Quedah Merchant*.

It was now early February 1698 and Kidd's time was running out on the Indian Coast. The monsoon season was coming: the northwest wind would die away to that of a shallow breath ushering in the torrential rainy season and strong southwest monsoon. If Kidd didn't leave then he would be locked into the coast for the entire season until October. But he couldn't stay on the coast because there was nowhere friendly enough for him to carry out the major repairs needed to keep the *Adventure Galley* afloat. It would not survive the torrential rains, high winds and heavy seas of the monsoon season. So he had to leave.

Around this time they took a small Portuguese ship which Kidd decided to keep as an escort and it was towed by the *November* (formerly the *Rupparell*). Kidd's crew plundered this unfortunate vessel while Kidd turned a blind eye, presumably because of the fight he'd had against the two Portuguese warships.[39]

Kidd continued to use Caliquilon as his base, trading with the local merchants and presumably the renegade East India Company employee. Johnson stated in his account of Kidd disposing of the cargo from the *Quedah Merchant* that 'he soon sold as much of the cargo as came to near ten thousand pounds'. He also exchanged some of the cargo for provisions and supplies. 'By degrees he disposed of the whole cargo, and when the division was made, it came to about two hundred pounds a man, having reserved forty shares to himself, his dividend amounted to about eight thousand pounds.' The Indian merchants freely traded with him, coming out in boats to buy his goods or meeting the boats from the ship on shore to trade with him. However, Johnson paints a bad picture of Kidd when he states that as the pirate was preparing to leave he took the goods the Indians gave him without paying them.

It may be that he did this because he was in a hurry to leave. The monsoon season was almost upon him, his ship was leaking and another group of ships had been seen heading his way. 'One evening they sighted a group of five ships bearing down on them, but darkness intervened.' Shortening his sail Kidd decided to wait until the morning to see who these ships were. When the sun came up Kidd could see that the largest of the ships was still nearby and that it was an East India Company ship, the *Dorrill*. 'Her companions were two Dutch ships, a Portuguese ship and the *Blessing*, a small company ship.'[40]

Was Kidd in the middle of some transactions when these ships hove into view? This is not what Johnson states. 'He made no scruple in taking their goods, and setting them on shore without any payment in money or goods, which they little expected; for as they had been used to deal with pirates, they always found them men of honour in the way of trade.' Perhaps Kidd didn't have a choice and Johnson in his account took a small incident and blew it up out of proportion to thrill his readers.

Kidd turned away from this group of ships as quickly as he could. The haste of his departure is seen in the fact that the *November* cut lose the Portuguese prize it was towing, which we know from the account of William Jenkins.[41]

Ritchie provides us with another illustration of Kidd's pressing need to leave with the incident where he decided to chase another East India Company ship, the *Sedgewick* in a particularly calm sea. He should have been able to catch up with this ship using the oars aboard the *Adventure Galley* but he couldn't so he gave up the chase. 'If Kidd could not capture a fully loaded merchantmen, he might was well leave the Malabar Coast.'[42] The *Adventure Galley* was still Kidd's only fighting ship and with it being so leaky and unable to catch a merchantman he wouldn't have much of a chance in an open fight so he had to find landfall in a place where he could spend time doing major repairs or scuttle the ship altogether. 'The said Galley was so leaky that they feared she would have sunk every hour, and it required Eight men every Two Glasses to keep her free; and was forced to woold her round with Cables to keep her together.'[43]

The teams of eight men manning the pumps came largely from a Moorish ketch the crew of the *Adventure Galley* had captured and stripped of everything practical that they would need for the long voyage across the Indian Ocean. Kidd allowed Captain Wright and Captain Parker to board the ketch and sail to freedom. Dickers now took over from Parker as master to guide Kidd across the ocean. As they headed out into open sea Kidd was now in command of a small flotilla consisting of the *Adventure Galley*, the *Quedah Merchant* and the *November*. Having been through so much hardship just to get the two prizes he now had there was no way Kidd was going to leave the Malabar Coast without them. Ahead of them were months at sea as they crossed the Indian Ocean heading for the pirate haven of Sainte Marie off Madagascar.

Mutiny in Africa

Early in April 1698 the sea-ravaged *Adventure Galley* arrived at the island of Sainte Marie. For two months the ship had struggled across the Indian Ocean, the pumps below decks worked constantly. The crew and Kidd were exhausted. The only saving grace was that they had not seen another ship, for they were in no condition to engage them. The *Adventure Galley* was on its last legs. The poor construction, long periods at sea, battle damage and the sea worms had taken their toll and now the ship was falling apart.

The island of Sainte Marie had originally been populated by Jewish and Arab traders some centuries before but by 1596 the Dutch and the Portuguese arrived. In 1643 the French also arrived and the many coves and little bays made the island a perfect place for pirates. Men such as Thomas White, Thomas Tew and David Williams were known to have used these coves and inlets as their bases to hide their ill-gotten gains and careen their ships without any prying eyes. There was also one other pirate who regularly used the island as his base and whom Kidd already knew: Robert Culliford.[1]

The island is about ten miles from the northeastern coast of Madagascar. Sainte Marie is a long, narrow strip of land with a bulge in the middle and an excellent harbour at the southwestern end that attracted the pirates to the island. The climate is very hot and humid, with October being the best month before the weather deteriorates. It was in the season of bad weather that Kidd and his little fleet were approaching, with temperature averages around 80°F and the average monthly rainfall around 23 inches. Ships approaching the island were met by seas frothed by heavy rain, low dark cloud and dim light that made landfalls appear to just loom up out of the gloom.

By the time they approached the island the *Quedagh Merchant* had been renamed as the *Adventure Prize* and Kidd had put George Bullen, the chief mate, in command of the *Prize* along with some of his other more trustworthy men while he remained aboard the *Adventure Galley*. His fleet of three ships was spread out, with the *November* some distance behind him and the *Adventure Prize* even further away.

Even after selling a large portion of the cargo on the Malabar Coast, there was still a lot left, most of which was the shares belonging to the crew, and it could not all be carried by the *Adventure Galley*. The smaller items such as the locked chest of precious gems and gold Kidd kept aboard the *Adventure Galley* but much of the cargo still remained aboard the *Adventure Prize*, which is confirmed in Hugh Parrot's deposition. He stated under oath that 'when she (the *Quedah Merchant*) arrived at Madagascar, they took out of her all the Bale Goods and shared them among the Galley's Company'.[2]

A few days into April the *Adventure Galley* rounded the northern tip of the island and slowly approached the harbour. The entrance was very narrow and quite vulnerable to whatever was moored in the harbour. Kidd had no idea who might be there so he approached with as much care as his leaking ship would allow.

As feared, another large ship lay moored in the harbour, its guns trained on the entrance. As Kidd brought the *Galley* through the entrance and ordered the anchor to be dropped, a boat full of heavily armed swarthy Europeans approached the ship. They turned out to be pirates that Kidd either knew or who knew of Kidd and knew that he had a commission to hunt pirates. Kidd also knew some of these men because they had been shipmates aboard the *Blessed William*. The man in charge of these pirates was Robert Culliford, who had stolen the *Blessed William* out from under him and left him stranded in Antigua.[3]

In many ways Culliford's life had mirrored Kidd's and been just as eventful. He'd left the *Blessed William* at the Nicobar Islands in the Bay of Bengal and returned to New York. He'd joined William Mason on the *Jacob* and they'd sailed that to India. With Mason, Culliford left the *Jacob* at Mangalore where he offered his services to the East India Company as a gunner serving until 1696 aboard the merchantman *Josiah*.

Some historians suggest that Culliford led a mutiny in June 1696 to seize the *Josiah* while others say he was part of the mutiny. At any rate the mutineers seized the ship and sailed to the Nicobar Islands and while ashore another ship seized the *Josiah* from the mutineers and left them on the beach.[4] Culliford and his men were soon rescued by a ship bound for Bombay where Culliford again offered his services to the East India Company: 'a further indication of the company's desperate need for European sailors, who were cut down in frightful numbers by disease', Ritchie states in his book. Culliford then joined the *Mocha Frigate*, an English East India Company merchantman boasting 40 cannon, a crew of 130 and weighing in at 150 tons.

Ritchie states that Culliford was part of a gang that seized the *Mocha Frigate*, killed the captain and turned pirate. At this point Ralph Stout became captain and they sailed for the Malacca Strait where they captured four ships, including a Portuguese merchantman which they plundered. After this they sailed to the Indian Ocean, arriving at the Maldives Islands to refit but instead ended up looting and burning the local villages.

During a watering expedition in June 1697 Stout was killed and the crew elected Culliford as captain, voting to head for China. On the way towards the Malacca

Strait they took another heavily laden Portuguese ship and as they reached the Strait and began sailing through it Culliford decided to go after an East India Company merchantman, the *Dorrill*.

For three days they chased the merchant ship, trading shots with her, until finally Culliford brought the *Mocha Frigate* alongside but before he could fire his guns the *Dorrill* fired first, completely surprising Culliford. As cannonballs whistled through the air and smashed into the deck, shards of wood flew everywhere. Another shot smashed his main mast, forcing Culliford to pull away before any more damage was taken. He needed to repair his ship before heading for China but, unlike Kidd, Culliford was lucky. As he retreated out of the Strait of Malacca he captured two small Javanese ships and a 300 ton Chinese merchantman. In order to plunder the Chinese ship properly they headed for southern Burma where they anchored in Cape Negrais. But a safe place was needed to repair and refit the *Mocha Frigate* so once the plundering of the Chinese ship was finished they set sail for Sainte Marie 'where they could rest and refit in peace'.[5]

So in the harbour at Sainte Marie the anchor was lowered and Kidd waited for the rest of his ships to arrive. It is at this point that events become unclear. In Kidd's account he states that 'there was a pirate ship, called the *Mocha Frigate*, at Anchor, Robert Culliford, Commander thereof; who with his Men left the same at his coming in, and ran into the Woods'. However, ship's surgeon Robert Bradinham testified that Kidd told Culliford and his men that he was a pirate like they were, 'and went aboard with them and swore to be true to them. He took a cup of bumbo and swore to be true to them and assist them; and he assisted this Captain Culliford with guns, and an anchor to fit him to sea again.'[6]

Joseph Palmer testified that when they arrived at Madagascar and saw the *Mocha Frigate* Kidd said to the crew of that ship after they'd accused him of coming to hang them that he would do them all the good he could. 'And Captain Culliford came aboard of Captain Kidd and Captain Kidd went aboard of Captain Culliford.' Indeed Palmer went on to testify that on the quarter deck the two captains drank together and Kidd said 'Before I would do you any harm I would have my soul fry in hell.'

Getting back to Kidd's account, he claims he wanted to attack Culliford's ship and take it as a prize. Not only did he have a commission to attack pirates and here was one ripe for the taking but he also had a score to settle with Culliford who had taken his first command away from him.

But with the *Adventure Galley* being on its last legs he knew any attack would fail so he had to wait for the other ships to arrive before he did anything. Taking Culliford to Boston with the huge *Mocha Frigate* would have been a feather in Kidd's cap and perhaps Kidd felt it would have excused any crimes he was accused of. So he waited.

According to his account Kidd says the 'Lesser Prize' arrived on 6 May 1698, which would have been the *November*, and it sailed right past the *Adventure Galley*, running aground on the shore. According to Kidd the *November* was 'ransacked and sunk by the mutinous men' that Kidd had put aboard. The crew of the *November* after ransacking the ship poured over the side and went ashore to mix with the natives, especially the women, and to mingle with Culliford's crew.

A few days later the *Adventure Prize* arrived. Over this time most of the crew of both the *Adventure Galley* and the *November* were mingling onshore with the natives and Culliford's crew, as well as buying liquor and women from Edward Welch, a local trader originally from New England who had a fortified compound some four miles from the harbour.

Now with his main prize in the harbour Kidd summoned the crews to the main deck of the *Adventure Prize*. A little over a hundred men arrived and Kidd then told them he wanted to take the *Mocha Frigate*, 'having sufficient Power and Authority to do so'.

Kidd states in his account that the men refused to take Culliford. After so long at sea with very little to show for it they wanted their money, not more promises about how great it would be if they sailed into Boston with the *Mocha* and Culliford. Kidd and his crew were once again at odds. Indeed the response from the crew was that 'If he offered the same, they would rather fire Two Guns into him, than one into the other.' In this case the 'other' was Culliford.[7]

The vast majority of the crew, Kidd tells us, voted with their feet and deserted. 'Thereupon ninety-seven men deserted and went into the *Mocha Frigate*; and sent into the Woods for the said Pirates, and brought the said Culliford and his Men on board again.' This is according to Kidd. No other testimony covers this incident. In the trials virtually every witness states that Kidd was on friendly terms with Culliford and that no one heard Kidd say he wanted to attack Culliford. Only one person in his deposition supported Kidd's account and that was Gabriel Loff, who stated under oath that 'the generality of the men refused saying, they would sooner shoot him, than into the said *Mocha Frigate*: and they went aboard the said Frigate'.

One thing that everyone agrees on is that the majority of Kidd's men deserted him and went aboard Culliford's ship. That left Kidd with less than a third of his crew, which included the sick, injured and cabin boys. Kidd puts the number at thirteen but if we include the Moors he had manning the pumps on the *Adventure Galley* then the number is higher, but probably no more than twenty or thirty men in total. There was no way Kidd could sail even one of his ships or attack Culliford. To make matters worse the *Adventure Galley* was in such a bad way that he could not possibly sail her home or even out of the harbour. This harbour was going to be her final resting place and there was nothing he could do to prevent it.

Again we have differing accounts of events. Kidd states that the crew went on a rampage and ransacked both the *Adventure Galley* and the *Adventure Prize* as they had done the *November* which they later burnt. But William Jenkins stated under oath that the loot taken from the *Adventure Prize* was shared according to the agreements.

Whereupon each of the said Galley's Company, being then about 115 in Number, shared, one with another, three Bales and some loose goods, besides about Two Thirds of a Bale: And Captain Kidd had Forty Shares. The Bales contained Callicoes, Romalls, Muslins, some Silks, some striped, some flowered and some plain. After sharing of the Goods, Ninety and upwards of the Company belonging to the *Galley* deserted and went to the *Mocha Frigate* and Captain Kidd with the Men that remained with him, carried their Shares on board the Prize Ship, and run the Galley onshore, being very leaky, and having stript her of her Furniture, set her on Fire to get her Ironwork.

According to Kidd, at some point he and some of his most trusted men had walked inland four miles to Welch's house carrying Kidd's chest. When this was done we don't know but we do know it was done before the *Mocha Frigate* left. No one else makes mention of this.[8]

Kidd tells us that in both the *Adventure Galley* and the *Adventure Prize* the mutinous crew grabbed anything that wasn't nailed down.

For the space of four or five days, the Deserters sometimes in great numbers, came on board the *Adventure Galley* and *Adventure Prize* and carried away great guns [cannons], powder, shot [cannonballs and small-bore balls for hand weapons], small arms [muskets and swords], sails, anchors, cables, surgeons' chests [including medicinal alcohol and medicines], and what else they pleased.

Indeed, the surgeon Robert Bradinham also deserted, carrying off the surgeon's chest containing ointments, drugs and surgical tools, according to Kidd.[9]

Kidd doesn't give us a reason as to why the crew turned on him in such vast numbers. The assumption we can make is that it was for all the hardship they'd endured and that they wanted paying rather than to try and take the *Mocha Frigate*. They wanted their money then and there. But just about every other deposition tells us they were paid. Indeed Johnson states that as Kidd 'had divided the money before he now made a division of the remainder of the cargo'.

It seems from the depositions and trial transcripts that the only person who talks about the crew rampaging through the ships was Kidd. The witnesses against Kidd testified that he ordered the cargo to be hoisted out of the *Adventure Prize* at Sainte Marie. Chief among these witnesses was Joseph Palmer, who said 'Captain Kidd ordered the goods to be hoisted out.' Kidd replied by asking, 'Did I order the goods to be hoisted out?' 'Yes,' Palmer stated, 'you did.' 'My lord, it was the mutinous men that did it. There were 95 men that deserted my ship, and took away what they pleased: we could not stand in defence of anything.'

The other witness against him was Robert Bradinham, the ship's surgeon, who also stated that the 'Captain divided out the shares.' Kidd responded by saying 'he tells a thousand lies'. To back up his statement about the men taking what they wanted Kidd asked Bradinham the following: 'Did not you come aboard my ship and rob the surgeon's chest?' 'No, I did not', Bradinham replied.

If we believe what Kidd says in his account and at the trial the mutinous men went ashore with their goods to sell whatever they could but the only real wealth around was with Edward Welch. According to Kidd the mutinous men decided to attack him in his cabin one night to slit his throat. Kidd tells us that he was warned of this attempt and kept his guard. The night he was warned of the impending attempt on his life he barricaded himself in his cabin, 'with Bales of Goods; and having about Forty small Arms, besides Pistols ready charged, kept them out'.

Unable to get into to kill Kidd the men realized that the real prize lay in his chest which was kept up at Edward Welch's house. The mutinous men rowed ashore as quickly as they could and made their way to Welch's house where they found Kidd's heavy chest. Smashing it open they found 40 pounds of plate, 10 ounces of gold, 370 pieces of eight, Kidd's journal and 'a great many Papers that belonged to him, and the People of New York that fitted him out'.[10]

If we take Kidd's account at face value then presumably the men were hoping to find a chest full of jewels. We know that Kidd had jewels with him when he was arrested because Bellomont inventoried his possessions, which were largely gold, silver and jewels. However Kidd makes no mention of the chest of jewels in his account.

So Kidd claims that when the men broke open his chest they took everything in it including all his papers and the journal. Presumably these were either destroyed or burnt on the spot. 'He is the only one who claims this happened, so the story is suspect, particularly because it was one that benefited Kidd.'[11]

Under the articles of his agreement Kidd was supposed to keep a detailed record of his voyage as part of being in regular correspondence with Edmund Harrison and ultimately with Bellomont. Without this detailed journal Kidd had to write another much shorter account of his actions when he arrived in Boston.[12]

This raises some interesting questions. First did Kidd actually make a detailed journal as he was supposed to or was he lying about it? Did the men really destroy his journal out of hate for Kidd and out of spite because they couldn't get to him themselves to string him up or is he lying about that too? What if Kidd destroyed the journal himself? If the incident at the Maldives that Barlow wrote about in his report is true, where several natives were killed and maimed by Kidd's men and Kidd ordered one of the natives to be tied to a tree and shot, then that plainly puts him into the realms of piracy even if it was rough justice for the death of one of his own men. If his journal detailed this action it could incriminate him and prove that he was a pirate. 'With that journal destroyed, there was no official record of his travels, thus one of the major pieces of evidence against him no longer existed.'[13]

Also, if Kidd felt that it was so important to hide the journal in his chest and to have that chest lugged four miles inland to Welch's compound, then why not do the same with the French passes from his two prizes? Why didn't he keep them in the chest as well or why not keep the journal close at hand?

The passes were crucial to Kidd's defence. They proved that he was still operating as a legitimate privateer according to his commission and agreements. If Kidd felt keeping the journal in his chest safely ashore was the safest course of action wouldn't he have felt the same about the passes? But if the journal incriminated him and he destroyed it himself he could make up whatever story he liked and would only need to produce the passes to show his innocence. 'He would claim thereafter that the crew had forced him into every illegal deed he committed.'

Unable to get to Kidd, the mutineers joined Robert Culliford as pirates in a situation that almost mirrored Kidd's loss of the *Blessed William*. Yet again, Culliford had come out on top, now having the majority of Kidd's crew at his disposal. There is another point of view that suggests that Kidd was glad his men deserted 'because it meant that fewer witnesses would return home with him'.[14]

On 15 June 1698 the *Mocha Frigate* left the harbour at Sainte Marie with a crew of 130 men (95 of them formerly the crew of the *Adventure Galley*) to plunder any ship from any nation that they chose to attack. Kidd was left stranded on the island with two ships and not enough men to man one of them.

Before the mass mutiny the *Adventure Galley* had barely been afloat, with teams manning the pumps around the clock to keep the ship on the water rather than under it. Perhaps one of the reasons the men mutinied was so they could be aboard a ship that didn't leak and was seaworthy? When the men deserted to Culliford they took with them the men who had been manning the pumps. 'Without them the ship could never remain afloat. It was pushed up on the beach and burned so that the iron fittings could be recovered.'[15]

Across the harbour, the Indian-built larger *Adventure Prize* was Kidd's only lifeline. But he was going to have to wait for the winds and tide to be right before he could sail home. This would give him and those of his remaining crew enough time to agree on a story about what took place on Sainte Marie. That story had to be believable because it was the only thing that would protect them from the authorities and the gallows. Unfortunately, for Kidd the story wasn't good enough.

While he waited for the winds and tides to turn so he could sail away other ships came into the harbour and Kidd was able to increase his crew to some degree. For example, Edward Davis was a boatswain on the merchant ship *Fidelia* travelling from London on a trading voyage to India. Commanded by Tempest Rogers the ship stayed in the harbour for five weeks, according to Davis's deposition, and sailed away when he was still ashore. Kidd took advantage of the situation and signed Davis onto the *Adventure Prize*. Davis said he was left on the island by Tempest Rogers and 'being desirous to get off, entered on board the Ship; whereof Captain Kidd was Commander, to work for his Passage'.

Another individual who joined Kidd at Sainte Marie was James Gilliam, alias James Kelly, alias Sampson Marshall, a hardened pirate who preferred the life at sea. He'd left England in 1680 and had been moving from ship to ship ever since. It's highly likely that Kidd put Gilliam to work as soon as he signed on.[16]

As he waited to set sail Kidd must have taken stock of his situation. On the plus side he had the massive 400 ton *Adventure Prize* (formerly the *Quedagh Merchant*), several thousand pounds worth of gold, silver and jewels as well as thousands of pounds worth of bales in the hold. He also had the French passes taken from the *November* and *Adventure Prize*, which proved that he had taken the ships legally according to his privateering commission.

On the downside, Kidd had personally been beaten by the same man twice. He had virtually no crew. The ship he had was also a liability in that he had few cannon to defend himself, not enough men to man the few guns there were, and the ship was ungainly, huge and not very manoeuvrable. For any American port that Kidd sailed into its Indian design would be so different from any other ships people were used to seeing in their harbours that he might as well have hung out a sign saying 'I'm a Pirate.'

Throughout the voyage, Kidd had fallen foul of the East India Company and the Royal Navy, along with the navies and trading companies of Portugal, France and the Netherlands. Although Kidd had been busy getting the *Adventure Prize* ready for sailing surely he would have had the time to write another account, if not a complete journal, of what went on, with various incriminating bits removed, so that he could present that journal and the passes as proof of his innocence?[17]

Perhaps this is where his arrogance and naiveté come through? At this time he couldn't have known the effort that the East India Company was putting into gathering evidence and building a case against him. He must have heard the stories being circulated about him and must have been aware that he was already branded a notorious pirate. Perhaps he believed that he had the *Adventure Prize* and the French passes and they would be enough to prove his innocence?

If he felt he didn't need a sound defence then that would explain why he didn't write one. Perhaps he felt that all the witnesses who mattered had sailed away with Culliford and so would never be part of his life again? He had no idea he would find himself in the dock with some of those very men.

9

The Most Infamous Pirate Ever

Kidd landed here this day seven night; and I would not so much as speak with him but before witnesses. I thought he looked very guilty and to make me believe so he and his friend Livingston (who posted hither from Albany upon news of Capt. Kidd's design of coming hither) and Campbell aforesaid began to juggle together and embezzle some of the cargo; besides Kidd did strangely trifle with me and the Council three or four times that we had him under examination. (Lord Bellomont)

The East India Company was out to get Kidd. To them he represented everything that had been going wrong with the company for some time. Letting Avery slip through their hands had been a disaster from which the company had not recovered. During the 1680s the company had declared incredible dividends from the profits it made. For a ten-year period between 1678 and 1688 the yearly value of its imports from Asia back to England exceeded £400,000. Prosperity of this magnitude made it the most powerful economic institution in England and certainly one of the most powerful in the world. The company was able to build political friendships during this time by buying influence with the monarchy and the politicians.[1]

But with King William's War and the success of the French privateers attacking and plundering East India Company ships, their fortunes started to turn. A trade depression hit the company hard. For example, from 1689 to 1699 the imports from Asia the company was able to ship fell to a little more than £134,893.[2]

The East India Company backed the Tories but when the political climate changed this caused serious problems for them. In England with Whig dominance rising, a consortium of English textile manufacturers started attacking the company because they resented the wide variety of Indian fabrics that were being imported. This came to a head in 1696 when a bill was introduced into Parliament to restrict the wearing of cloth from India. While the company tried to fight the bill the textile workers in England rioted and in 1701 the bill was finally passed, dealing the company a major blow.

Coupled with this was the explosion of piracy into the East. This wasn't a problem until 1691 when a very large ship belonging one of the leaders of the

Gujarati merchants, Abd-ul-Ghafur, was captured and plundered by pirates at the mouth of the Hoogli River at Surat. Ghafur demanded that the governor and the emperor force the English East India Company to compensate him for his loss, claiming that the pirates were English. There was no evidence of this but on 27 August 1691 English trade was stopped and the English were confined to their factory. Ghafur's asking price was 700,000 rupees or £78,750, which the Company said they would not pay until they knew for sure it was English pirates who had done the deed. It turned out that the pirates were Danish but the governor kept the English locked in their factory until 2 December 1691.

For a few years the company was left to trade in peace until Avery arrived in 1695. His arrival was spectacular: Avery captured and plundered the *Ganj-i-Sawai* and he and his men stripped it of everything. When it finally limped into the harbour at Surat the crew and passengers had many stories to tell about English pirates. Accounts of the women being violated and holy men being killed infuriated the local people who rioted and set siege to the English compound. President Samuel Annesley and sixty-three company employees were arrested by the Governor Ahmanat Khan and thrown in jail for eleven months. Khan had them released on 27 June 1696 but kept their trade embargoed until they agreed to protect all Indian shipping. Finally, after suffering severe losses, they agreed to Khan's demands; all the while the Dutch and the French had been reinforcing the idea that all pirates were English.[3]

The piracy continued. Ghafur lost another ship in the Persian Gulf, local brokers for the company lost ships in the Babs, while five pirates were said to be cruising in the Red Sea. The losses mounted as the captains of merchant ships refused to leave port because the risks were too high that they would be captured. Then the company lost the *Josiah*, the *Gingerlee* and the *Mocha Frigate*, all from crews who mutinied and took the ships away from their captains.[4]

Before Kidd even arrived in the Red Sea the company's officials in Bombay and Surat knew all about him. This information was based on the report that Warren filed at the Cape of Good Hope as well as from captains who had met Kidd in Johanna. Captain John Clarke as we already know wrote a lengthy report about his dealings with Kidd. All of this information on Kidd was sent to the highest ranking company man, Sir John Gayer, who was based in Bombay. When Jonathan Tredway, Nicholas Anderson and Benjamin Franks deserted Kidd they were put through rigorous interrogation by company officials in Surat and these reports were sent to London. In the meantime, Gayer wrote a series of reports that sensationalized Kidd, branding him another Attila the Hun of the high seas. In short, Kidd represented everything the company hated about the unknown and unseen pirates who were tormenting it.

When the *Quedah Merchant* was captured the company again felt the sting of rage from not just the governor but also the emperor himself. The passengers who Kidd set free were a bedraggled lot. Those Muslims and Armenians told exaggerated stories of their capture and the hardships they'd suffered under Kidd. They reported Captain Wright's refusal to fight Kidd and they reported that Kidd had shown them his Royal Commission from King William of England that gave him the right to take the *Quedah Merchant* because of its French pass. Again the populace rose up against the English when stories about Kidd and other pirates were circulated and again the English were forced to take refuge behind the walls of their factory in Surat.[5]

In December 1698 the emperor ordered the European companies to compensate all those victims of piracy and to ensure that all Muslim trade was protected. If they didn't the entire European community would be expelled. In Surat Ahmanat Khan made sure the brunt of this edict fell on the English. He stopped their trade again, had their Muslim brokers beaten, sent soldiers to watch them and ordered the people not to sell them food. In the meantime the French and the Dutch managed to distance themselves from the whole thing, convincing Khan they had nothing to do with piracy, and were freed after paying bribes to him.

When the English did surrender they were ordered to compensate everyone on the *Quedah* who had been victimized by Kidd as well as being ordered to convoy ships from Surat to the Spice Islands. But the next Mocha convoy was attacked by pirates, even though it was being protected by Dutch ships. Ghafur lost another ship and three more were captured. The company was blamed for this attack although they had nothing to do with it.

Having had enough the emperor ordered that all English East India Company factories be closed and their trade stopped. The factory at Surat was plundered to compensate Ghafur, while other company factories were overrun. It was a terrible time for the English East India Company and the beginning of the end for Kidd. 'He came to be identified with the most disastrous years in the company's history.'[6]

Kidd was important to the company because of their inability to arrest and hang Avery. Even though they managed to capture six of his men, Avery slipped through their fingers. The six men were put on trial in London and the trial was meant to be a signal to all the Indian authorities that England and the English East India Company did not tolerate pirates. Unfortunately, for the company officials attending the trial, the jury found the six men not guilty. This was a massive setback but a new trial was convened and the men were found guilty and hung. The effect in India was minimal. The six men were faceless: they were not Avery and the company needed a major figure to put on trial and hung. Kidd was that figure. 'He had form and shape, a past and a future and impressive value as a symbol of all the afflictions besetting the company, afflictions it no longer had any intention of enduring.'[7]

While Kidd had been on his voyage a change had taken place in the English government's policy towards piracy. At the beginning of the decade, in the early 1690s, the constraints of King William's War meant the best the government could do was issue a pardon for those pirates who turned away from their piracy. In the middle of the decade Kidd's voyage to attack piracy was mounted as the government's concern increased. But once he was at sea more measures came into being, a new law was written, those officials in the colonies who looked the other way were recalled and using the navy to protect commerce was greatly increased. In England, a campaign was mounted to make sure that action was taken against piracy. Into this new resolve against piracy Kidd was sailing.

There is no exact date as to when Kidd left Sainte Marie but most sources believe that it was sometime in November 1698 when the wind and tides would have been right for Kidd to set sail towards the West Indies where he arrived in April 1699. Kidd would have had a slow voyage due to the lack of crew to sail the *Adventure Prize* properly and most importantly to the fact that the ship was so ungainly and slow in the water – nothing like the *Adventure Galley*. The wreckage of that ship lay on the beach at Sainte Marie.

King William's War ended in 1697 and the East India Company pressed for naval power to be used to hunt down pirates like Kidd. A squadron of ships, under the command of Commodore Thomas Warren, was dispatched to hunt him down. In a letter to the Council of Trade and Plantations dated 23 December 1698 Secretary of State Sir James Vernon wrote that the pirate stronghold at Sainte Marie should be destroyed.

Warren and his fleet sailed south with the aim of capturing Kidd when he reached the Cape of Good Hope or preferably to get him while he was just out of harbour from Sainte Marie. Warren had the authority to offer a pardon to all those pirates who turned away from piracy but this pardon did not include Kidd and a handful of others. It may be that some of the pirates who did surrender to the authorities and took advantage of the pardon could provide them with information on Kidd's whereabouts. Indeed, they may even have turned pirate hunters themselves.

There was a steady trade between merchants from New York and pirates on Madagascar. This is how mail would be carried between the two destinations. In 1698 four ships left New York heading for Sainte Marie but by November of that year only one had reached Madagascar. This was the *Nassau* under the command of Captain Giles Shelley, a friend of Kidd's. Of the other three ships, we know from High Court of the Admiralty papers held at the Public Records Office that two ships were taken by pirates. The third ship, the *Margaret*, was captured by an East India Company merchantman, the *Loyal Merchant*, with the incident being mentioned in that ship's log. The capture of the *Margaret* must have been quick because her captain didn't have time to throw his papers overboard. Amongst these papers were letters to Kidd.[8]

One of those letters was from James Emot, fellow Scot and Kidd's friend. Emot basically told Kidd not to believe any of the rumours about Lord Bellomont being upset with Kidd. The tone of the letter was reassuring. 'His Lordship did assure me that he ever has a good opinion of Captain Kidd,' Emot wrote. 'I mention this more largely lest these false reports should reach you and thereby put you after measures than what you formerly proposed to me."[9]

Both Livingston and Bellomont wrote Kidd letters asking him to return and Bellomont assured Kidd that he could return to New York rather than going first to Boston as his contract stated. Ritchie tells us that at this time the practice was to send multiple letters via different ships so it is likely that Kidd received this message, though we can't be completely sure. However, it provides some reason for Kidd to return to New York rather than simply disappearing with his loot as other pirates did.

Kidd left Sainte Marie, sailed around the southern tip of Madagascar down the African Coast around the Cape of Good Hope and out into the Atlantic Ocean without getting anywhere near Warren's squadron which was trying to find him. But Ritchie states that Warren died during the voyage so the squadron never reached Sainte Marie and must have been in some disarray.

Once he was safely round the Cape Kidd sailed north up the African Coast and didn't encounter a single ship. At Annobon Island Kidd briefly stopped to take on water and provisions for the long voyage across the Atlantic. Approximately 220 miles west of Equatorial Guinea, this island has an area of less than seven square miles with a crater lake in its centre. With as much provisions as they could carry the *Adventure Prize* left the African coast, heading off across the Atlantic Ocean towards the Caribbean Sea.

After five months, at the beginning of April 1699 Kidd made landfall at Anguilla Island off Barbados, the most easterly island of the Lesser Antilles, and for Kidd it was quiet enough for him to take on fresh food and water. Anguilla was a British colony and when Kidd went ashore to get fresh food he also got some very disturbing news. On 23 November 1698 the English government had sent an alarm to the colonies in the West Indies declaring him a pirate and ordering the colonies to hunt him down and capture him. The alarm also stated that Kidd was one of the few pirates not to be offered a pardon. By the time Kidd arrived this general alarm would have reached most of the colonies in the West Indies.

Kidd still had thirteen loyal men who had been with him almost from the beginning. These were the men left after the mass mutiny at Sainte Marie. But the rest of the crew that Kidd had managed to scrape together must have been scared stiff to have heard the news that Kidd had been declared one of the most notorious pirates that ever lived. What if they were recognized as one of his crew? 'This put them in such consternation that they sought all Opportunity to run the Ship on Shore upon some Reef or Shoal, fearing Kidd should carry them into some English port.'[10]

Kidd had very little room to manoeuvre. Very few ports were open to him and he knew that the Royal Navy and the East India Company were out to get him. He needed a safe refuge to resupply and think about his options. He set sail for the island of St Thomas, a Danish colony that often used as a base for pirates, and about the only island in the Caribbean that wasn't held by the English, the French, the Spanish or the Dutch. Today it is part of the US Virgin Islands.[11]

When he arrived at St Thomas the news was just as bad. In his account he wrote 'My brother-in-law Samuel Bradley was put on shore, being sick; and five men went away and deserted and we heard the same news that we had been Proclaimed Pirates.' When Kidd arrived offshore he sent a message to the governor of St Thomas, John Lawrence, asking permission to enter the harbour. Lawrence sent a Dutchman Peter Smith to Kidd's ship to find out what he was doing in the area. 'If an honest account he might come in and if otherwise to go away.'[12]

Kidd wanted Lawrence to immediately dispatch a sloop up to Nevis to let them know that he was there, presumably to see if his old friend Codrington would vouch for him. 'Kidd was desirous to buy a sloop, but Smith would not sell him one. Then Kidd desired him to supply him with the value of two hundred pounds of provisions and that he would give him for it a sloop-load of bales of muslin and other goods. But Smith refusing to do it went ashore.'[13]

He stayed forty-eight hours at St Thomas, then set sail for the island of Mona between Puerto Rico and Hispaniola.[14] Hispaniola is today the island that is shared between Haiti with the Dominican Republic. The island of Mona (Moona according to some depositions) was originally settled by the Arawak Indians and at Kidd's time was a haven for pirates and privateers. As the *Adventure Prize* entered the harbour approaching sails were spotted and a single-masted sloop came up fast towards them. It was the *St Antonio*, out of Curacao, an island off the coast of Venezuela.[15] In his account, Kidd refers to this island as Curaso while other accounts and depositions refer to it as Curacao. The *St Antonio*, under the command of Samuel Wood, was heading for Antigua. It was owned by Henry Boulton.[16]

Kidd had a problem. His ship was far too big and too noticeable for him to continue his journey and worse he couldn't persuade the men remaining with him to sail the *Adventure Prize* all the way up to Boston: 'I could not persuade the Men to carry her for New England; but Six of them went and carried their Chests and things on board of Two Dutch Sloops bound for Curaso; and would not so much as heal the Vessel, or do anything.'

He made an agreement with Boulton to despatch the *St Antonio* to Curacao 'for Canvas to make Sails for the Prize, she not being able to proceed; and she returned in Ten Days'. It was at this point that his men refused to continue with the *Adventure Prize* to Boston so Kidd needed a new ship. He then moved the *Adventure Prize* to 'St Katharina, on the South East Part of Hispaniola, about Three Leagues to Leeward of the westerly end of Savona', and turned the giant ship into a floating market.[17]

It didn't take long for word to get around that Kidd was selling exotic goods from the East Indies. One small ship after another came alongside and each would pack their holds with the goods Kidd was selling. The two men who benefited the most from Kidd's sale were Henry Boulton and Curacao merchant William Burt.[18]

While Kidd lay at Hispaniola he traded with Boulton and Burt 'to the value of 11,200 Pieces of Eight; whereof he received the sloop *St Antonio* at 3000 Pieces of Eight and 4200 Pieces of Eight by Bills of Exchange drawn by Boulton and Burt upon Messieurs Gabriel and Lemont, Merchants of Curaso'.[19]

In his deposition, Hugh Parrot claimed he'd been robbed of half of his share, which amounted to a total of 400 pieces of eight, while the other half he lost gambling aboard the *St Antonio*.[20] Peter Smith's testimony stated that Burt (Burke) purchased 130 bales of muslin from Kidd and sailed back to St Thomas where the cargo was put ashore but seized by Governor John Lawrence (Laurents), along with the vessel that carried it. 'And said Burke left in the Governor's hands five thousand pieces of eight security for the vessel and went away with her to Barbados.'.[21]

Kidd bought the *St Antonio* from Boulton for 3,000 pieces of eight because he needed a new ship, something small and fast and indistinguishable from many other sloops. The *St Antonio* fitted the bill perfectly.[22] So he and his remaining crew transferred all the cloth, muslin, silks, jewels and gold they'd not sold to the much smaller vessel.

Gabriel Loff testified that Kidd left the *Adventure Prize* with Boulton, stating that Kidd 'leaving the said Boulton, with Seventeen or Eighteen Men, on board the ship, the said Captain Kidd, with several of his Company, proceeded in the said Sloop towards New York and the discourse was, that Captain Kidd was to return to the Ship again within the Space of Three Months'.[23]

Indeed, Samuel Wood, master of the *St Antonio* stated that Kidd provided Boulton with instructions 'to dispose of the Goods, for the Account of himself and the Owners of the *Adventure Galley*'. Wood also stated that Boulton paid Wood's wages and those of his crew when he sold the *St Antonio* to Kidd. From his deposition it would appear that Wood continued to act as master for the sloop as he states that he set sail for 'New York; and breaking our boom-iron put into Delaware Bay to get it mended; and at Horekills they landed a chest belonging to one James Gilliam'.[24]

Gabriel Loff stated that Gilliam's chest was taken ashore and that Gilliam did not follow but stayed with the ship. Crewman Richard Barlycorne confirms this in his account, except he says that James Gilliam 'carried' two chests ashore.[25]

While Kidd anchored at Horekills his actions were being noticed. In a letter received at the Council of Trade and Plantations (Board of Trade) on 30 July 1700 it stated that a 'parcel of pirates' were settled here.

> So that when any pirates come near this Bay, they send their boats ashore there, and get intelligence and supplies from these men. When Capt. Kidd was in this Bay, he sent his boat ashore every day and was supplied, and these men went constantly on board him, and brought ashore with them

great quantities of East India goods. The whole intrigue of this roguery hath all been lately discovered.[26]

Perhaps this is why Kidd only stayed at Horekills for two days – he couldn't afford to hang around too long.

After spending such a short time in Horekills, Kidd and his crew were soon back on the open sea, the ship rocking with swell as they sailed further up the coast around the tip of Long Island into Oyster Bay. Here Kidd's friend Mr Emot came aboard and took a letter from Kidd to New York. From there Kidd sailed to Gardiner's Island for the first of two visits.

Gardiner's Island is located between the two prongs on the eastern end of Long Island. It was reputedly purchased in 1638 from the Nantucket Indians for the sum of a large black dog, powder and shot and had been owned by the Gardiner family since 1639 when the King of England granted ownership and the title Lord of the Manor by Royal Patent. Only thirteen square kilometres, the island's main products at the time were wheat, corn, tobacco, livestock and fruit.

Around June 1699 Kidd anchored off the island and sent Emot ashore to borrow a boat to carry him to New York, according to Gardiner's deposition. 'That evening I saw a Sloop with six Guns riding at anchor off Gardiner's Island.' At this point, Gardiner had no idea who Kidd was. Two days after this unknown ship arrived off the island Gardiner went aboard 'to inquire what she was'. No sooner had he come aboard the *St Antonio* than Kidd inquired after the health of his family and Kidd told Gardiner that he intended to meet Bellomont in Boston.

Gardiner also stated in his deposition that there were two other sloops tied up close to Kidd's ship. 'There was a New York Sloop, whereof one Coster is Master, and his Mate a little black man, who as it was said, had been formerly Captain Kidd's Quarter-Master.' Gardiner didn't know who the mate was but he stated that the third sloop, also from New York, was under the command of Jacob Ferrick. The significance of this is that while Gardiner was on board the *St Antonio* he saw several bales of goods, chests and other items being transferred from the *St Antonio* onto these other sloops. The three ships remained together for three days and then the two New York sloops sailed away.[27] To some degree this is confirmed in the depositions of Gabriel Loff and Edward Davis who state that goods were transferred to a sloop under the command of Captain Coster.

William Jenkins has a slightly different account of what went on between the three ships. Under oath he stated that 'there was a sloop said to belong to New York, whereof one Hendrick, a Dutchman, a young man, was either Skipper or one of the Company, into which sloop there was sent two or more Bales, One of them being Bengal Silks, all belonging to one Humphrey Clay, and Four or more Chests belong to said Humphrey Clay, English Smith, Gabriel Loff and Martin Skinke.' This sloop was bound for Martha's Vineyard, an island south of Cape Cod; but having received the new cargo it turned back and headed for New York.

Gardiner stated that Kidd gave him three Negro children, two boys and a girl to take with him back to his island and keep until he came for them. About two hours after Gardiner returned with the children Kidd sent his boat over with two bales of goods along with another Negro. 'And the morning after, the said Kidd desired me to come immediately on board, and bring Six Sheep with me for the said Kidd's Voyage to Boston.'

Kidd also asked Gardiner for a barrel of cider which Gardiner graciously gave. Other goods changed hands, including some 'Muslins and Bengals' for John Gardiner's wife, which he took as payment for the cider and sheep. Kidd's crew also gave gifts to Gardiner's men, 'some inconsiderable Things of small Value, which, were Muslins for Neck cloths'. We must remember that Gardiner had no idea that Kidd had been proclaimed a pirate, though he must have had some suspicion of him. After all, it couldn't have been a common occurrence for a sloop to be anchored off his island and for him to receive gifts from that sloop that were clearly from East India. Still, Gardiner stated he knew nothing of Kidd's predicament 'and if he had, he durst not have acted otherwise than he has done, having no Force to oppose them'. As the *St Antonio* pulled away from the island, Kidd saluted his friend with four cannon blasts.[28]

Kidd sailed for Block Island, eight miles off the coast of Rhode Island, where he delivered two guns, each weighing 200 pounds, to a family which Jenkins refers to only as Sands.[29] What was Kidd up to? Kidd knew he was proclaimed a pirate and that he was a hunted man. Perhaps he was forming an escape plan so if things went badly with Bellomont he could abandon the *St Antonio* and equip another ship with extra firepower to fight his way out. Was he also spreading his treasure around so that he might have something to bargain with if he did need to flee quickly?[30] Samuel Wood's account confirms that the guns were put ashore here.

In the various accounts from Kidd and his crew one name keeps popping up – the lawyer Mr Emot. He was supposedly Kidd's friend and he seems to have spent a great deal of time shuttling from ship to shore acting as Kidd's envoy. 'Mr Emot came from New York to them whom they took in and stood for Rhode Island and put him on shore there and at Mr Emot's return went to Gardiner's Island,' Wood stated in his deposition.

On 13 June 1699 Emot met with Bellomont. 'He came late at night to me and told me that he came from Captain Kidd who was on the coast with a sloop, but would not tell me where.' According to Bellomont, Emot said that Kidd had 60lb weight of gold, about 100lb weight of silver, seventeen bales of cloth and that he'd left behind a great ship with its holds stuffed with goods 'to the value of £300,000'.

The offer was that, if Bellomont would give Kidd a pardon, then the captain would bring in the goods he had and go and get the remainder of the goods he'd left down in Hispaniola. To sweeten the deal, 'Mr Emot delivered me that night two French passes which Kidd took on board the two Moors' ships, which were taken by him in the seas of India, or as he alleges by his men against his will.'

Bellomont would later describe Emot as 'a cunning Jacobite . . . and my avowed enemy'.[31]

Two days after this meeting Bellomont sent Duncan Campbell, a fellow Scot and the postmaster of Boston, along with Mr Emot to Kidd to invite him to come into port. In addition to this, Bellomont briefed the Council of Massachusetts Bay on 17 June 1699 on the information he had received from Emot regarding Captain Kidd.[32]

Bellomont states that a letter was drafted to Kidd and approved by the Council on 19 June. Campbell was again sent to Kidd with the letter advising Kidd to come ashore and surrender himself where he would be given a fair hearing and, providing he could supply proof of his innocence, could hope for a pardon.[33]

Kidd sent his reply to Bellomont on 24 June 1699 and in it he stated that he'd avoided writing to Bellomont earlier because 'the clamours and false stories that have been reported of me made me fearful of writing or coming into any harbour till I could hear from you'.[34]

Clearly his intentions in this letter were to come into the harbour once he knew how Bellomont felt. However, he didn't mention the death of Gunner William Moore or the acts of piracy that took place at Motta, the Maldives or the kidnapping and imprisonment of Parker. He must have hoped that none of the crew who deserted him at Sainte Marie had made it back to Boston to testify against him. But as we have already seen, the East India Company were no laggards in building their case against him so it is possible that Bellomont may already have had information from them about Kidd.

One of the first things he mentions in his letter is the mass mutiny of his men to Robert Culliford 'who went away to the Red Seas and committed several acts of piracy as I am informed, and am afraid the men formerly belonging to my galley, that the report is gone home against me to the East India Company that I have been the actor'.

Pleading his innocence he claimed that he was always protecting the interests of the owners of the *Adventure Galley*, even when faced with difficult circumstances, which he would later clarify in his account and that he never once acted contrary to the King's Commission.[35] 'A sheet of paper', wrote Kidd to Bellomont, 'will not contain what may be said of the care I took to preserve the owners' interest and to come home to clear my own innocence.'

Kidd made two visits to Gardiner's Island and on the second visit he had his wife and children aboard with him. Also on board were two other men, as Gardiner stated in his deposition: 'one Thomas Clark of Setauket, commonly called Whisking Clark, and one Harrison of Jamaica, Father to a Boy that was with Captain Kidd'.[36]

Bellomont also confirms the fact that Kidd now had his wife with him, which made Bellomont feel confident that Kidd would not flee because he wouldn't want his family in harm's way. 'Another reason why I took him not up sooner was that he had brought his wife and children hither in the sloop with him, whom I believed he would not easily forsake', Bellomont wrote in his letter to the Council of Trade and Plantations received on 20 September 1699.

During Campbell's visits to Kidd while he was at Block Island, Kidd gave Campbell a wide variety of expensive and luxury items such as some handkerchiefs, three-quarters of a pound of tea and some gold, including some rare Arabian gold. On the second visit, Campbell received 190 pieces of eight from Kidd, 'New York Money, which he (Kidd) said, was his Wife's towards his Charges and some things he had bought for him.' Kidd also gave Campbell a few pieces of muslin, a gold chain and two pieces of speckled calico for Campbell's wife. In her account Sarah Campbell said she received 'a Gold Chain, three Pieces of Muslin, a Piece of India Silk as a Present from Captain Kidd', which her husband delivered to her. She claimed that nothing else belonging to Kidd was stored in her house, so denying any knowledge of any attempt at embezzlement.[37]

Both Duncan Campbell and Bellomont make reference to Kidd giving Campbell a gift for the Countess of Bellomont which was a gilt gold box later valued at £55 in Boston. Under advice from her husband, Lord Bellomont, she kept the box in case refusal might offend Kidd but then later the box and any other gifts from Kidd were handed over the Council as evidence.[38]

Kidd continued to distribute his loot to various places with various merchants. Whether he was selling the wares or just giving them away or asking individuals simply to look after the goods is uncertain. For example, between his two visits to Gardiner's Island he met up with another sloop out of New York commanded by Captain Cornelius Quick. Both ships anchored off Gardiner's Island where two chests of goods were transferred by Kidd over to Quick's vessel and Gardiner believed there were several more bales transferred between the two ships.

As the sun was setting, Gardner watched Quick's sloop sail away for Oyster Bay, where it stopped. The same sloop under Quick's command was seen landing the same goods at Nassau Island (just off Long Island) according to a later report and there Quick was seized by the authorities.[39]

The Kidd legends and myths say that he buried treasure on Gardiner's Island worth as much as £20,000, which included gold dust, bars of silver, rubies, diamonds, candlesticks, porringers and pieces of eight. In today's money this would be worth millions to anyone who finds it. But is it true? Bellomont stated in his letter that 'I heard by the greatest accident in the world the day that Captain Kidd was committed that a man had offered £30 for a sloop to carry him to Gardiner's Island, and Kidd having owned he had buried some gold on that island.' Bellomont goes on to say that Kidd never mentioned any gold or jewels during his questioning. 'Nor, I believe, would he have owned the gold there but that he thought he should himself be sent for it.'[40]

Bellomont had to be sure if the story was true so he dispatched a messenger directly to Gardiner demanding him to deliver any treasure that Kidd or any of his men had left with him. The messenger arrived swiftly and Gardiner handed over some gold, silver and jewels, 'and by my direction delivered it into the hands of the Committee. If the jewels be right, as 'tis supposed they are, but I never saw them nor the gold and silver brought by Gardiner, then we guess that the parcel brought by him may be worth £4,500.'

Was this the hidden treasure that the man who offered money for the sloop was after? Bellomont stated that this man was one of Kidd's men so it is highly likely that Kidd did tell him that he'd buried some treasure on the island. Was this it? There is no evidence to suggest that the treasure that Gardiner handed over to the committee was buried treasure. In fact, Bellomont goes on to say that Gardiner couldn't bring everything over because Kidd had left six bales of goods with him and one of them was twice as big as the others 'and Kidd gave him particular charge of the bale and told him it was worth £2,000'.

If Kidd buried any treasure on Gardiner's Island it wasn't this we've just mentioned because he states in his account that he left 4,000 pieces of eight which were locked in a box, nailed, corded and sealed in the care of Mr Gardiner, 'and he took no receipt of it of Mr. Gardiner'. Kidd also stated that he left bales and chests of goods containing muslins, latches, Romalls and flowered silks, in Gardiner's care and while some of his crew put goods ashore elsewhere he didn't. Of course Kidd doesn't mention any buried treasure. Perhaps he was counting on Bellomont giving him a pardon so he could clear his name and sail away a rich and free man and spend the rest of his days living in luxury with his family?[41]

As with so many things in Kidd's story there are contradictions: Gardiner's version is slightly different in terms of what Kidd and his crew gave him for safekeeping. He stated that Kidd gave him a box of gold intended for Bellomont, a chest, a bundle of quilts, four bales of goods, while two members of Kidd's crew gave him two bags of silver weighing 30 pounds, a bundle of gold and gold dust and presents in the form of a sash, a pair of worsted stockings, and a bag of sugar. These two crewmen he states were named Cook and Parrot. With these transactions concluded Kidd sailed away from Gardiner's Island heading for Boston.[42]

While all of this was taking place, a New York registered ship the *Nassau* under the command of Captain Giles Shelley (who has already been mentioned) returned from Madagascar. According to a deposition made by crewman Theophilus Turner, a sighting had been made of a ship off the coast of Sainte Marie which was believed to be the *November*, left there by Captain Kidd and also the bottom of the burnt-out *Adventure Galley*.[43] One of Kidd's old shipmates was on board the *Nassau* – Robert Bradinham, one of the many deserters who left the *Adventure Galley*.[44] He would later prove to be a key witness against Kidd at his trial. So now, unfortunately for Kidd, there was a man who could tell Bellomont his version of the truth of what went on aboard the *Adventure Galley*.

On 30 June 1699, as Kidd sailed for Boston, he spotted the sails of another sloop on the horizon. Boston-based mariner Thomas Way commanded this sloop. Having left the Bay of Compeach he had now run across the *St Antonio* in the shoals of Nantucket. Both ships were heading for Boston so they decided to sail together. Along the way Kidd transferred more goods over to Way's ship. Way provided a detailed account of all the goods that Kidd transferred over.[45]

This cargo included three firearms, a pair of stilliards (scale for weighing gold), a Turkish carpet, a clock and a bag of canvas sealed with two seals 'which he said contained Pieces of Eight that his Wife brought with her from New York; to bear her Expenses'. Kidd also gave Way a bundle of his wife's clothes 'and desired me to carry up for him; which I accordingly did'.

According to Way's deposition it seems Kidd called for that bundle of clothes and the bag of money soon after they arrived in Boston. If both ships were going to Boston why did Kidd ask another captain to take a bundle of his wife's clothes to the same place he was going unless that bundle of clothes also included the bag of money? Way definitely states that Kidd asked for the bundle shortly after arriving in Boston which he delivered to Kidd. He also states that on the day Kidd was arrested he came to Way's house 'with a Negro boy, and fetched away the said Bag of Money'.[46]

There is also another question here as well. Both Way and Campbell said they had received pieces of eight from Kidd, who claimed that it was his wife's money he was giving away. Why would he give away his wife's money? Was Kidd that much of a fool to be giving away money like that or was he giving them tokens out of the thousands he had and going around saying the money was his wife's when it was really plundered money?

Before stopping in Boston Kidd dropped his anchor just off Tarpaulin Cove a beach on Naushon Island, part of the Elizabeth Islands south of Cape Cod. Two barrels and a bale of goods were landed here by Kidd.[47] After this brief stop Kidd set sail again, steering the *St Antonio* for Boston.

When Kidd arrived in the harbour at Boston and dropped anchor he sent Duncan Campbell two bales of goods, two bags of sugar and other items. What was he up to? In those days support was more often than not bought rather than earned, so perhaps he was trying to build some good support for himself. By spreading his wealth around he may have been simply hedging his bets so that if his ship was seized he wouldn't lose everything in one go.

As soon as he heard that Captain Kidd was coming to Boston, Robert Livingston left his home in Albany, climbed on his horse and headed for Boston, to try to get as many details as possible from Kidd about his fateful voyage. He claimed that Kidd told him the sloop *St Antonio* contained forty bales of goods, some sugar and about eighty pounds of plate. Kidd also told him that there were forty pounds of gold hidden somewhere between Boston and New York, and that only he knew where it had been hidden, which we can assume means that Kidd was going to use that information as a bargaining tool. He further informed his backer that the goods were for the owners of the *Adventure Galley*.[48]

Kidd later admitted to Livingston that several chests and bundles of goods belonging to his crew had been transferred from his sloop into other sloops. He also admitted to giving 100 pieces of eight to Duncan Campbell. Campbell said it was 190 pieces of eight.

Livingston stated in his deposition that Kidd admitted to hiding forty pounds of gold, some plates and 300 or 400 pieces of eight on Gardiner's Island. Livingston then goes on to say that Kidd presented him with a Negro boy around the same time as he presented Duncan Campbell with his human gift. With all these gifts coming from Kidd to people such as Campbell, Gardner and Livingston amongst others, the suspicion that embezzlement was taking place could not be ignored so around 12 July 1699 Bellomont questioned both Campbell and Livingston concerning any accusations of embezzlement and collusion with Kidd.[49] 'I know no further Disposal, made by the said Kidd, his company, or Accomplices, of any Good, Gold, Money or Treasure whatsoever', Livingston stated.

10

Arrested

At the heart of Kidd's case is a single question – did he turn pirate? Right up until his death he maintained his innocence and blamed his crew for his downfall. Indeed, in his final speech from the scaffold he stated that 'but several others, who instead of being his Friends (as they promised) had traitorously been Instrumental in his Ruin'.[1] Some historians believe that Kidd was part of a conspiracy that went right up to Westminster. But Bellomont did try to deal as fairly with Kidd as he could: 'The promise I made Captain Kidd in my letter of a kind reception and procuring the king's pardon is conditional, that is, provided he were as innocent as he pretended to be.' We shall see that Bellomont gave Kidd more than one opportunity to clear his name and to provide some form of evidence in his defence. No one who stood up and corroborated Kidd's version of events in their entirety. All the evidence was overwhelmingly against him.

In earlier chapters we stated that Kidd sailed back into a different political climate. Let's take a look at that political climate in 1699. The Parliament of the day was made up of two political parties, the Whigs and the Tories. Each of the parties was made up of wealthy businessmen, landowners, some nobility, all of whom were interested in keeping the nation prosperous. This, of course, meant that they would remain prosperous and powerful. The voting system in Parliament was nothing like the system we have today. To be elected into a seat the member had to be a man of the right social and business class, with a certain reputation and standing. Very few at the time had the right to vote: women had no say in this system, nor did the majority of men. It was for the select few. MPs often were in somebody's pocket, such as a wealthy landowner or businessman, and votes were often bought. Before the rise of industry the system favoured the men who inherited large estates but as industry began to grow and more men became wealthy from running banks, mines, smelting firms, shipbuilding and other industries they were able to enter this world of politics and influence.

The Tories wanted to expose the men behind Kidd in their bid to gain power and to deal with the piracy problem at the same time. Exaggerated stories about Kidd were circulating around London and this was their chance to attack the men in the shadows, such as Lord Shrewsbury and Lord Somers, who were Kidd's backers.

Kidd was originally sent out on his voyage in 1696 to tackle the piracy problem. We have already seen the difficulties caused to the East India Company by Avery's antics and later piracies on the Great Mogul's fleet. 'The situation was, in fact, becoming desperate; neither on sea nor on land was the company's property safe; both trade and credit were suffering accordingly.'[2]

In an earlier chapter we saw that two of Kidd's men jumped ship at Carwar because they believed he was turning to piracy. These men were arrested and sent home to England for questioning. With them went a letter from the company dated 18 November 1698 to the Lord Justices that accused Kidd of piracy in the plundering of the *Quedah Merchant*. That he had French passes the company could not know or perhaps didn't want to know. The squadron commanded by Commodore Warren was sent out to get Kidd. A letter to all the governors of the American colonies was sent by Rear Admiral John Benbow on 23 November, calling for the capture and arrest of Captain Kidd and his accomplices, so that he and 'his associates [might] be prosecuted with the utmost rigour of the law'.

Once the public heard of these moves by the Lord Justices and the government the rumours started flying. Some of the stories suggested that the four Whig backers behind Kidd's expedition had sent him to go pirating for their own personal gain. Some of the stories that circulated included the fact that Kidd had turned pirate and taken a ship of the Great Mogul to the value of £400,000 and then been captured by a French ship who duly sent him to the Great Mogul clapped in irons. This was untrue of course. Another story, dated 3 August 1699, that appeared in the press suggested that Kidd's capture was incorrect and that he had sunk the *Adventure Galley* and then gone aboard a Portuguese vessel 'and sailed directly to Darien where the Scots receive him and all his riches'.[3]

A story dated 5 August 1699 suggested that Kidd had not sailed to Darien but was at Nassau Island near New York, where he gave Livingston £30,000 to pay off his partners and £20,000 to get him a pardon. Twelve days later another story about Kidd appeared in the papers stating that he had given the Dutch governor of St Thomas 45,000 gold pieces of eight if he would protect him and his crew for a month. The story continues that the governor refused and Kidd then purchased another ship. Another rumour which appeared in the press on 22 August 1699 suggested that Kidd had surrendered to Lord Bellomont. At least this rumour turned out to be true.[4]

But even with Kidd arrested public fears in England were not allayed. Weren't there four very influential Whig backers behind Kidd and could they not easily ensure that he would get away free? The fear was that these four Lords, one of whom was the Lord Chancellor (Lord Somers), would ensure that Kidd wasn't brought to justice to hide their own culpability. To ease the public's fears HMS *Rochester* was despatched in September 1699 to New York to bring Kidd back for trial. Unfortunately, the ship ran into a terrible storm for several weeks and limped back to port, badly damaged in need of repair. The press fuelled a public outcry that the return of the *Rochester* was a trick set up by the four Lords to ensure Kidd remained free.

The government were so concerned that they ordered an investigation into the return of the *Rochester*. While this was taking place the East India Company sent a deputation from the company's board to the Lord Justices demanding a speedy trial of Captain Kidd and that all the goods he had taken and passed around to people be rounded up and sent back to the rightful owners, in particular the riches he'd taken from the Great Mogul's ship, the *Quedah Merchant*.

The House of Commons set up an inquiry and called for everything relating to Kidd's voyage. On 2 December 1699 copies of Kidd's commission and the grant of pirate goods to Bellomont were presented to the House along with nominees of the four great lords. An entry in the Journal of the House of Commons dated 16 March 1700 (volume xiii) stated that Kidd could not be tried, discharged or pardoned until the following session of Parliament which was in recess at the time of this entry. The same entry went on to state that 'the Earl of Bellomont, governor of New England, may transmit over all communications, instructions and other papers, taken with, or relating to, the said Captain Kidd'.

The House was anxious to bring Kidd to them in person in the hope that he might provide them with the evidence needed to incriminate the four lords. In this atmosphere it made no difference if Kidd was guilty or innocent: he had turned pirate and that was that.[5]

When Kidd had begun on his journey the Whigs had been rising in power but now that was starting to wane and they no longer wanted anything to do with him. They saw him as a liability to their reputations and standing. The four lords couldn't deny outright their involvement in the expedition but they could insist that he'd gone against his commission and turned traitor.

On the streets embellished and exaggerated stories about Kidd freely circulated. It seemed that every act of piracy was associated with William Kidd. Piracy in those days could be said to be similar to terrorism today. Captain Kidd was the number one criminal who had to be brought to justice; he was the chief symbol of all that was wrong with the maritime trade and was the reason why goods failed to arrive and prices were so high.

Putting Kidd on trial would send the right messages not just to the people but also to India, where this was probably more important. The people saw him as one of the most notorious pirates that ever sailed the high seas and for the establishment he was guilty and there was only one sentence for murder and piracy – death by hanging. It was now up to Kidd to prove he was innocent.

According to Ritchie, Kidd had his first opportunity to clear himself when he met privately with Bellomont at the end of June 1699. Bellomont was subject to a number of influences. First he was under orders to arrest Kidd. But if he did that he would be violating the contract he and Kidd had signed with the four Whig lords who were his sponsors. At the same time Bellomont was in America because of the poor state of his finances: 'which had not improved in New York – a source of great concern to him'.

So now here was Kidd presenting a way out for Bellomont. Kidd claimed to have £10,000 with him, plus another £30,000 in the West Indies. Ritchie states that these figures meant that Kidd's voyage had made £40,000 for the partnership. After costs were deducted 'of approximately £6,000 the partners would net £34,000, with certainly no more that £5,000 going to Bellomont'.

In a letter dated 17 March 1700 Bellomont wrote to Secretary Vernon suggesting that in his role as vice admiral he would get a third of any treasure he seized from criminals or pirates, which meant that if he arrested Kidd he'd get £13,000. If he took this route, Bellomont would be fulfilling the orders of the Tory government about capturing Kidd and that meant he was also protecting his American position, according to Ritchie.

The first official meeting with Kidd was when he appeared before Bellomont and the Council in Boston on 3 July 1699. He was asked for a full account of the goods he'd seized and a full account of his voyage. Bellomont sent some men aboard the *St Antonio* to ensure the cargo Kidd told them he had remained where it was.

Bellomont and the Council gave Kidd until the following day to complete his narrative. At the appointed time Kidd arrived but without the narrative, telling the council he had not yet had time to finish it. He was given an extension until the next day. Again Kidd did not have the narrative available. The Council gave him until 6 July 1699 to complete the narrative. The day came and Kidd arrived in the morning, again pleading he hadn't had enough time to complete his account of the voyage. However this time the council and Bellomont insisted he return at five that afternoon with his narrative finished.[6]

Bellomont was getting increasingly worried about Kidd escaping so when Kidd arrived at the correct time he was arrested outside Bellomont's door. 'I was so much upon my guard with Kidd,' wrote Bellomont, 'that, he arriving here on Saturday the 8th of this month, I would not see him but before witnesses; nor have I ever seen him since but in council twice or thrice that we examined him, and the day he was taken up by the constable, it happened to be by the door of my lodging and he rushed in and came running to me, the constable after him.' Bellomont shows the concern he had that Kidd might escape: 'I observed he seemed much disturbed, and the last time we examined him I fancied he looked as if he were upon the wing and resolved to run away, and the gentlemen of the council had some of them the same thought with mine, so that I took their consent in seizing and committing him.'

Bellomont and the Council then appointed a committee of people they could trust to go and search Kidd's ship and lodgings. In his letter he set out the items that were found. 'They searched Kidd's lodgings and found made up in two seabeds a bag of gold dust and ingots of the value of about £1,000 and a bag of silver, part money and part pieces and pigs of silver.' Bellomont swore he'd not looked at or 'meddled with' the treasure but put it all into the safekeeping of the Council and the special committee.

Some weeks before Kidd had been arrested another pirate, Bradish, had escaped from the jail in Boston because the jailor was related to him and aided in his escape. Bellomont was determined to ensure that Kidd did not escape. He managed to get the council to agree to put the jail into the care of the high sheriff of the county with an annual salary of £30 just to keep Kidd safe. 'He has without doubt a great deal of gold, which is apt to tempt men that have not principles of honour', Bellomont wrote. Bellomont also ordered Kidd to be put in solitary confinement.

After Kidd's arrest and incarceration the Committee uncovered a great deal of wealth held by Captain Kidd which was made up of 1,111 ounces of gold, 2,353 ounces of silver, 17 ounces of precious stones, fifty-seven bags of sugar and forty-one bags of other goods. All this was inventoried by Bellomont, the Council and the special committee which had collected them from a wide variety of places, including a box and a chest held by Kidd, found in Duncan Campbell's house where Kidd and his wife and daughter were lodging, and items obtained from John Gardiner and from the *St Antonio*.[7]

On 20 July 1699, two mariners, Carsten Luerse and Hendrick Vanderheal, members of the crew of a sloop registered in New York, declared that they had received four bales and four chests of goods from Captain Kidd's sloop around Gardiner's Island. They declared that two of these were put into the care of Justice White and Dr Cooper, both residents of Oyster Bay, one to each, with the rest sent ashore at Connecticut. These goods were seized by the high sheriff of Queen's County on Nassau Island and the two crewmen were ordered to surrender the remaining goods.[8]

Over the next few days the Committee received accounts from people connected with Kidd about his movements and the whereabouts of the goods he'd been distributing. These included: Duncan Campbell and his wife Susanna of Boston, crewman Gabriel Loff of Long Island, Andries Henlyne, John Pero and Jacob Rateere of the sloop *Mary* from Curaso, Captain Nicholas Evertse of St Thomas, William Jenkins from Bow, London, who joined the *Adventure Galley* in Plymouth, Richard Barlycorne and Robert Lamley, both crewmen on the *Adventure Galley*, William Cuthbert, Captain Samuel Wood, captain of the *St Antonio*, Thomas Way from Boston, Robert Livingston from Albany, Edward Davis another *Adventure Galley* crewman, Hugh Parrott from Plymouth, who joined the *Adventure Galley* at Johanna Island, John Gardiner from Gardiner's Island, Abel Owens (the cook on the *Adventure Galley*), and Samuel Arris (the steward on the *Adventure Galley*). By now Kidd had finished his narrative and that was also examined. Bellomont made a full account of the proceedings on 26 July 1699 which also included the two French passes.[9]

According to Bellomont, the inventory and the French passes were sent along with his letter to the Council for Trade and Plantations. 'One of these passes wants a date in the original as in the copy I send.' Bellomont asked for directions on what to do with Kidd. 'As the law stands in this country a pirate cannot be punished with death. Therefore I desire to receive orders what to do with Kidd and those men of his I have taken.'

During his examinations in Boston by Bellomont and the Council Kidd repeatedly mentioned that a great ship waited for him in the West Indies to return and claim her cargo. In his letter to the Council for Trade and Plantations Bellomont wrote that 'I was advised by the Council to dispatch a ship of good countenance to go and fetch away that ship and cargo', referring to the *Adventure Prize*.

> I had agreed for a ship of 300 ton, 22 guns, and I was to man her with 60 men to force (if there had been need) the men to yield, who were left with the ship. I was just going to seal the writing, when I bethought myself 'twere best to press Kidd once more to tell me the truth. I therefore sent to him two gentlemen of the Council to the gaol, and he at last owned that he had left a power with one Mr. Henry Bolton, a Marchand of Antigua, whom he had committed the care of the ship to, to sell and dispose of all the cargo. Upon which confession I held my hand from hiring that great ship, which would have cost £1,700 by computation. To-morrow I send the sloop Kidd came in with letters to the L.G. of Antigua, the Governors of St. Thomas' Island and Curacao to seize and receive what effects they can that was late in the possession of Kidd and on board the *Quedagh Merchant*.[10]

Bellomont also included with his letter the depositions of two mariners who had just come from the West Indies who confirmed that the cargo had been sold but also added a more alarming bit of news that the great ship had been burnt 'and without a doubt t'was by Kidd's orders, that the ship might not be an evidence against him, for he would not own to us her name was the *Quedah Merchant*'. According to Bellomont it was Andries Henlyne who brought the news of the cargo being sold and it was Nicholas Evertse's report that said that the *Adventure Prize* had been consumed by fire on 29 June. Evertse stated he saw two ships loading up from the larger ship, which was then engulfed in flames. Was this an accident? We don't know but Bellomont sent the *St Antonio* to the area to search for the cargo that had been removed from the *Adventure Prize/Quedah Merchant* prior to the fire. Kidd claimed that there were vast riches in the hold of the giant ship but now they were gone and Bellomont was in pursuit.

The *St Antonio* never arrived. The legal sale of the *St Antonio* to Kidd by Boulton wasn't as legal as Bellomont thought and the rightful owners of the ship tried to seize it back so the crew of the ship never searched for the cargo that

Boulton sold on Kidd's behalf.[11]

In early 1700 Bellomont tied up as many loose ends as possible and had his orders regarding what to do with Kidd. He was to be sent back to sea, destination England, but not as a captain – as a prisoner. So on 1 February 1700 HMS *Advice* arrived in Boston to take Kidd back to England to stand trial. Twenty days later, while HMS *Advice* still remained in Boston, Joseph Palmer surrendered to Bellomont. Palmer is the one person who testified at Kidd's trial that he murdered his gunner. He is the one who stated that Kidd paced up and down and then struck William Moore – clearly an act of murder.

On 10 March 1700, Kidd began his last Atlantic crossing, this time in the bowels of the naval ship. Ironically, the same ship had been part of the flotilla he had encountered around the Cape of Good Hope when he was sailing towards India. Then he was on a mission that could have given him wealth, honour, fame and position. It had turned out to be a mission to the gallows.

11

At the Old Bailey

And so Kidd sat in misery in a small bitterly cold cabin in the steerage compartment of HMS *Advice* as it rode the waves, rolling and pitching with the movement of the sea. High winds and torrential rain battered the ship as it headed for England, ice swirling around the deck, the cold seeping into men's bones. Several times the *Advice* tried to enter the English Channel in order to land Kidd in London but the terrible weather beat them back. In the end, the captain of the *Advice* Captain Robert Wynn landed at Lundy's Island. 'He sent letters to the government advising them of his arrival.'[1]

By this time, early in 1700, the Whigs had lost a great deal of their influence. The four lords who backed the project were all out of office, now replaced by Tories or by Whigs who were not the political dynamos that the four lords had been. Secretary Vernon wanted Kidd brought to face the Commons before the end of the session, then be speedily tried and executed, so the letter from Wynn was not good news. He asked if the Privy Council could send one of the King's yachts out to meet the *Advice* and bring Kidd into London. The Privy Council agreed and told the Admiralty to send the yacht. It turned out to be the *Katherine*, the very yacht to which Kidd had failed to dip his flag when he left on his momentous voyage. The irony could not have been lost on him.

When the *Katherine* rendezvoused with the *Advice* Kidd, who was ill, was brought on board the yacht and isolated below decks as the ship sailed for Greenwich. Was he wondering how things had turned out so badly? Did he think only about his family and not his own fate? Did he think about the one act that had sealed his fate three years earlier?

His refusing to lower his colours when he passed the King's yacht had set off a series of events that found him where he was now, rotting in confinement on the *Katherine*. His confidence and exuberance as he left London must have seemed a lifetime ago.

Now he was on the journey that would see him tried for murder and for piracy. If he was found guilty there would be only one sentence. Over the centuries since his death Kidd's trial has been hashed and rehashed. Many believe he was a scapegoat, a victim of his own character and circumstance and that the trial was nothing but a sham. Others believe he was guilty. The condemnation of Kidd took place in eight stages, four of which were the four trials he had before he was sentenced, while the first of the eight stages were the hearings he had with Bellomont and the Council in Boston.[2]

He arrived in England on 13 April 1700 and the following day the next stage in his condemnation took place when the Admiralty sent their barge to Greenwich to bring him to the Admiralty Building for a private hearing. Before the interview could take place the Admiralty wanted to examine the papers that Bellomont had sent from America via the *Advice*. With most of the Lords of the Admiralty present, the boxes of papers relating to Kidd were opened and Secretary Vernon ordered that the contents of the letters be read aloud, including those from Bellomont to himself.

As the barge moved down the River Thames Kidd must have wondered what lay in store for him. When the barge was moored up Kidd, still under guard, was transferred to a sedan chair and taken to the new Admiralty Building beside Whitehall Palace. It was 1600hrs when Captain Kidd, his clothes filthy, ill from the voyage and looking nothing like the proud arrogant captain he'd once been, arrived at the Admiralty for questioning. For seven hours Sir Charles Hedges, the Chief Justice of the Admiralty, with Admiral Sir George Rook, the Earl of Bridgewater and other dignitaries interrogated Kidd. In his book, *Under the Black Flag*, David Cordingly states that Kidd repeated his arguments that he had only taken two ships. 'He claimed that his crew had forced him to commit piracy and had robbed him and destroyed his logbook and all his records.'

By 2300hrs that evening the lords of the Admiralty had heard enough and a transcript of Kidd's testimony was read to him for him to sign and then sealed by the each of the lords present. He was then committed to Newgate Prison to be kept in close confinement. He could only be visited by a physician and could have paper only to write to the Admiralty. Why he wasn't committed to the Admiralty's own jail, the Marshalsea, isn't clear but perhaps it was because the Lords of the Admiralty were viewing the case as a political one rather than a military one? Or perhaps they didn't have jurisdiction over Kidd's case at all? He was led away from the Admiralty and taken to Newgate Prison, which Cordingly describes as 'a nightmarish place in which to be confined'.

A forbidding stone building on the corner of Holborn and Newgate Street in London the prison was built to house criminals while they waited for trial and execution. Here every conceivable type of criminal was housed from cut-throats to petty thieves and prostitutes. 'Wives and children were allowed to visit, and there was a relaxed attitude toward gambling, drinking and sex, but this was offset by the severe overcrowding, the stinking smells and the shrieks and screams of the inmates.'[3]

In this hell hole Kidd's health went rapidly downhill. His harsh conditions were lifted slightly when the keeper at Newgate reported to the Admiralty that Kidd was in a fever, suffering tremendous pain. He was allowed to have visits by two of his relatives in the presence of a keeper and given fresh clothing, bedding and better care. The physician was allowed in to see him as well. But as soon as Kidd showed signs of regaining his health the visits were stopped. He complained bitterly about this and told the Admiralty that he probably would not last the year if he was not able to have a small allowance and be able to go to chapel and have his visits restored. The Lords of the Admiralty in their great generosity decided to give him a pittance for an allowance, allow him the visit of only one of his relatives, Mathew Hawkins, with a keeper always present. Very occasional supervised visits to the chapel were also allowed. He was allowed to exercise under guard but was not allowed to talk to anyone while he was exercising.[4]

In the meantime the prison remained a cesspit of squalor and disease where Kidd spent almost a year before the third stage of his condemnation took place. On 27 March 1701 Kidd was brought before the House of Commons for questioning, the only pirate ever appear in the House of Commons. The elections of 1700 had brought in more Tories so they now controlled the House of Commons and they were determined to punish the Whigs, especially the four backers of Kidd's expedition. The men they were after were men like Lord Orford, Shrewsbury, Somers and Romney. Sadly there are no records of what took place during the questioning of Kidd before the House but one commentary stated that Kidd repeated his earlier testimony that he had never met Somers or Shrewsbury but had met Orford and Romney.

During this questioning, the transcript of the seven-hour interrogation he'd had with the Admiralty was read out. But at the end Kidd maintained that his two main contacts were Bellomont and Livingston. Here we could ask if he actually knew who all the backers were: otherwise, why couldn't he provide the House with the information they wanted? In the end he was sent back to Newgate prison, only to be brought back to the House on 31 March for more questioning. It was announced on 28 March 1701 that Captain William Kidd was to stand trial at the Old Bailey.

Preliminary Proceedings – 8 May 1701 (Old Bailey, London)

Almost two years after Kidd was arrested in Boston on 6 July 1699 he found himself facing the first of his four trials at the Old Bailey. These trials took place over two days but preliminary proceedings were held before the first trial.

Over the two years that Kidd had been in prison, the prosecution had built its case against him. Cordingly states: 'In many ways Kidd's trial was not typical. He was kept in prison for nearly two years before trial which was very unusual in piracy cases.'

In the late seventeenth and early eighteenth centuries it was standard practice for the defendant to conduct his or her own defence. Regardless of the defendant's understanding or experience of the law, they had to cross-examine their own witnesses and make their own opening and closing remarks. Any legal representation that the defendant had could only be consulted on specific points of law. However, the prosecution was entitled to as much legal representation as it desired. Instead of being innocent until proven guilty, prisoners were guilty until proven innocent.

For this fact alone it could be said that Kidd had an unfair trial and certainly by today's standards that's true, but since this was the way the courts worked then everyone else who stood before the courts had equally unfair trials.

Those of Kidd's crew who had been captured and arrested were brought back to London by Admiral John Benbow. Henry Boulton, the man who had sold the *St Antonio* to Kidd and to whom Kidd had given the safekeeping of the *Adventure Prize/Quedah Merchant* had been tracked down and was brought to England to give his evidence for the prosecution. One of the Armenian merchants (probably Coji Baba) who had lost everything when Kidd captured the *Quedah Merchant* was brought to London by the East India Company to add his version of events to the prosecution if needed. In addition,the papers relating to Kidd that Bellomont had sent to London, depositions from crew members and anyone who had dealings with Kidd were all assembled and brought back to provide evidence for the prosecution. Although it had taken almost two years for the Crown to build its case, Kidd was given only two weeks.[5]

Robert Ritchie states in his book that Kidd peppered the Admiralty board with requests to have more freedom of the prison and to have visits. These requests were initially ignored so Kidd wrote to the Commons to ask for writing materials and more visits. 'George Churchill carried this request to the Commons because the Admiralty refused to make an independent decision', Ritchie states. The Commons relented and allowed Kidd to be 'treated like any other prisoner'. They also allowed him to have the papers sent over by Bellomont and ordered the Commons clerk to accommodate Kidd's request.[6]

Five days after Kidd's request most of the documents he needed arrived but 'missing from the documents sent Kidd were a "blue-skinned" book naming his owners and containing his accounts, the instructions sent by the Admiralty relating to his letter of marquee, the letter sent by Bellomont as he approached Boston and the vital French passes', Ritchie tells us.

Everything was found except the French passes, which were in London and found in the twentieth century in the archives of the Board of Trade. These archives were created from the Board's own records and from the records of the office of the Secretary of State. 'The finger points at Vernon, who had access to the papers at the time and kept some of them in his office.'[7]

Secretary Vernon knew that Kidd would base his defence on the French passes so it is possible that he deliberately kept them from him but there is no direct evidence to support this. Bellomont sent every piece of paper he had concerning Kidd to London so he didn't misappropriate the passes.

Kidd was charged with five counts of piracy and one of murder; even if he did have the French passes they could only be used as evidence for the piracy charges, not for the charge of murder. 'It must be remembered that Kidd was charged with piracy in respect of five separate vessels; as regards three of these ships it was never suggested that any French passes existed, and so the issue of those indictments was not, and could not be, affected by the non-production of the documents.'[8]

To those individuals who suggest that Kidd did not have a fair trial there is some cause for concern. For the two ships where the passes could have helped Kidd they were not available to him. 'It cannot be denied that a gross injustice was done to Kidd by the Admiralty in not handling those papers over to him or to his advisors, as ordered by the House.'[9]

But did this result in a miscarriage of justice? The evidence for murder appears solid and Kidd had the five indictments for piracy against him. 'A study of the evidence for the prosecution clearly reveals that the ships were Moorish, that the owners were Moors, and that Kidd knew it.'[10]

Defendants could not give their own evidence on the crime of which they were accused, which meant that Kidd could call upon his fellow prisoners as defence witnesses for the charge of murder but not for the charges of piracy as they were facing the same charges. The only other people he could call upon were crew members who had deserted at different times and places throughout the voyage but their testimony was at best unreliable and at worst antagonistic. His options were limited, to say the least.

From the court transcripts we know that the following men were on the jury: William Broughton, Thomas Hanwell, Daniel Borwell, Humphry Bellamy, Nathaniel Rolston Snr, Joshua Bolton, Benjamin Pike, Joseph Marlow, Benjamin Travis, Stephen Thompson, Thomas Cooper, Robert Gower, Robert Clement, Thomas Sesson, William Goodwin, Robert Callow, and Thomas Haws. The number of men on the jury would reduce down to twelve for each of the trials and the members of the jury would change for each trial, while the prosecuting council would remain the same throughout.[11]

David Cordingly suggests that Kidd's trial was unusual even by the standards of the day. 'The most extraordinary array of legal dignitaries was that assembled in London for the trial of Captain Kidd and nine members of his crew.' For the Crown were Sir John Hawles, the Solicitor-General, Dr Newton, the Chief Advocate to the Admiralty, Mr Coniers, Mr Knapp and Mr Cowper. Kidd had some representation, in Dr Oldish and Mr Lemmon, but could only turn to them for matters directly related to points of law. Charged for piracy along with Kidd were Nicholas Churchill, James Howe, Robert Lamley, William Jenkins, Gabriel Loff, Hugh Parrot, Richard Barlycorne, Abel Owens and Darby Mullins.

This was a high-profile case and, while there is no evidence to suggest it, the court room was probably packed. It would have been hot and stuffy. Windows, if there were any, would not have been open because of the stench and noise from the streets of London outside.

The preliminary hearings began with the empowerment of the grand jury and the charges were read out against the prisoners. When it came time for Kidd to hold up his hand and enter a plea, Kidd refused to do so. Instead he asked for the trial to be delayed because he wanted to speak to his counsel on a matter of law. The Clerk of the Court, Dr George Oxenden, replied, 'What matter of law can you have?' He was interrupted by the Clerk of Arraigns, Sir Salathiel Lovell, who said, 'How does he know what it is he is charged with? I have not told him.'

Then Lovell added, 'You must let the Court know what those matters of law are before you can have counsel assigned to you.' Kidd replied they were matters of law. Pressed again by Lovell, Kidd changed tack and asked for a delay so he could get his evidence ready. Lovell insisted Kidd tell the Court what his point of law was. Kidd changed tack again, asking that both his counsel be heard. Lovell replied: 'what you have to say may be heard when you have pleaded to your indictment'.

Now Kidd asked for the French passes to be provided to him. Lovell replied that the trial would not be delayed and demanded that he plead. Kidd responded by continuing to ask for the trial to be delayed because 'I am not really prepared for it'. 'Nor never will, if you can help it,' Lovell replied. 'You have had reasonable notice,' Oxenden said. 'You knew you must be tried and therefore you cannot plead you are not ready.'

Kidd again asked for counsel to be heard and again he was rebuffed, with Lovell demanding he plead. Kidd again asked for counsel to be heard. Mr Lemmon interjected saying that 'he ought to have his papers delivered to him as they are material in his defence'. 'You are not to appear for anyone till he pleads and that the Court assigns you for his counsel.'

Kidd said his papers had been seized and asked for a delay in the trial until he could get the passes he needed. Then he asked again for his counsel to be heard. Again he was told he had to plead first. 'It is a hard case when all these things shall be kept from me,' Kidd said. 'And I am forced to plead.'

For several minutes the stand-off continued. 'Are you guilty or not guilty?' the Court demanded. 'I insist upon my French papers, pray let me have them', Kidd replied. 'Guilty or not guilty?' demanded the court. 'I cannot provide that plea without access to all the documentation', Kidd replied again. 'Guilty or not guilty?' was the response. Under the threat of a judgement against him that he would be an accessory to his own death if he didn't plead, Kidd finally relented raised his hand and entered a plea of not guilty.

The First Trial – 8 May 1701 (Old Bailey London)

With Kidd having pleaded not guilty at the preliminary proceedings, the first trial began once the judges entered and sat down. Arrayed against him were six of the top legal judges in London: Lord Chief Baron Ward, Baron Hatsell, Mr Justice Turton, Mr Justice Gould, Mr Justice Powell and Sir Salathiel Lovell. Once again Oxenden read aloud the charges against Kidd, this time related to the murder of William Moore.

William Kidd, hold up thy hand. Thou standest indicated in the name of William Kidd, late of London, mariner, the jurors of our Sovereign Lord the King do, upon their oath present: That William Kidd, late of London, mariner, not having the fear of God before his eyes, but being moved and seduced by the instigation of the devil, on the thirtieth day of October, in the ninth year of the reign of our Sovereign Lord, William the Third, by the grace of God, of England, Scotland, France and Ireland, King, Defender of the Faith, by force and arms, upon the high seas, near the coast of Malabar, in the East Indies, and within the jurisdiction of the Admiralty of England, in a certain ship, called the *Adventure Galley* (whereof the said William Kidd then was commander), then and there being, feloniously, and of his malice aforethought, then and there did make an assault in and upon one William Moore, in the peace of God and of our said Sovereign Lord the King, to wit, then and there being, and to the ship aforesaid, called the *Adventure Galley*, then and there belonging; and that the aforesaid William Kidd, with a certain wooden bucket, bound with iron hoops, of the value of eight pence, which he the said William Kidd then and there had and held in his right hand, did violently, feloniously, voluntarily, and of his malice aforethought, beat and strike the aforesaid William Moore in and upon the right part of the head of him the said William Moore, a little above the right ear of the said William Moore, then and there upon the high seas, in the ship aforesaid, and within the jurisdiction of the Admiralty of England aforesaid, giving the said William Moore, then and there with the bucket aforesaid, in and upon the aforesaid right part of the head of him, the said William Moore, a little above the right ear of the said William Moore, one mortal bruise; of which mortal bruise the aforesaid William Moore, from the said thirtieth day of October, in the ninth year aforesaid, until the one and thirtieth day of the said month of October, in the year aforesaid, and within the jurisdiction of the Admiralty aforesaid, did languish, and languishing did live; upon which one and thirtieth day of October, in the ninth year aforesaid, the aforesaid William Moore, upon the high sea aforesaid, near the aforesaid coast of Malabar, in the East Indies aforesaid, in the ship aforesaid, called the *Adventure Galley*, and within the jurisdiction of the Admiralty of England aforesaid, did die; and so the jurors aforesaid, upon their oath aforesaid, do say, that the aforesaid William Kidd feloniously, voluntarily, and of his malice aforethought, did kill and murder the aforesaid William Moore upon the high sea aforesaid, and within the jurisdiction of the Admiralty of England aforesaid, in manner and form aforesaid, against the peace of our said Sovereign Lord the King, his Crown and dignity.[12]

He pleaded not guilty to the charge of the murder of William Moore.

Facing the judge and jury Kidd stood alone with no legal knowledge or experience. It was up to him to conduct his own defence and if he was declared guilty of murder he would be hanged, regardless of whether he had committed acts of piracy or not. Execution was the standard punishment for murder. This time, twelve men made up the jury: Nathaniel Long, John Ewers, John Child, Edward Reeves, Thomas Clerk, Nathaniel Green, Henry Sherbrook, Henry Dry, Richard Greenaway, John Sherbrook, Thomas Emms and Roger Mott.[13]

While Kidd had to prove that he did not murder Moore but had killed him accidentally in a fit of rage and had not meant to kill him, which meant the charge could be downgraded to manslaughter, the prosecution had to prove that he had committed murder. They had two key witnesses. The first was Joseph Palmer.

In order for Kidd to be found not guilty of murder the evidence hinged on whether there was mutiny aboard at the time. Kidd's anger was as a result of several attempts at mutiny but the incident took place almost two weeks after Kidd met with the *Loyal Captain* and let her go, according to Palmer. Palmer related the conversation between Kidd and Moore where Kidd called his gunner a 'lousy dog' and Moore replied that if he was a lousy dog Kidd had made him so and brought him and the rest of the crew to ruin. Palmer testified that Kidd picked up a wooden bucket with iron hoops on it and struck Moore on the side of the head.

Furthermore, he claimed the assault that claimed the gunner's life had occurred after the captain had paced up and down a few times rather than instantly after the gunner accused him of carrying them to ruin. Under these circumstances, this could not possibly have been committed in a moment of rage so it was murder.

Kidd's cross-examination of Palmer may have made things worse. He asked Palmer what Moore was doing at the time. 'He was grinding a chisel,' Palmer replied. 'Was there another ship?' 'Yes,' replied Palmer. 'A Dutch ship.' 'What were you doing with that ship?' 'She was becalmed.' Kidd then said that the ship was close by and some men wanted to take her but he refused and that Moore said that he, Kidd, always got in the way of the men making their fortunes by refusing to take these ships. Kidd then directly asked Palmer if there was mutiny onboard. 'No', Palmer said. 'There was no mutiny; all was quiet.'

One of the jurors then asked Palmer why Kidd struck Moore and Palmer replied because he wouldn't take the *Loyal Captain* two weeks beforehand. Palmer was then asked by the Court if he knew of any other reason why Kidd would strike Moore and Palmer answered that he didn't.

The next prosecution witness was Robert Bradinham. His testimony was as damning as Palmer's. First he said that after Kidd hit Moore the gunner said that 'Captain Kidd has given me my last blow.' Bradinham maintained that Kidd heard these words and said: 'Damn him, he is a villain.' Bradinham then added that two months later Kidd said to him that he wasn't sorry about the death of his gunner because 'I have good friends in England that will bring me off for that.' He also stated that the blow to the head showed a small wound but had fractured the skull which he believed was the reason why Moore died, although it took him a day to die.

In his defence Kidd was allowed to call some of his crew. The cook, Abel Owens, spoke first. He testified that after Moore said that Kidd had brought them all to ruin that Kidd replied: 'I have not brought you to ruin, I have not done an ill thing to ruin you; you are a saucy fellow to give me these words.' At that point Owens said that Kidd hit Moore with the bucket.

Again, the point of whether or not there was mutiny at the time of the incident was raised and Owens was asked directly if Moore was making mutiny before Kidd hit him and Owens, like Palmer, replied that he wasn't.

Another juror asked Owens if Kidd threw the bucket at Moore or picked it up and struck the gunner with it. 'He took it with the strap, and struck him with it,' Owens replied. 'Did I not throw it at him?' Kidd cried. 'No; I was near you when you did it.'

Unfortunately for Kidd Richard Barlycorne's testimony was confusing and contradictory. He stated that there was mutiny aboard when the *Loyal Captain* was within sight of the *Adventure Galley*. When pressed he said that this was not when Moore was killed. He also stated that Moore was sick in bed well before the blow was given and that the doctor said that the blow was not the cause of his death.

To clarify the issue, the court recalled Bradinham and he was asked if the blow caused Moore's death and the doctor replied 'I never said that the blow which Moore received from Captain Kidd was not the cause of his death. Moore was not sick at all before he received the blow.'

The third witness for the defence, Hugh Parrot, testified that the incident between Moore and Kidd took place at least a week after the *Loyal Captain* had been let go. He said that, at the time when the *Loyal Captain* was alongside, there were the beginnings of mutiny as some men wanted to take the ship but Kidd told them that if they left the *Adventure Galley* they would never come aboard again and that he would force them into Bombay where they would be brought before the council there. Parrot then said that when the incident with Moore took place he wasn't on deck so 'I understood afterwards that the blow was given, but how I cannot tell.'

The Court then asked Kidd if he had anything to say. He replied by saying, 'it was not designedly done, but in my passion, for which I am heartily sorry'. But he had nothing else to add. The Lord Chief Baron then read the charge to the jury and a little later Kidd was found guilty.

The Second Trial – 9 May 1701 (Old Bailey, London)

The next day the second trial took place with Kidd in the dock with other prisoners Nicholas Churchill, James Howe, Robert Lamley, William Jenkins, Gabriel Loff, Hugh Parrot, Richard Barlycorne, Abel Owens and Darby Mullins. The charge against them all was piracy and robbery of the *Quedagh Merchant / Adventure Prize*.

This time the jury was made up of John Cooper, John Hall, John James, Peter Parker, Caleb Hook, Robert Rider, Peter Walker, William Hunt, John Micklethwait, Richard Chiswell, Abraham Hickman and George Grove.[14]

Each of the defendants pleaded not guilty to the charges and the case rested on whether or not the ship had been taken legally.

Bradinham was again witness for the prosecution and he related the entire incident of the taking of the *Quedah Merchant* and the subsequent division of the spoils. When Kidd cross-examined him he asked him if he'd seen the French passes and Bradinham replied, 'You told me you had French passes, but I never did see them.' Kidd asked him again and Bradinham replied: 'I never saw any; but I only said I heard you say you had them.'

Without the French passes, Kidd really had no defence against the charge of piracy. When the *Quedagh Merchant* was approached by the *Adventure Galley*, the latter ship was flying French flags, a common ruse that privateers and navies used in times of war. But as far as the Court was concerned, the fact that Kidd was flying French colours which prompted the *Quedagh Merchant* to display a French pass showed his intentions were not honourable.

Bradinham was then cross-examined by the other prisoners. Churchill, Jenkins, Howe, Barlycorne and Mullins all asked him if they ever disobeyed their captain's orders and he replied they didn't. Each in turn asked if they had a share of the goods from the ship and Bradinham said they had. Then Palmer took the stand for the prosecution and related the events that led up to the mass mutiny on Sainte Marie.

When pressed by Kidd about the French passes he too said he'd heard of them but had never seen them. 'I did hear you say that you had French passes but never saw them.'

Kidd's commissions were then read out in Court, one commissioning him as a privateer and the other to cruise for pirates. The Court asked Kidd if he could prove that there were French passes aboard the *Quedah Merchant*. 'My lord, these men said they heard several say so.' 'But all came from you.'

The Lord Chief Baron then asked Kidd 'Now that you have had the commissions read, what do you excuse yourself by?' Kidd denied having given the order to share the goods from the ship, saying he wasn't there when it took place. He was then asked why he didn't take Culliford and Kidd replied that most of his men had gone ashore.

Mr Justice Powell said: 'But you presented him with great guns and swore you would not meddle with them.'

Going back over the testimonies, Lord Chief Baron added that Kidd had said to Culliford that he would 'fry in hell before I will do you any harm'. Kidd's reply was: 'that is only what these witnesses say'.

In his defence Kidd claimed he didn't have the French passes that would prove his innocence but he was incapable of providing any witnesses to confirm his side of the story. He had character witnesses but none who could corroborate the events that took place regarding the *Quedah Merchant*.

The Third Trial – 9 May 1701 (Old Bailey, London)

That same day the third trial was held on two counts for piracy. This time the jury was made up of William Smith, Benjamin Hooper, John Hibbert, John Pettit, William Hatch, Joseph Chaplain, Peter Gray, Robert Comfort, Thomas Hollis, William Ford, Thomas Stephens and John Dodson.[15]

The first indictment was for the taking of a Moorish vessel some fifty leagues from Carwar and, though the ship isn't named, Captain Parker is named by Bradinham as its commander so we can assume it was the *Mary*. In his testimony for the prosecution Bradinham stated that Captain Parker and a Portuguese linguist were brought aboard by Kidd, who also took out 'some of the men and bound their hands behind them, and ordered them to be drubbed with a naked cutlass'.

Bradinham then said that Kidd took the cargo of pepper, coffee, Arabian gold, clothes and several other items but let the ship go, while keeping Parker and the Portuguese aboard. This testimony ties in with other reports we've seen that Kidd kept Parker as a prisoner to act as his pilot.

The second indictment was for the piracy and robbery of a ship some four leagues from Calicut on 27 November. This again is not named, but described as a Moorish vessel, out of which was taken apparel and tackle worth £500, eleven bales of cotton worth £60, two horses worth £20 each and fifty Indian quilts worth £5.[16] This would have been the ship that the crew later renamed the *November*, commanded by Captain Michael Dickers.

Bradinham testified that Dickers told him he was a Dutchman and that he took up arms under Captain Kidd. He also said that all of the prisoners were aboard the *Adventure Galley* when both these ships were taken. He continued by saying that when they got to Sainte Marie Kidd was very friendly with Culliford and he ordered that all the goods they'd plundered be hoisted out of the ships and shared with the crew. 'The captain divided out the shares.'

'He tells a thousand lies,' Kidd declared.

Kidd then asked if Bradinham had a share and he replied he had. 'Did you not then come aboard my ship and rob the surgeon's chest?' 'No I did not.' 'Did I not come to you when you went away and met you on the deck and said, "Why do you take the chest away?"?' 'No, I did not do it.'

'He is a rogue!' exclaimed Kidd.

Then it was Palmer again for the prosecution and in his testimony he too stated that Kidd had taken a Moorish ship commanded by Parker. He testified that when they got to Sainte Marie Kidd ordered the goods to be shared out and that he was on friendly terms with Culliford.

In his defence Kidd could only call a character witness, Colonel Hewetson, an old friend with whom he had served in the West Indies when he was in command

Captain Kidd on a legal
Cuban one peso coin.
Author's collection

A battle of small
arms fire from
the deck of a
pirate ship.
*Copyright David
Barlow and
reprinted by kind
permission*

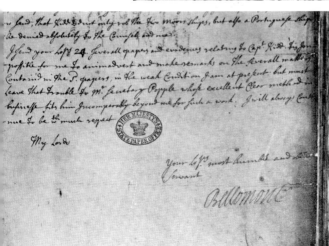

A letter from Lord
Bellomont announcing
Kidd's arrest. *Now held in
the National Archives at Kew*

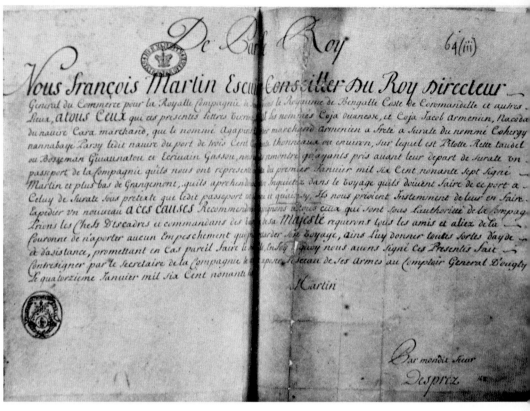

French pass from the *Quedah Merchant. Now held at the National Archives in Kew*

French pass carried by the *Maiden. Now held at the National Archives in Kew*

Burying treasure as
Kidd's legend suggests.

Careening a ship. *Copyright by David Barlow and reprinted by kind permission.*

Kidd's privateering commission. *Now held at the National Archives at Kew*

A pinnace at sail after leaving the mother ship in the background. *Author's collection*

A replica galleon from an earlier century, anchored in modern Bristol harbour, showing the type of vessel early explorers used on voyages similiar to Kidd's epic journey in the late seventeenth century. *Author's collection*

Captain Kidd's signature. *Held at the National Archives at Kew*

Boarding the *Quedah Merchant*. *Copyright by David Barlow and reprinted by kind permission.*

Pirate Sir Henry Morgan as he appears on a legal Cuban one peso coin. *Author's collection*

Battle at sea between a pirate ship (left) and a merchantman. *Author's collection*

A contemporary
portrait of Kidd from
an unknown source.

An example of a gun deck on a large warship.
The gun deck on the Adventure Galley would
have looked similar to this.

Captain Kidd's body after
he was executed he was
strung up by the Thames
River as an example to
other criminals.

A two-masted modern sailing vessel similar to a sloop but smaller and now used for pleasure cruising rather than commercial trade.
Author's collection

Two modern sailing vessels tied up together. While these two modern sailing ships have sails they also have engines for navigating in harbours. These vessels are not used solely for trade as they would have been in Kidd's day.
Author's collection

of the *Blessed William*. Hewetson did his best for Kidd, claiming that the captain would rather have himself shot dead than turn pirate. But Hewetson's description was of a character several years previously and it carried little weight with the jury and the judges.

Nicholas Churchill, James Howe, Gabriel Loff, Hugh Parrot, Abel Owens, Darby Mullins and Captain William Kidd were found guilty of piracy and robbery on both counts. The apprentices Richard Barlycorne, Robert Lamley and William Jenkins were found not guilty.

The Fourth Trial – 9 May 1701 (Old Bailey, London)

For this trial the jury changed again and consisted of Joseph Watson, Joseph Viller, George Ashby, Edward Fenwick, Gilbert East, Thomas Humfrevil, Thomas Plaisted, Samuel Rown, Marmaduke Bludder, John Scot, John Reynolds and Richard Drew. One interesting point in this trial is that Kidd's old nemesis Robert Culliford was also in the dock charged with piracy.[17]

Again there were two indictments for piracy. The first was on a Moorish ship taken about four leagues from Calicut. From this, the plundered goods were apparel and tackle valued at £50, thirty tubs of sugar candy valued at £15, six bales of sugar valued at £6, and ten bales of tobacco valued at £10. The final indictment was for an act of piracy on a Portuguese ship twelve leagues from Calicut. The cargo of this ship consisted of two chests of opium to a value of £40, eight bags of rice to the value of £12, ten tons of bees wax to the value of £10, thirty jars of butter to the value of £10 and half a ton of iron to the value of £4.[18]

Abel Owens, Nicholas Churchill and James Howe claimed the protection of the King's Pardon to these two indictments, while the rest of the prisoners pleaded not guilty, but their pleas were overruled by the court. 'It was adjudged that they could not be entitled to the benefit of the said proclamation, because they had not in all circumstances complied with the conditions of it.'[19]

In the dock with Culliford were some of his crew, all of them accused of piracy and robbery, especially of the ship *Great Mahomet* and all its cargo and passengers. Culliford, Nicholas Churchill, James Howe, Darby Mullins and John Eldridge all pleaded not guilty to all counts. Culliford and Robert Hickman also pleaded not guilty to taking another two ships. Remember that most of Kidd's men had left him at Sainte Marie and gone aboard Culliford's ship, so it isn't surprising to find some of them indicted alongside Culliford.

The trial transcripts state that Culliford retracted his not-guilty plea and changed it to guilty under the King's Pardon. All the other prisoners followed Culliford's lead and changed their pleas to guilty under the King's Pardon, except John Eldridge who was tried alone and found guilty.

By some strange twist of fate Culliford that day was spared the gallows. Indeed, the transcripts say he was 'set aside'. It must have filled Kidd with fury and deep despair to know that his nemesis had once again beaten him – this time escaping the clutches of death.

Only Richard Barlycorne, William Jenkins and Robert Lamley were found to be not guilty or acquitted while all the rest (Nicholas Churchill, James Howe, Gabriel Loff, Hugh Parrot, Abel Owens, Darby Mullins, Robert Hickman, John Eldridge, and of course William Kidd) were found guilty of piracy and robbery. Kidd was found guilty of murder. It was almost two years from arrest to trial for Kidd and his crew members but it took only two days for the entire proceedings to be played out.

Mullins tried to plead for mercy, saying he served under the King's commission so if he'd disobeyed his captain he would have endured extreme punishment. 'The men were never allowed to call their officers to an account, why they did this or why they did that, because such a liberty would destroy all discipline.' 'Acting under the commission justifies what is lawful but not what is unlawful', the court replied. Mullins added that if the men were in danger of obeying unlawful commands from the officers and punished for not obeying them or if they were allowed to dispute orders then there would be no command at sea. His complaints fell on deaf ears and the court said that the fact that he had taken his share of the plunder and been involved in the mutinies showed that he'd paid no obedience whatsoever to the commission.

Nicholas Churchill, James Howe, Abel Owens, Darby Mullins and Robert Hickman all claimed that they had attended under the King's Pardon, which was countered by the Court, claiming that they were not within its wording; Gabriel Loff consistently claimed he was innocent; Hugh Parrot claimed that he had surrendered to Lord Bellomont because he was innocent; and John Eldridge claimed he had been falsely accused.

Kidd maintained his innocence to the last. In his account of Captain Kidd, Johnson tells us that Kidd said: 'I went out in laudable employment and had no occasion to go a-pirating. The men mutinied against me and ninety-five left me at one time and set fire to my ship.'[20]

In Johnson's account of Kidd, published in his book *A General History of the Most Notorious Pirates* a little more than two decades after Kidd's death, he claims that Kidd also said that the two prizes were 'taken by virtue of a commission under the broad seal, they having French Passes'. At the end of the proceedings Kidd said that 'I have been sworn against by perjured and wicked people.'[21]

For all the men found guilty the sentence was death by execution as the clerk stated. 'You shall be taken from this place where you are, and be carried to the place from whence you came, and from thence to the place of execution, and there be severally hanged by your necks until you be dead. And the Lord have mercy on your souls.'[22]

The incident with Parker shows that Kidd was not as innocent as he claimed to be. He kidnapped Parker and held him prisoner below decks to act as his pilot for the waters along the Indian coast. Did he order the men on the *Mary* to be beaten with cutlasses? Did he have a man tied to a tree and shot? Did he turn pirate? Much of the evidence suggests he did. If so, then why did he maintain he was innocent right up until the very end? His last words about being sworn against by perjured and wicked people have eerie echoes to Lee Harvey Oswald's claim that he was a patsy in the assassination of JFK.

The Devil's Jig

The day Kidd died was 23 May 1701. He had lived longer than Lord Bellomont who had battled gout for many years before finally succumbing.[1] In the hope of a stay of execution Kidd wrote to Robert Harley, the Tory Speaker of the House of Commons. In his letter he said that if he was set free he could recover £100,000 he had hidden in the West Indies which he would hand over to the government. But Kidd had had his chance and failed to make an impact. Harley ignored his request. Ever since, the letter has fuelled the passions of treasure hunters around the world.[2]

Now began an even more difficult task than bringing the pirates to justice: the distribution of the wealth that Kidd had plundered and that Bellomont had seized. The line of people to whom Kidd owed money increased regularly. Indeed, India merchant Coji Babba wanted to recover all the goods he'd lost taken from the *Quedah Merchant*. He managed to get an audience to see Kidd but it was fruitless. All he could do was file a claim and hope that he would be reimbursed. Some of the widows of the crew of the *Adventure Galley* also met with Kidd about their husbands' share of the loot. But they too would have to wait and place themselves at the mercy of the courts.

Paul Lorrain was the pastor of Newgate and was responsible for the spiritual well-being of the prison population. In this case, he urged the pirates, including Kidd, to repent their sins. After they had been condemned he visited them twice a day on the run-up to the execution. On 18 May 1701 he gave two sermons in the chapel to a packed audience. Ritchie describes the scene in his book, stating 'the attractions at these services were the condemned, who were made to sit in the front pews, facing a coffin draped in black'.[3]

Lorrain continued to urge the men to repent and finally Mullins and Eldridge confessed their sins, succumbing to his cries for repentance. Kidd remained unmoved. Perhaps, as Ritchie suggests, he was expecting a last-minute reprieve and so didn't see the need to repent anything. The only person who did get a last-minute reprieve from the King was Eldridge.

The execution of a pirate, or a group of pirates, was a public event, a popular past-time, and something of a holiday treat. To watch someone convicted of piracy strung up by the neck, their legs thrashing in the air, until they were dead was the equivalent of a good day out.

Kidd's journey to meet his maker began with a procession of the accused in wooden horse-drawn carts that left Newgate and headed out onto Holborn and turned east towards the City of London and the Thames. Normally they would head towards Tyburn but the Admiralty Court Execution Dock was in Wapping so they turned east.[4]

As the crowds gathered, street peddlers sold their wares to citizens whose minds were caught up in the enjoyment of a day's entertainment. 'The very poor and the very rich and every social group in between came to witness the drama of the last moments of the condemned.' Shopkeepers would ensure they had signs up inviting passers-by into their premises with offers of special low prices.[5] Along the way people would give the condemned liquor while others would abuse them. According to Lorrain's account Kidd arrived at the gibbet drunk: he'd either been given alcohol on the way or had been drinking most of the night.

By the time the procession reached Execution Dock, there was a huge crowd. Execution Dock had been used by the Admiralty for disposing of its criminals who'd been sentenced to death for the previous 270 years. Since the Admiralty could only claim jurisdiction over crimes at sea, the actual gallows were located off land, on a makeshift platform, where the tide regularly ebbed and flowed around posts in the ground.[6]

Criminals had the chance to speak to the crowd who usually only cared about how long it would take these public enemies to die. Allowing them to speak was to give the convicted felons a chance to repent their sins and state that their sentence was justified. It rarely worked out that way.

Once the executioner had secured the noose around their necks they would drop only a short distance. Instead of the swift death by having their necks broken by a long rope, the pirates would die slowly from asphyxiation. As a further humiliation and deterrent, their bodies would then be left to dangle or be bound to the nearby posts until the tide had washed over them three times before they were removed.

The number of men executed that day varies depending on the source. Ritchie states that only Kidd, Eldridge and Mullins were to be hanged, along with two French pirates, while the rest were to wait to see if clemency was forthcoming. Johnson, however, states that 'Wherefore about a week after, Captain Kidd, Nicholas Churchill, James How, Gabriel Loff, Hugh Parrot, Abel Owens and Darby Mullins, were executed at Execution Dock, and afterwards hung up in chains, at some distance from each other, down the river, where their bodies hung exposed for many years.'

When Kidd was given a chance to say a few last words, he blamed everyone except himself, including his crew and Bellomont. When the steps were kicked away, the men fell. Legs danced as the pirates choked to death. The crowd cheered and applauded.

Kidd looked up. He was still alive. His rope had broken. Kidd was too disorientated with alcohol to know that he may have had a new lease of life; but it wouldn't have mattered if he did. A new noose was prepared.[7] Kidd was man-handled back into position. The execution was carried out again. If the rope broke again, it surely would be seen as divine intervention. This time, and to the delight of the cheering crowd, the rope remained intact and Kidd danced in thin air until he was strangled by the weight of his own body.

Like the others that were hanged, his body was secured until three tides had covered him. He was by then covered in congealed grime. The body was then coated in tar – to delay the decaying effect and to deter birds pecking it – and encased in a metal cage, specifically built just large enough to hold a dead man's bloated body in a standing position. The cage was suspended at Tilbury Point, where any ship entering or leaving the River Thames would have a full view of it and the dead captain inside. The sight was a warning against anyone choosing a life of piracy.

Kidd's Legacy

What did Kidd leave behind other than his family? His widow, Sarah Bradley Cox Oort Kidd was also under suspicion and put in jail by Bellomont, who seized all the property she had in Boston. But he had no evidence against her and so she was released. She began slowly to reacquire her property and managed to get some of the loot that Kidd had left behind. Perhaps he distributed the booty to so many different places to help his wife in acquiring it? In 1703 she remarried and she died in 1744 in New Jersey in her mid-seventies, having outlived four husbands and raised five children. It took her three years to unravel the red tape surrounding her property and be allowed back into her own home.

Aside from his family, Kidd's biggest legacy is the treasure rumoured to be scattered all over the world. It is a legend that still persists today and fuels the romantic myth of the flamboyant pirate Captain Kidd; but there is nothing at all glamorous about Kidd's sad story. In his letter to Parliament, Kidd explained that he'd hidden treasure worth £100,000, but was he bluffing? It is one aspect of Kidd's story in which the jury is still out and that's what brings a sense of wonder and excitement to his story to this day, along with great speculation.

There is also the theory that Kidd hid his treasure along the coast somewhere between Gardiner's Island and Block Island. He was met by his wife and Emot the lawyer when he first arrived in the waters around New York. We've seen that Kidd unloaded cargo onto sloops that met with him around Gardiner's Island and Block Island, where some of his crewmates unloaded their chests as well.

Sarah sent a bag of several pieces of eight with Thomas Way, while Thomas Paine of Jamestown, Rhode Island, was given an unknown amount of gold to take away for safekeeping. Several pounds of gold were given to Thomas Clarke by Kidd and Clarke took those to a Major Jonathan Selleck in Stamford, Connecticut, who was accused of receiving more than £10,000 from Kidd.[1]

We know that Kidd left several bales of cloth and a chest with Gardiner, along with a box of gold. Most of this was tracked down once Bellomont had arrested Kidd and locked him up. Gardiner sent Bellomont several bags of gold and silver while Bellomont sent out men to track down Way, Paine and Clarke to seize any loot they had and question them about Kidd's activities.

Bellomont sent £14,000 of Kidd's loot that he'd reclaimed back to England on

HMS *Advice* but whether there was any more is something we will never know. 'If there was a substantial amount, it was surely in the hands of some individual and subsequently spent', Ritchie writes in his book. An interesting point to note is that the £100,000 Kidd claimed was the exact value quoted in the Articles of Agreement originally signed by Livingston, Bellomont and himself.[2]

So Kidd left behind two mysteries, the possibility of buried treasure which may or may not be true and the mystery of the wrecked ships, specifically the *Adventure Galley* and *Adventure Prize*.

In 2007, a wreckage was discovered off the coast of the Dominican Republic which is believed to be the wreck of the *Quedah Marchant/Adventure Prize*. The spot is certainly very likely and as it seems to have been found relatively intact it has raised the question whether the ship really did burn as Captain Evertse claimed in his account. Was he simply stating this to throw Bellomont and others off the trail so he could return sometime later to scavenge for Kidd's lost loot? Maybe the wreck is an entirely different ship; but the find does add further intrigue into Kidd's story.

Perhaps one good thing that comes out of Kidd's story is the fact that when Queen Anne came to the throne she donated around £6,471 of the monies seized from Kidd towards the establishment of Greenwich Hospital.

Annexe A – Crew Members Who Served with Kidd

The following list shows some of the more notable people who served with Captain Kidd aboard different ships.

Robert Culliford	First mate (*Blessed William* – mutinied against Kidd and became a pirate)
Henry (James) Mead	Second-In-Command (*Adventure Galley* – died on Mohelia Island)
Abel Owens	Ship's cook (*Adventure Galley*, *Adventure Prize*)
William Moore	Gunner (*Adventure Galley* – killed by Kidd)
John Walker	Quartermaster (*Adventure Galley*)
Robert Bradinham	Ship surgeon (*Adventure Galley* – prosecution witness against Kidd)
Armand Viola	Ship's surgeon's mate (*Adventure Galley*)
John Brown	Crewman (*Blessed William*, *Adventure Galley*)
John Weir	Passenger (*Adventure Galley*, *Adventure Prize*)
Saunders Douglas	Lookout (*Adventure Galley* – died on Mohelia Island)
Richard Barlycorne	Cabin boy to Captain Kidd (*Adventure Galley*)
George Bullen	Chief mate (*Adventure Galley*), Acting Captain (Adventure Prize)
John Parcrick	Crewman (*Adventure Galley*)
Samuel Bradley	Crewman (*Adventure Galley*)
Benjamin Franks	Passenger and crewman (*Adventure Galley* – deserted in India)
Hugh Parrot	Gunner (*Adventure Galley*, *Adventure Prize*)
Robert Lamley	Apprentice to Abel Owen (*Adventure Galley*)
William Jenkins	Apprentice to George Bullen (*Adventure Galley* – a resident of Bow, London, and joined at Plymouth)
Gabriel Loff	Crewman (*Adventure Galley* – a resident of Long Island and joined at New York)
Nicholas Churchill	Crewman (*Adventure Galley* – joined at Mohelia Island)

Ventura Rosair	Crewman (*Adventure Galley* – joined at Mohelia Island)
Nicholas Alderson	Crewman (*Adventure Galley*)
Jonathon Treadway	Crewman (*Adventure Galley* – deserted in India)
Joseph Palmer	Crewman (*Adventure Galley* – prosecution witness against Kidd)
Michael Dickers	Master (*Adventure Galley* – joined at Malabar Coast)
Pierre LeRoy	Crewman (*Adventure Galley* – joined at Johanna Island)
Darby Mullins	Crewman (*Adventure Galley* – executed with Kidd)
John Hales	Gunner (*Adventure Prize* – joined at Sainte Marie)
Dudley Raynor	First mate (*Adventure Prize* – joined at Sainte Marie)
James Gilliam	Passenger (*Adventure Prize* – joined at Sainte Marie)
John Dear	Deckhand (*Adventure Prize*)
John Fishelis	Deckhand (*Adventure Prize*)
John Elms	First mate (*Adventure Prize*)
Michael Calloway	Boatswain (*Adventure Prize*)
Samuel Arris	Steward (*Adventure Galley*, *Adventure Prize*)
Alexander Gordon	Mate (*Adventure Galley*)
Alexander Milbourne	Boatswain (*Adventure Galley*)
Walter Dorman	Gunner (*Adventure Galley*)
John Peake	Carpenter (*Adventure Galley*)
Arnant Fielde	Ship surgeon (*Adventure Galley*)
John Oate	Cook (*Adventure Galley*)
Arthur Pearse	Midshipman (*Adventure Galley*)
Edward Buckmaster	Crewman (*Adventure Galley*)
Edward Davis	Crewman (*Adventure Prize*)

Annexe B – Legend

Here is everything advantageous to life.

(William Shakespeare, *The Tempest*)

What fuels a legend? Notoriety and wonder. A classic case, aside from Kidd is that of Dick Turpin. The romantic highwayman and the long ride to York, all so exciting and romantic, really didn't happen. And Captain Kidd? Buccaneer of the high seas that hid a fortune in gold and was also hanged, like his highwayman counterpart, for his crimes. Sounds so glamorous; but it's only the hanging we can be sure of for both men with regard to the legend.

In searching for the truth regarding Captain Kidd, we have to ensure that no one feels we have left any truths out regarding hidden treasure. The legend of Kidd – like Dick Turpin – is a strong one and, therefore, cannot be broken down by a single book after generations of hearsay. What we have written here is the story of Captain Kidd who took on a bad deal, risked everything and, in the face of evidence, committed acts that could only be seen as illegal. He did his best to stay within the law, within his commission. Yes, he made some bad decisions along the way, but that is his story. It has nothing to do with burying gold on treasure islands and having swashbuckling sword fights, as depicted in Hollywood movies. In fact, there is a whole book's worth of information on how Hollywood has twisted the already exaggerated facts regarding pirates and outlaws, not just the story of Captain Kidd.

It is strange that we glamorize criminals: Ned Kelly, Jessie James and the Kray Twins are classic examples. But what about Kidd, was he really a criminal? In the eyes of the law – to this day – he is and, therefore, to all law-abiding citizens he should remain so, until some intelligent spark tries to clear his name. And why should anyone do that, what purpose would it serve? Bringing down the legend would bring perspective to Kidd and piracy at a time where the average person in the street thinks it all jolly good fun, full of mystical sea creatures and loveable rogues.

It is up to the biographers and historians to examine legends, perhaps in modest tomes like this, to tell the basic story and let people begin to understand that certain characters are not as black as they have been previously painted. There's a lot to be said in making your own mind up and not believing all you read in novels and see on films, however entertaining.

'Avast there!' cried Silver. 'Who are you, Tom Morgan? Maybe you thought you were Cap'n here, perhaps. By the powers, but I'll teach you better! Cross me, and you'll go where many a good man's gone before you, first and last, these thirty years back – some to the yard-arm, shiver my sides! And some by the board, and all to feed the fishes. There's never a man looked me between the eyes and seen a good day afterwards, Tom Morgan, you may lay to that.' (Robert Louis Stevenson, *Treasure Island*)

Annexe C – Timeline of Kidd's Maritime Career

Listed here is a sequence of events in Captain Kidd's maritime career that we can be certain of.

3 October 1695	Investors into the mission of Adventure Galley located
10 October 1695	Articles signed between Kidd, Livingston and Bellomont
4 December 1695	*Adventure Galley* launched in Deptford
11 December 1695	Commission presented to Captain Kidd as a privateer
26 January 1696	Commission presented to Captain Kidd to seize pirates
25 February 1696	Kidd receives his sailing orders from Bellomont
27 February 1696	*Adventure Galley* begins its first voyage commanded by Captain Kidd
1 March 1696	*Adventure Galley* stopped and some of the crew pressed into RN service
1 April 1696	Admiral Shovell attacks Calais. Private ships allowed to leave England
10 April 1696	*Adventure Galley* arrives at the Downs
May 1696	*Adventure Galley* captures French fishing vessel in Atlantic Ocean
4 July 1696	*Adventure Galley* arrives in New York
6 September 1696	*Adventure Galley* departs from New York with its newly formed crew
8 October 1696	*Adventure Galley* arrives at Madeira
19 October 1696	*Adventure Galley* passes Bona Vista
24 October 1696	*Adventure Galley* arrives at St Jago
12 December 1696	William Kidd sails with Captain (or Commodore) Warren at the Cape of Good Hope
18 December 1696	William Kidd sneaks away from Warren
28 January 1697	*Adventure Galley* arrives at Toliara, Madagascar
29 January 1697	Kidd sights *Loyal Russell* and Mr Hatton dies in his cabin

25 March 1697	Deadline for Kidd to return to England
10 April 1697	*Sceptre* commissioned as a pirate hunter by the East India Company
25 April 1697	*Adventure Galley* sails to the Red Sea[2]
Mid-August 1697	*Adventure Galley* leaves the Red Sea
9 September 1697	*Adventure Galley* arrives at the coast of India
20 September 1697	Kidd commits his first alleged act of piracy, attacking the *Mary*[3]
October 1697	Two crewmen desert at Carwar and spread stories of piracy
30 October 1697	William Kidd attacks William Moore
31 October 1697	William Moore dies from his wound
27 November 1697	Kidd commits his second alleged act of piracy
28 December 1697	Kidd commits his third alleged act of piracy
20 January 1698	Kidd commits his fourth alleged act of piracy; on a Portuguese ship
30 January 1698	Kidd takes *Quedagh Merchant*, the fifth alleged act of piracy
1 April 1698	Kidd reaches Sainte Marie (St Mary's Island) with *Adventure Galley*
1 April 1698	Kidd encounters Robert Culliford
7 April 1698	*Adventure Prize* arrives at Sainte Marie
6 May 1698	*November* arrives at Sainte Marie
15 June 1698	*Mocha Frigate* sails with most of Kidd's crew aboard
September 1698	Kidd leaves Sainte Marie in *Adventure Galley*
18 November 1698	East India Company reports Kidd's acts of piracy
20 November 1698	The order is issued to track and seize Kidd
23 November 1698	Letter sent to colonial governors to seize Kidd on sight
April 1699	Kidd arrives in the West Indies
15 May 1699	Kidd abandons *Adventure Prize* and leaves in *St Antonio*
15 May 1699	President of Nevis Council sends HMS *Queenborough* to catch Kidd
27 May 1699	HMS *Queenborough* abandons the search mission
9 June 1699	Kidd arrives at Oyster Bay
19 June 1699	Bellomont writes to Kidd, inviting him to come ashore
24 June 1699	Kidd replies to Bellomont, stating that he will come ashore
25 June 1699	Sarah Kidd visits her husband aboard the *St Antonio*
29 June 1699	*Adventure Prize* is reported destroyed by fire
30 June 1699	Kidd encounters Thomas Way
2 July 1699	Kidd lands at Boston
3 July 1699	Kidd visits Bellomont

6 July 1699	Bellomont has Kidd arrested
17 July 1699	Bellomont receives letter from Captain Evertse about *Adventure Prize* burning
3 August 1699	Captain Carey sails to recover Kidd's treasure
1 February 1700	HMS *Advice* arrives in Boston to collect Kidd
21 February 1700	Joseph Palmer (prosecution witness against Kidd) surrenders to Bellomont
10 March 1700	HMS *Advice* leaves Boston with Kidd onboard
16 March 1700	House of Commons decides to question Kidd, but not until the next session
11 April 1700	Kidd is transferred to King's yacht *Katherine*
13 April 1700	Kidd arrives in England as a prisoner
14 April 1700	Kidd is presented to the Admiralty Board
28 March 1701	Kidd is presented to the House of Commons
8–9 May 1701	Kidd stands trial for murder and piracy
23 May 1701	Kidd executed

Annexe D – Articles of Agreement

Below is a copy of the articles of agreement between Captain William Kidd, Commander of the *Adventure Galley*, and John Walker, Quartermaster, dated 10 September 1696:

> The Captain shall receive for the ship, the finding her in wear and tear, 35 shares, and five full shares for himself and his commission of such treasure etc. as shall be taken by sea or land. (ii) The Master shall receive two shares and the Captain shall allow all the other officers a gratification above their own shares as he shall deem reasonable. Other arrangements for rewards, fines and compensations, e.g.: (6) 100 pieces of eight for the loss of a finger or toe; (8) 100 pieces of eight for the man who shall first see a sail, if she prove to be a prize; (10) that man that shall prove a coward, or (11) that shall be drunk in time of engagement before the prisoners then taken be secured, shall lose his share. Signed, William Kidd. Subscribed and agreed to by the ship's company;

Starboard Watch	Larboard Watch
Robert Bradinham	Henry Meade
George Bullen	John Warker
Alexander Milberry	(Quartermaster)
William Beck	Henry Olive
John Torksey	William Moore
George Sinkler	Alex Gordon
John Wier	John Finely
Samuel Bradley	Joseph Palmer
Peter Hammond	John Smith
Archibald B. Bohanan	Barnet Higgins
William Skines	William Bowyer
Edward Collins	William Turner
Edward Roberts	Walter King
Peter B. Rouse	Edward Spooner
Ellis Strong	Robert Smithers
Yoer oovrall	Thomas Purdeg

Thomas Hobson
John Pears
Joseph Budden
William Rowles
Jan Spons
John Jonson
Hendrick Albert
John Browne
Cornelius Orwyn
John Marten
Nicholas Jennings
Andries Jeaniszen
William Wellman
Charles Bathurst
John Davis
Thomas Fletcher
Edward Buckmaster
William Hunt
Hercules Bredsteed
Jan de Roodt
John West
John Fling
Daniel Mokoricke
Henry Sanders
Edward Graham
Aldris Saerdenbreech
George Tarpole
John Burton
Ebenezar Milker
James Alger
William Percy
Nicholas Tredgidgen
Phillip Cunninghame
James Carr
Robert Hunt
John Hunt, Junior
William Whitley
William Arnett
Neschen
Isaac Ambros
John Hunt, senior
William Weakum

John Kemble
Hugh Washington
Robert Ruderford
Richard Basnet
Jacob Cornelijs
Morgan Harris
Peter Lee
Michael Calloway
Ery Geyseler
John Fletcher
Clexfidders [sic]
Humphrey Cley
Jacob Horran
John Watson
Henry Bainbridge
Nicholas Tuder
Harman Buger
Bernard Looman
Hendrickus Cregier
Peter de Roy
James Betles
Henry Pietersen
Casper Spreall
David Carsson
Noah East
James How
David Mullings
Samuel Taylor
John Collings
Henry Evertse
Joseph Hill
Richard Wildey, senr.
William Wildey, junior
Thomas Wright
Peter Smith
Gabriel Loff
Alexander Mumford
William Holden
Patrick Dinner
William Bowyer, Senior
Peter Fewb
Robert Clem.

Jacob Conklin
Benjamin Franks
Isaac Dernes
Samuel Aires
John de Mart
Simon de Woolf
John Parerick, negro
John Roberts
Govert Baners

Mich. Evens
Andrew How
English Smith
Aba. Coucher
Jonathan Tredway
Andrew Calwell

Annexe E – Letters Concerning Kidd

3 December 1699

In a letter written by Mr R Yard, Secretary to the Lords Justice, to Mr Lowndes of the Treasury, a copy of Kidd's commission and warrant was enclosed in order for the Lord Chancellor to put the great seal on to it.

> The commission is not now with it, nor is the warrant, but there is a copy of a grant of all ships' merchandize, &c. captured by Captain William Kidd, of the ship 'Adventure,' galley, from Thomas Too, John Ireland, Thomas Wake, and William Mace or Maze, or other pirates since the 13 April 1696, made by the King to Richard Earl of Bellomont, Edmund Harrison, merchant, Samuel Newton, gentleman, William Rowley, gentleman, George Watson, gentleman, and Thomas Renolls of St. Martin's, who had been at the expense of fitting out the ship.

12 April 1700

A letter from Mr Burchett to William Popple, secretary to the Board of Trade, discussed several packets sent by Bellomont to the Board of Trade.

> Several pacquets sent from New England by my Lord Bellomont in H.M.S. Advice, among which are some directed for the Lords of the Council for Trade and Plantations, and yourself, they desire that their Lordships will appoint some proper person to receive the said packets from them to-morrow morning, and I do believe it will be expected that the said packets should be opened and read in their presence, as the Secretary of State did theirs this morning, that if anything relates therein to Capt. Kidd the pirate, the same may remain here till such time as he shall be examined.

1 December 1699

> Order of the House of Commons, that a copy of the Privy Seal and of the indenture and commission under the Great Seal of England granted to Capt. Kidd, and of the petition and all other papers upon which the same were granted be laid before this House, as also such representations as were

made by the merchants relating to pirates and an account of what Captain
Kidd has done abroad and what has been done thereupon here.

21 November 1699

Secretary Vernon wrote to the Secretary of the East India Company, one Mr
Blackburn, concerning Kidd's actions.

I laid to-day before the Lords Justices your letter of the 18th inst., with the
enclosed advices from India, concerning the piracies committed by Captain
Kidd. They ordered that instructions be given to the commander of the
squadron, now going to the East Indies for the suppressing of the pirates,
that he use his utmost endeavours to seize Kidd and his vessel, if he be still
in those seas, in order to bring him and his accomplices to condign
punishment; and they directed instructions to be sent to the earl of
Bellomont for securing Kidd with his ship and associates, in case he return
to New York, where he has his family settled, and from whence he is said
to have carried the greatest part of his crew; and the like instructions will
be sent to the rest of his Majesty's colonies in America. Their Excellencies,
finding by these advices how much Capt. Wright, the commander of the
Quedah Merchant, misbehaved in yielding up his ship to Kidd without
making any resistance, and in sharing with him in his piracies by taking to
his own use some part of the plundered goods that belonged to his
freighters, are of opinion that Wright ought to be apprehended and made
answerable; and will give orders accordingly, unless the company have
anything to object. If there be anything more that the company judges
proper to be done for vindicating the honour of the nation against the
calumnies raised in India, and for the security of the factories there, I
desire you will let me know it.

Annexe F – Pirates and Privateers: Kidd Compared

The story you have read gives us a glimpse into what made Kidd tick. From his early days as a privateer in the West Indies when he was employed by Codrington it seems he was man prepared to do what was right. His refusal to let ships pass them by without attacking them shows us he had some moral fibre but that begs the question why he took such an enormous risk with his last voyage.

Like every other privateer of the time he must have been out to find the main score, the big haul, while also doing the King's business. He signed two agreements and in the second agreement he agreed to pay a Performance Bond of £20,000 if he failed in his mission to capture and plunder rich French or pirate ships. Why? He must have believed that he could fulfil his mission. His arrogance, confidence and belief in himself can be seen throughout the voyage every time he had to impose his will on his crew to keep them on the lawful path.

But perhaps there was something more. His wife was wealthy; the property he lived in was her inherited property. True he had some money and a ship when he married her but, if we accept Richard Zack's claims that she had more money than he did, then we might be able to see some motivation for Kidd to take the risks he did.

Was Kidd looking for that one big prize that would give him the money he needed to buy a house for his family that would be of his own making? If so, he wouldn't need to be tied to anyone, even his wife? Remember that women in those days didn't have the same status as men did. Very few had property. They were not the equals of men. So not having property or the kind of money his wife had may have been one of the prime motivations for Kidd to take such a drastic risky mission. Until he took on the mission there was nothing to suggest that the man was reckless or prepared to take such huge risks.

Perhaps the best way to look at Kidd is to look at some of his contemporaries and peers – other privateers operating around the same time – privateers who did turn pirate and did so very successfully.

There is a common thread in looking at these other privateers turned pirate. Most of these men were not comfortable on land, or with life on land, yet they all dreamed of making a big score so they could settle somewhere and, presumably, buy property or build assets of some sort.

What we've seen of Kidd is that his arrogance, overconfidence, naiveté and bad luck caused his downfall. It's true he did capture a prize ship and he did get a chest of jewels, gold and silver, but he never had the chance to enjoy them and use them to buy property. We've seen that he distributed some of the goods he'd captured among many other people and places, possibly in the hope that once he'd cleared his name he could return to where he'd hidden the loot and sail into the sunset a rich man. Why didn't he just sail away?

Some privateers who turned pirate around the same time as Kidd did just that. One was Captain Henry Avery, who was in many ways a typical pirate. He was apparently, according to what documentation there is, rather short and fat – the complete antithesis of Johnny Depp prancing around as Captain Jack Sparrow. For all that, however, he was a typical pirate, according to Daniel Defoe's account of him in his *The General History of the Pyrates*. Defoe also wrote *The King of the Pyrates*, which appears to be based on interviews that he had with Avery.

Avery, also known as John Avery, Long Ben or Captain Bridgeman, like most pirates had a career that was short and in his case successful. According to Defoe, Avery was born in Plymouth in 1653 and went to sea early in his life with the Royal Navy. He served for some time as midshipman on HMS *Kent* and HMS *Rupert*. However, by 1694 Defoe tells us he was aboard a privateer where he was the second mate. This ship had been hired to plunder and raid the Spanish colonies. Defoe refers to this vessel as the *Duke*, but David Cordingly in *Under the Black Flag* suggests it was called the *Charles*.

Defoe wrote of Avery, 'Being a fellow of more cunning than courage, he insinuated himself into the good will of several of the boldest fellows on board the other ship as well as that which he was on board of: having sounded their inclinations before he opened himself, and find them ripe for his design he, at length, proposed to them, to run away with the ship, telling them of what great wealth was to be had upon the coast of India.'

For months they'd been in the port of Corunna without action of any kind while their captain had a love affair with the bottle. On the evening of 7 May 1694, at 2200hrs, while Captain Gibson, drunk as usual, lay sleeping it off in his cabin, Avery and the men quietly went about securing the ship, weighed anchor and put to sea, 'without any disorder or confusion'. Gibson was still sleeping it off in his cabin while Avery, now in command, slowly sailed out of the bay towards the open sea.

Defoe stated that Gibson woke to the motion of the ship and the sounds of the tackles being worked. He summoned Avery to find out what was happening. When Avery entered with two other men Gibson said, 'What's the matter, what's going on?'

'Nothing,' Avery replied calmly.

'Come man, something's the matter with the ship, does she drive? What weather is it?' Gibson, now fully awake, was worried a storm had torn the ship from her anchor and she was drifting. Avery soothed his fears by replying, 'No, no. We're at sea with a fair wind and good weather.'

'At sea? But how can that be?'

Avery laid the facts before Gibson: 'I am Captain of this ship now, and this is my Cabin, therefore you must put on your clothes and walk out. I am bound for Madagascar with a design of making my own fortune and that of all the brave fellowes joined with me.'

Gibson's alarm grew as the realization began to sink in (according to Defoe's account). But Avery told him that if he wanted to join them, he, Avery, would make Gibson one of his lieutenants; but if he didn't want to join him then Gibson would be put into one of the boats and sent ashore to safety. Gibson chose the latter and was rowed away from his former ship. That out of the way, Avery continued sailing for Madagascar.

Before we continue with this story let's look at the differences and the similarities between the two men and the events in their lives. Both men served aboard privateers before turning to piracy. Both men were able seamen; but Kidd had commanded the *Blessed William*, while Avery had no command until he seized the *Charles/Duke*. The main difference is that Avery chose the road to piracy early while Kidd tried to avoid going down that road.

Avery renamed his ship the *Fancy* and sailed south towards Madagascar; Kidd was also in this area but not at the same time. Along the way, Avery plundered three English ships in the Cape Verde Islands and captured two Danish ships near the island of Principe, on the west coast of Africa. Kidd, as we have seen, did his level best to avoid English ships but had the bad luck of regularly running into ships of the Royal Navy or armed merchantmen of the English East India Company. With the exception of one action Kidd did his best to get away from East India ships whenever he encountered them. Avery had no qualms about attacking English ships.

He continued round the Cape of Good Hope heading for Madagascar. Finally, after several months at sea, they dropped anchor at the northeast corner of the island and went ashore for provisions, water and wood. Avery had a plan that at one time Kidd had tried but failed. But then he had been after pirate ships.

The pilgrim fleet of Muslim ships that sailed from the Indian port of Surat across to the mouth of the Red Sea at Mocha, then on up to Mecca every year, was a ripe target for pirates. These ships were loaded with treasure and wealthy passengers and merchants. Usually, the merchants sailing with the pilgrims would trade their wares, cloth and spices for gold and coffee. The Great Mogul often sent his own ships with the fleet. Avery's plan was a simple one: to intercept the fleet and plunder what he could.

Remember that Kidd parked himself in the same area and ran across a pilgrim fleet but no pirates. His mission was to catch pirates or French ships. He was following the pilgrim fleet in the hopes of picking off any pirates also shadowing the fleet. Kidd shadowed a pilgrim fleet when he was in the area but ended up empty-handed, capturing no pirate ships and no French ships; had he turned pirate then he would have had a great opportunity to capture one of the Mogul's ships. How different would his story have been had he turned to piracy then, as his crew wanted and captured a heavily laden pilgrim ship? We will never know.

But this was what Avery was planning to do. It was September 1695 and the *Fancy*, with Avery commanding, was cruising off Mocha. Avery had fitted the ship with more cannons so she now boasted 46 guns with a crew of more than 150 men. While Avery cruised the area, more pirate ships joined him as they waited for the fleet to arrive. Kidd sailed for Mocha in May 1697.

Unlike Kidd, Avery had luck on his side. The first of the pilgrim fleet of ships to be plundered was the *Fath Mahmamadi*, which the pirates stripped of gold and silver. A few days after this ship was plundered, the lookout on the *Fancy* far above the deck sighted a white sail on the horizon and Avery ordered the men to put on as much sail as they could to catch it. The ship they were chasing belonged to the Great Mogul himself. The *Ganj-i-Sawai* (later referred to as the *Gunsway*) was a massive vessel of 40 guns. The captain, Muhammed Ibrahim, must have felt confident that he could defend the huge ship against any attackers because he also had 400 muskets, so anyone trying to board would be in for a surprise.

Avery got round that problem altogether by a lucky shot. As the small fleet of pirate ships approached, Avery ordered his guns to open fire on the *Ganj-i-Sawai*. The first broadside smashed into the Muslim ship's mainmast, sending it crashing down onto the deck. One of the cannon exploded sending shrapnel and splinters in all directions, mowing down men and causing carnage. The fight lasted two hours and was very one-sided. When the pirates boarded the vessel they met with little resistance.

On board the vessel was one of the Great Mogul's daughters and her various attendants, several slave girls and many wealthy merchants. Though Avery claimed that no harm was done to the women this was later refuted when one of his crew was captured and confessed at his trial that they embarked on an orgy of plunder, torture and rape, while the two vessels lay tied together becalmed on the Arabian Sea. These atrocities apparently lasted for days.

Avery now having made his fortune with this one act of piracy decided to retire so he left the other pirate ships and headed for the West Indies. He arrived at the Bahamas on Providence, where he presented the governor of the day with his ship and several ivory tusks. From that moment on, he seems to have slipped into obscurity, with legend saying he lived out his life in luxury on a tropical paradise. Others say he died in obscurity, poverty-stricken in the village of Bideford in Devon.

However, there are discrepancies in this story. In his book, David Cordingly uses Captain Charles Johnson's text. Many people believe that Johnson and Defoe are the same person. Johnson wrote *A General History Of The Most Notorious Pyrates* but his account does not tie in with Defoe's. For example, Defoe writes that Avery was joined by two other pirate sloops before they sighted the *Ganj-i-Sawai*, which he does not mention by name. He doesn't mention the plunder of the first of the pilgrim ships and says that it wasn't Avery's first few shots that brought down the mainmast. 'Avery only cannonaded at a distance and some of his men began to suspect he was not the hero they took him for. However, the Sloops made use of their Time and coming one on the Bow and the other on the Quarter of the ship, clapt her on board and enter'd her upon which she immediately struck her Colours and yielded.'

Cordingly, using Johnson's account as his source, suggests that Avery just slipped away from the rest of the pirates but Defoe's version of events has him double-crossing the other pirates in the two sloops. Avery did this by making a proposal to the commanders of the two sloops that all the loot should be kept aboard his ship, which was far larger than the two sloops. The reason for this, he suggested, was in case the two sloops should fall into the hands of the navies in the area, or worse succumb to storms at sea and be lost. Since the loot was carried on all three ships, if one ship was lost everyone lost part of their share.

The other captains quickly agreed to this as Defoe states, 'For they argued to themselves that an Accident might happen to one of the Sloops, and the other escape, wherefore it was for the common Good.' The booty was duly loaded aboard Avery's ship and the three vessels kept company over the next day. But by nightfall, Avery slipped away from the sloops, leaving the other pirates with no booty at all.

Avery decided to go to America because he wasn't known there. He landed (as we have seen) at Providence first, where several men went ashore and dispersed, living on their ill-gotten gains. Avery stayed for some time and then moved on towards New England where he thought he could settle. At this point Avery got worried. He had in his possession large amounts of jewels taken from the Muslim ship. Many of these were diamonds. He started to worry that if he landed in New England and was questioned about where he got so many diamonds he would be found out. Defoe said he sailed to Ireland where he stayed for a while and from there contacted people he could trust to see if he could sell the diamonds with no questions asked. He then sailed to Bideford in Devon and met up with two Bristol merchants who essentially swindled him out of his fortune.

So, like Kidd, Avery was left with nothing. He died a beggar despite the single act of piracy that brought him his fortune. Defoe's version implies that he was easily swindled by these merchants.

Why was Avery so afraid? Here's what Defoe says: 'As soon as the News came to the Mogul, and he knew that they were English who had robbed them, he threatened loud and talked of sending a might Army with Fire and Sword, to extirpate the English from all their settlements on the Indian Coast.' We know that the Mogul bayed for Avery's blood and was prepared to wage a war to rid himself of the English. We also know from Cordingly's account and Defoe's account that the East India Company officials did their best to pacify the Mogul. 'However, the Great Noise this Thing made in Europe, as well as India, was the occasion of all these Romantick stories that were formed of Avery's greatness' (Defoe).

Avery was operating less than two years before Kidd arrived on the scene. Now we have a conundrum. Did Avery really commit the atrocities he was said to have committed on the Mogul's daughters and her attendants as well as the slave girls and the rest of the passengers and crew? Did the East India Company make every effort to find Avery and his crew?

It's highly likely that Avery's actions had such repercussions that they were a key factor in Kidd's downfall because the East India Company, smarting from losing Avery, were determined to get Kidd. So Avery was successful in virtually one hit. Kidd took years before he could get his treasure and lost his ship and his crew. Neither of the two men ended up living in luxury.

One pirate did live in luxury and, though he has a small entry in Johnson's work, he does have a rather large chapter in Defoe's. This pirate was Thomas Tew. At the time he must have been a notorious pirate because his name was listed with four other pirates in the agreement that Kidd signed giving him the commission to go and attack pirates.

Like Kidd and Avery, Tew began his sea career as a privateer. He was a contemporary of Kidd and Avery and operated out of Bermuda. Indeed, it was the governor of that colony that gave Tew the commission to sail directly to the River Gambia, in Africa, and to liaise with the agents of the Royal African Company in order to seize a French factory on the coast at Goorie. Johnson's account doesn't say what this factory was making or why the governor of Bermuda would want the factory taken, nor does Defoe's account.

Tew was sailing in company with Captain George Dew; but Dew was caught in a violent storm on the voyage and sprung his mast. He turned back to refit, leaving Tew to press on. But Tew didn't get to his destination either. He rounded the Cape of Good Hope and, once there, headed for the entrance to the Red Sea. Defoe writes that at this point Tew turns away from his commission and turns pirate. He captures one of the pilgrim ships and, although it had 300 soldiers on board, Tew boarded her and took her. This ship, which Defoe doesn't name, was richly laden and Defoe suggests that each of the crew of Tew's ship got £3,000 a piece.

The prisoners they'd captured on this ship told Tew that there were at least five other ships just as rich about to pass the same way. Now both Tew and Avery did something that Kidd rarely did: consult the crew. The first time Tew did this was before when they decided to forsake their commission and set sail for the Red Sea to intercept the pilgrim fleet and capture a rich prize. In Defoe's account he writes that Tew gathered his crew on the main deck and put a resolution to them: 'Wherefore he was of the Opinion, that they should turn their thoughts on what might better their circumstances: and if they were so inclined he would undertake to shape a course which should lead them to Ease and Plenty.'

The crew were more than happy to steer this course. Tew then asked his crew to choose a quartermaster who would consult with him on behalf of the crew. Defoe writes that this was common practice onboard privateers and pirate ships. He states 'the quarter-master's opinion is like the Mufti's among the Turks: the Captain can undertake nothing which the quarter-master does not approve'. Indeed, Defoe likens the quartermaster to a humble imitation of the Roman tribune, who speaks for and looks after the people, in this case the crew. So Tew steered towards Madagascar.

Eventually Tew left Madagascar and sailed towards America. Again, Tew consults his crew and while most of them stayed behind, thirty-four decided to sail with their Commander. They still had most of the loot they had taken from the pilgrim ship, though they had spent some of it while they were at Madagascar. They arrived in Rhode Island without any fuss, without anyone knowing them and the crew dispersed throughout the area to live quietly and happily.

Although Tew had turned pirate he now reverted to privateer and decided to pay off his backers in Bermuda who had fitted out his ship and given him his commission to attack the French factory, which he never did. According to Defoe, Tew 'sent for his Owner's account fourteen times the value of their sloop'. From then on Tew lived quietly and peacefully in luxury for awhile, according to Defoe. He says that some of Tew's men who lived near him and squandered their money were continually pestering Tew to take another trip so they could rebuild their fortunes. 'He withstood their Request a considerable time: but they having got together (by the report they made of the vast riches to be acquired) a number of resolute fellows they, in a body, begged him to head them but for one more Voyage.'

The idea was to return to the straits of the Red Sea and attack the pilgrim fleet. Eventually, Tew gave in and they prepared a sloop and headed out to sea. Defoe stated that they did get to the Red Sea and engaged one of the Great Mogul's ships. However this engagement was not successful, as Defoe stated: 'A shot carried away the rim of Tew's belly, who held his bowels with his hands some small space; when he dropp'd it struck such a terror in the men, that they suffered themselves to be taken, without making resistance.'

Interestingly, this account of Tew's end does not appear in Johnson's account. Perhaps it was more of Defoe's fiction? But if we speculate that it was true or based on some form of truth then what do we have? Three seafaring men, each one starting out as privateers and all three at some point turning pirate – despite Kidd's protestations that he never was a pirate, in the eyes of the Royal Navy, the East India Company, the English Parliament and the rest of the world, he was. Each of them died without their treasure. Kidd distributed his, Avery was swindled out of his and Tew left his in Rhode Island to go to sea.

So is there a thread that runs through the stories of these three men that gives us a clue or insight into the mind of the pirate? For example, did Tew go back to sea because he missed the life, because he loved the sea so much and even though he was rich he was bored? Or was it arrogance that was the undoing of all three of them?

Let's look at the men themselves. First of all they were hard men. They were not scholars, not overly educated, though we know that Kidd could read and write. Presumably so could Tew and Avery, to some degree. The sea was their world but all of them went to sea to make a fortune to realize their dreams of living in luxury quietly somewhere on land. So the sea was the route they would take to make their fortune. If we look at arrogance then we know that Kidd's reckless arrogance brought him to the gallows, along with incredibly bad luck. But, from Defoe's account and Johnson's account, it seems that once Avery got onto dry land he was lost and didn't understand the ways of business. His arrogance could have been his belief that people would fall all over themselves for him because he had money. He was easily swindled.

Tew's arrogance may have been his belief that he could go back to sea and capture a juicy prize pilgrim ship again without loss of life as he did before. Unlike the others he had realized his dream and was living in luxury a wealthy man, so what could have induced him to leave all that and go back to sea if not his arrogant belief that he could do it again and make even more money?

What about other pirates who were Kidd's contemporaries, did they fare any better? Let's look at Captain Thomas White. Like the others, White began his career lawfully. His birthplace was Plymouth, like Avery, and he was one of the few successful pirates who did manage to live well on his earnings, though not in Europe where he wanted to be but in Madagascar.

Captain White was an educated man and went to sea at an early age. According to Defoe's account of White, he served onboard a man of war for some time then went to Barbados where he married and entered the Merchant Service. His plan, Defoe wrote, was to settle in Barbados with his family. He was given command of a brigantine called the *Marygold* and made two successful voyages, however on his third voyage out his luck ran out. He was captured by French pirates along with some English ships.

The French took the *Marygold* as she was in better shape than the ship they had and, once the prisoners had been secured, they sailed towards the coast of Guiney (Defoe's spelling), where they took another ship which was better than the *Marygold*. Transferring everything and everyone to the new ship, Defoe writes that they then burnt the *Marygold*. Defoe does not name the French pirate but he does say that the English prisoners were badly treated and some murdered, 'for they would set them up as a Butt or Mark to shoot at; several of whom were thus murdered in cold Blood by Way of Diversions'.

White had been marked out as one of these prisoners who would be shot by one of the French pirates on board. Luckily for White, he'd made friends with some of the other prisoners who knew the French were planning on killing White while he slept. 'He advised him (White) to lye between him and the ship's side, with intention to save him; which indeed he did, but was himself shot dead by the murderous villain, who mistook him for White.'

Presumably after this attempt White laid low and hid in the bowels of the ship with the other prisoners. The pirates cruised down the coast of Africa, rounding the Cape of Good Hope, making for Madagascar. Most of them were drunk and, as Defoe puts it, 'they knocked the ship on the head at the south end of the island'. The ship struck a reef at a place the natives called Elexa, the jagged rocks tearing great chunks out of the hull. This was White's chance. As water poured in, White and fellow officers Captain Boreman and Captain Bowen, along with other prisoners, managed to get up to the main deck, untie the long boat and jump into it as confusion and chaos reigned. The drunken pirates shouted and screamed as they slipped off the deck, some washed away by the water, others simply falling into it. Using broken oars that they found in the bottom of the long boat (as Defoe describes it) they managed to row away from the wreck towards the shore. They landed in Augustine Bay, were they were met by the King of the area, known as Bavaw, who apparently spoke good English. This king, or prince, we can assume was a native king because Defoe writes later that he gave them 'plentiful allowance of provision as was his Custom to all white men, who met with any misfortune on his coast'.

Somehow, White managed to end up aboard another pirate vessel that was captained by one William Read, who sailed along the coast of Madagascar picking up European pirates, either by force or voluntarily. Read then headed for the Gulf of Persia, according to Defoe, to intercept the pilgrim fleets. They took a single-masted vessel, which Defoe calls a grab. On board they found nothing but bale goods and threw them overboard but apparently learned afterwards that in one of the bales were considerable amounts of gold. Read died aboard the ship and was succeeded by another pirate. They took another French ship and headed back to Madagascar, setting sail for the River Mathelage on the west side of the island.

White lived ashore for some time before another ship came in, a pirate ship commanded by Thomas Howard called the *Prosperos*. This happened at Augustine and the evening that the *Prosperos* arrived some of the pirates decided to take her as a prize. Defoe tells us that White remained on the shore. Howard and his mate were killed putting up resistance and several others were wounded. At this point White was a free man and many of the pirates on shore pressed him to board the *Prosperos* and go with them.

He boarded the ship and was made quarter-master by the crew. They then met with a ship commanded by Captain Bowen and they all went aboard that ship, according to Defoe, presumably abandoning the *Prosperos*. When Bowen left that ship, White remained aboard. Defoe says that at Port Dauphin White took the ship's long boat (pinnace) and rowed into the harbour to pick up some of the crew who had been left behind. White and his men spent the night in the harbour and they woke up the next morning to find their ship was gone. 'He supposing her gone to the West Side of the island he steered that course in his boat with 26 men.'

Sailing back to Augustine they waited a week for their ship to arrive but it didn't. They took on provisions and headed for Mathelage (Dafoe) where Captain White and the native king were on friendly terms. They then headed for the north end of the island, determined to go round it and head for Sainte Marie island; but the currents were too strong and they were forced to turn back. At this point some of the men were for heading inland and walking across the island to the other side to catch their ship. White had a mini Kidd mutiny on his hands here; but unlike Kidd he put it to the men to see who would stay with him and who would go. The men who decided to leave did so and White took the remaining crew and they headed back to Mathelage.

After three months they got into their long boat and attempted to get around the currents in the north again; but poor weather and rough seas thwarted their attempts, so they put into a small harbour to wait it out. For a month White and his men stayed in the harbour until good weather finally arrived and they sailed around the northern tip of the island and down the eastern coast of Madagascar. It must be noted that all of this time, according to Defoe, they were using their long boat, which White had converted into a small sailing vessel.

They were heading for Sainte Marie and, when they did reach it, a canoe came out and they were handed a letter warning them that the natives were not friendly. Defoe wrote: 'The contents of the letter was to advise 'em to be on their guard and not trust too much to the blacks of this place, they having been formerly treacherous.'

It was here that they discovered the news of their ship. Their shipmates had given the ship away and settled at Ambonavoula on the southward side of Sainte Marie. White and his men were taken to Olumbah, which was a type of peninsula bounded by a river on one side and the sea on the other. White discovered through their native guides that some of his former shipmates were living here in one compound. The compound was heavily fortified with 20 cannons.

'The rest of them were settled in small companies of about 12 or 14 together, every nation by itself as the English, French, Dutch etc.' Defoe wrote. In this case there really was honour among thieves as the shares in the prizes taken for White and his men were there waiting for them 'and they found them all very justly laid by to be given to them'.

However, White persuaded some of the men to go with him and once again they set off in their long boat. They headed back to Mathelage where they took a French ship of six guns. This ship had been taken by pirates. White gathered them together and proposed they join him and his men and head for the Red Sea. Most of them agreed and White was unanimously made captain. Now commanding his ship, White headed away from Madagascar and steered for the pilgrim fleet.

We know from Defoe that Captain White's motivation was to return home and up until this point White had not been a pirate: he'd either been a prisoner or a spectator of pirate acts. At this point it appears that White goes on a rampage. Once they arrived at the mouth of the Red Sea, White took two small pilgrim ships, grabs, which were laden with provisions, drugs and had some money. After a fortnight, White let the two ships go. A few days later, the watch caught sight of a large sail on the horizon and White ordered the men to put on all sail so they could chase her. But the ship turned out to be a Dutch man-of-war, so White quickly ordered retreat and they managed to get away.

A few days after this they met a ship of 1,000 tons and 600 men, called the

Malabar. Defoe wrote this account of its capture: 'They kept company with all night and took her in the morning, with the loss only of their boatswain, and two or three men wounded. In the taking this ship they damaged their own so much, by springing their fore-mast, carrying away their bolt-sprit and beating in part of her upper works, that they did not think her longer fit for their use, therefore filled her with prisoners, gave 'em provisions, and sent them away.'

Presumably, White transferred his command to the *Malabar* and a few days afterwards they encountered a Portuguese man-of-war, which they chased and they blew away its main top-mast in the battle. Three days afterwards they captured a Portuguese merchant ship and boarded her. White had been flying the English flag as he approached the merchant ship who mistook the *Malabar* for an English East India Company merchantman. The Portuguese captain soon discovered he'd been duped but there was nothing he could do. White took this ship and everything of value that was on it.

Two days later, they captured the *Dorothy*, an English ship that came from Mocha. They took a considerable amount of money from the captain. The only Europeans, Defoe wrote, that were on board were the officers, and the rest were Moors.

By now they were building up a considerable sum. In the *Malabar* alone they'd plundered enough money and goods worth £200 per man. The next ship they plundered was a ketch of six guns a few days later. This ketch had two children aboard. White and his men took whatever provisions they needed along with 500 dollars, a silver mug and two spoons that belonged to the children. Discovering that this was all the children had to bring them up, Captain White gathered his crew together and told them it was wrong for them to rob innocent children. Unanimously, the crew decided to return what they'd taken and even gave the children a gift of 120 dollars, according to Defoe's account.

White then set sail towards the Bay of Defar where they captured another ketch, seized the vessel and put the crew ashore. They took 2,000 dollars from a French passenger and sold the ketch to the local natives for provisions. White decided to set sail for Madagascar and by this time the crew had fortunes of roughly £1,200, per man.

White built a house at Madagascar and took off the top deck of the ship to repair it. Presumably the weather had again turned against White and he decided to wait for better winds and currents before trying for home but he fell ill and died within six months of his return to Madagascar. Defoe states that White had a son by 'a Woman of the Country' and named three men of different nations in his will to be the guardians of his son, asking that he be sent to England on the first English ship that arrived to be brought up as a Christian. Several years after White died an English ship did arrive and the boy's guardians put him on the ship with the captain who brought him up.

What then are the similarities between White and Kidd? White was an experienced seaman, like Kidd, though not a privateer but a merchant sailor. He was captured by pirates and taken prisoner and was part of the pirate community, albeit at the bottom rung. But it was only when he was given the command by the pirates of the six-cannon French vessel that he turned to piracy. Why did he suddenly turn pirate? After all he'd experienced as a prisoner did he want that one shot at making a fortune so he could return home a wealthy man? Was he infected by the greed of the pirates and their need for money so he could purchase property back home? Of course we don't know but Defoe gives some interesting presumed facts. 'White took off the upper deck of his ship, and was fitting her out for the next season. When she was near ready for sea, Captain John Halsey came in with a brigantine, which being a proper vessel for their turn, they desisted from working on the ship and those who had a mind for fresh adventures, went on board, among whom Captain White entered afore the mast.'

This means that White went aboard Halsey's ship as a common sailor. They left Madagascar but Defoe does not tell us for how long nor how successful they had been nor where they went. But he does say that White returned to Madagascar and died six months later.

Of all the people we've looked at, White is the most successful pirate because he ended his days in his own house, with his wife and son, on his own land, a wealthy man. Of course the fact is that the land wasn't in England or Barbados – where he really wanted to be – but he had realized the pirate dream of making it big and living in luxury.

Kidd didn't do this. White didn't act recklessly. He was a prisoner so he must have done a lot of watching and waiting, turning things over in his mind and making friends of other prisoners. When he escaped and lived on Madagascar before turning pirate, he must have been talking with other pirates, persuading them to join him as well as joining with other pirate companies. In his actions at sea when he realized he couldn't beat the Portuguese man-of-war, he quickly backed off. It is our belief that White was the kind of man who looked for opportunities and grabbed them when they presented themselves. Instead of leaving with Captain Bowen he stayed aboard Bowen's ship, likely seeing this as an opportunity to gain control and finally head for home. After having spent so much time as a prisoner of the pirates he would have known where the best hunting grounds were for wealthy ships and so when he became pirate he took the opportunities to attack as many ships as he could.

These four men had much in common. They were all experienced sailors; they had all been legitimately employed before turning to piracy. But they were all after one thing – to make it big – to have that one shot at wealth and fortune. These men were not noblemen. It is likely they grew up in very mediocre surroundings and were enthused by stories of adventurers making fortunes on the high seas.

Further Reading

Bonner, Willard Hallam, *Pirate Laureate: The Life and Legends of Captain Kidd* (Rutgers University Press, 1947)

Botting, Douglas, *The Pirates* (Time Life Books, The Seafarers series, 1979)

Dalton, Sir Cornelius Nealen, *The Real Captain Kidd: A Vindication* (Duffield & Co., 1911)

Johnson, Captain Charles, *A General History of the Robberies and Murders of the Most Notorious Pirates* (1724, and 2 vols, 1726); introd. by David Cordingly (Conway Maritime Press, 1998)

Ritchie, Robert C, *Captain Kidd and the War Against the Pirates* (Harvard University Press, 1986)

The Trial of Captain Kidd, ed. Graham Brooks (William Hodge & Co., 1930)

Zacks, Richard, *The Pirate Hunter: The True Story of Captain Kidd* (Review, 2003; 1st publ. Hyperion, 2002)

Notes

Introduction

1. Captain Charles Johnson, *General History Of The Most Notorious Pirates* (Conway Maritime Press, 1998), 350.
2. Taken from William Hallam Bonner, *Pirate Laureate: The Life and Legends of Captain Kidd* (Rutgers University Press, 1947), p. xii.
3. Ibid.
4. Ibid., p. xv.

Chapter 1

1. Taken from William Hallam Bonner, *Pirate Laureate: The Life and Legends of Captain Kidd* (Rutgers University Press, 1947), 5.
2. Taken from Richard Zacks, *The Pirate Hunter: The True Story of Captain Kidd* (Review, 2003; 1st publ. Hyperion, 2002), 58.
3. David Cordingly, *Under the Black Flag* (Harcourt Brace & Co., 1995), 180.
4. Bonner, *Pirate Laureate*, 3.
5. Zacks states that the cargo of this vessel was made up of '50,000 pounds of tobacco, 2,500 leather hides, tons of dye-wood from Campeche, and 4,000 pieces of eight'. However, he does not name his source for this information.
6. Taken from Robert C Ritchie, *Captain Kidd and the War against the Pirates* (Harvard University Press, 1986), 29.
7. From Calendar of State Papers, America and West Indies, 550, nos. 17, 17/I, II.
8. From Calendar of State Papers, America and the West Indies, 550, no. 30, and Board of Trade, Leeward Islands, no. 43, pp. 148–55 and 171–7.
9. This entire account has come from Richard Zacks's book but he does not indicate which sources this came from. Most likely from letters by Codrington to the Board of Trade and Plantations. Zacks, *The Pirate Hunter*, 64.
10. From Calendar of State Papers, America and the West Indies, 789, received 3 July 1690.
11. Calendar of State Papers, America and the West Indies, vol. 13, 789, 1690, a letter from Governor Codrington to the Lords of Trade and Plantations.
12. From Calendar of State Papers, American and the West Indies, volume 13, 789/I, 1690, from an unknown officer aboard Heweston's *Lion*.
13. Zacks, *The Pirate Hunter*, 68.
14. Noted ibid., 69.
15. From Calendar of State Papers, America and the West Indies, vol. 13, 789/II.

16. Calendar of State Papers, America and the West Indies, vol. 13, 789, 1690, a letter from Governor Codrington to the Lords of Trade and Plantations.

Chapter 2

1. Taken from Robert C Ritchie, *Captain Kidd and the War against the Pirates* (Harvard University Press, 1986), 32. This reference Ritchie says is a statement from Kidd and is cited in virtually every history of Kidd.
2. Ibid.
3. Ibid.
4. Standard procedure on pirate ships, according to most sources, was that the crew elected the captain. While Mason was elected by the crew, it is likely that Culliford continued to provide advice and orders to Mason.
5. Noted in Richard Zacks, *The Pirate Hunter: The True Story of Captain Kidd* (Review, 2003), 73.
6. Indeed Richard Zacks says that he arrived 19 March 1691, while the date of 18 March was taken from Ritchie, *Captain Kidd and the War against the Pirates*. 79, 34.
7. Zacks suggests this was Fort William.
8. Ritchie, *Captain Kidd and the War against the Pirates*, 35.
9. This is according to Zacks, *The Pirate Hunter*, 82.
10. Ibid, 80.
11. Ibid, 87.
12. Taken from Ritchie, *Captain Kidd and the War against the Pirates*, 40.

Chapter 3

1. Calendar of State Papers, America and the West Indies, vol. 14, s. 621, 1699: a letter from Governor Lord Bellomont to the Lords of Trade and Plantations.
2. This entire section is taken from Robert C Ritchie, *Captain Kidd and the War against the Pirates* (Harvard University Press, 1986), 41, 47.
3. Richard Zacks, *The Pirate Hunter: The True Story of Captain Kidd* (Review, 2003), 95.
4. From Ritchie, *Captain Kidd and the War against the Pirates*, 44.
5. Ibid. for the facts in this entire section.
6. Ibid, 48.
7. Taken from Zacks, *Pirate Hunter*, 97.
8. We must be careful here as Zacks does not list his sources for these claims.
9. The various versions of this come from Ritchie, Zacks and the letters Bellomont wrote to the Lords of Trade and Plantations about Kidd.
10. The information on the Great Seal comes from the relevant page on Wikipedia. Much of the information on Lord John Somers comes from the relevant internet site on Wikipedia.
11. Ibid.
12. Ibid.
13. Ritchie refers to this man as Sir Edward Harrison. However, he is referred to

in more than one source as Sir Edmund Harrison so we will use that name.

14. *The Trial of Captain Kidd*, ed. Graham Brooks (William Hodge & Co., 1930), 13.
15. From the sailing orders from Bellomont to Captain Kidd.
16. Zacks, *Pirate Hunter*, 101.
17. *Trial of Captain Kidd*, ed. Brooks, 16.
18. Taken from Ritchie, *Captain Kidd and the War against the Pirates*, 53.
19. At the time, England and Scotland were still separate kingdoms. The formal union, creating the United Kingdom of Great Britain, occurred in 1701.
20. Articles of Agreement between Kidd, Livingston and Bellomont.
21. From a letter by Bellomont to the Council of Trade and Plantations dated 31 Aug. 1699, which is filed at Calendar State Papers Colonial Series (CSPCS) America and West Indies, vol. 17.
22. The place and date information for the launch comes to us from the narrative Captain Kidd wrote after his voyage, which is filed at CSPCS America and West Indies, vol. 17, s. XXV, and also reprinted in *Trial of Captain Kidd*, ed. Graham Brooks, 11. The state paper is available at the National Archives in Kew and at British History Online.

Chapter 4

1. This is rounded up from the original specification of 124 foot.
2. From file reference HCA 26/3/58 (located at National Archives).
3. According to official documents this was 3,200 square yards.
4. Undoubtedly, under extreme situations, the crew might have been more than happy to perform a role usually reserved for slaves.
5. This contradiction is included here because the only source that claims the ship was built specifically for the expedition is Richard Zacks's *The Pirate Hunter* (Review, 2003). He states that the ship was built in five weeks. The significance of this is that in less than a year poor workmanship would start to show as the ship began to leak.
6. Peter Earle, *The Pirate Wars* (Methuen, 2004).
7. The quotes and facts in this section come from Robert C Ritchie, *Captain Kidd and the War against the Pirates* (Harvard University Press, 1986), 58.
8. As it transpired, Edmund Harrison was destined to lose the most in purely financial terms.
9. From file reference HCA 26/3/58 (located at the National Archives).
10. Taken from Ritchie, *Captain Kidd and the War against the Pirates*, 59.
11. From the sailing orders from Bellomont to Captain Kidd.
12. Even after this, the dampening down of hostilities did not alleviate the fear of continued fighting. A couple of years later (on 6 July 1699) and at the end of Kidd's voyage, the agent for New York, T Weaver, was prompted to write to the Council of the Board of Trade and Plantations. This letter sought war-like supplies for defence, including 100 barrels of gunpowder, 20 pieces of cannon,

mortars and bombs. This is filed at Calendar State Papers Colonial Series (CSPCS) America and West Indies, vol. 17, s. 609. It can be found at the National Archives in Kew and at British History Online.

13. According to Richard Zacks this information came from Jeremiah Dummer, a Royal Navy surveyor.

14. Taken from Ritchie, *Captain Kidd and the War against the Pirates*, sourced as British Library Loan Manuscripts London, 29/207, fols. 47–8

15. Ritchie states the order was issued on 29 Feb. 1696 and is from Admiralty Papers, ADM 3/12 held at the Public Records Office, Kew.

16. Stories of people falling down drunk in the streets and waking up onboard ship at this time were common, but there are few accounts of people being recruited literally from the decks of other ships. However, desperate times called for desperate measures and Kidd's crew was decimated.

17. In Captain Kidd's account of his voyage, filed at Calendar State Papers Colonial Series (CSPCS) America and West Indies, vol. 17, s. 680, and reproduced in *The Trial of Captain Kidd*, ed. Graham Brooks (William Hodge, 1930), the captain makes a brief reference to the taking of some of his crew. According to him, they were pressed into service with the Fleet but no further reason is given. It is to others, such as Jeremiah Dummer, a Royal Naval Surveyor, that we turn to for a little more information. This account appears in several books such as Richard Zacks, *Pirate Hunter*, as well as in the online Wikipedia biography of Captain Kidd. The State Papers can be found at the National Archives in Kew and at British History Online.

18. Joseph Palmer would go on to become instrumental in the trial that convicted Captain Kidd. Kidd tells us in his account that there was a delay of 19 days before the mission could continue.

19. William Jenkins would remain with Captain Kidd throughout the remainder of the voyage. Jenkins joined the crew as an apprentice to George Bullen, who was himself the chief mate of the *Adventure Galley*. This is given to us in Calendar State Papers Colonial Series (CSPCS) America and West Indies, vol. 17, s. 680, part XI. We raise the question of where Jenkins joined the crew, although it is claimed in the account to be Plymouth because he claims to have joined some time after Christmas 1695. The State Papers can be found at the National Archives in Kew and at British History Online.

20. From the account of Captain Kidd filed at CSPCS America and West Indies, vol. 17, s. 680, part XXV.

21. Ibid.

22. Governor Hamilton of New Jersey wrote to Governor Fletcher on 28 Aug., explaining that he was losing some of his citizens to Captain Kidd. This is filed at CSPCS America and West Indies, vol. 14, s. 174.

Chapter 5

1. Calendar of State Papers Colonial Series (CSPCS) America and the West Indies,

vol. 18, s. 354. Letter from Bellomont to Council of Trade and Plantations.

2. Taken from Robert C Ritchie, *Captain Kidd and the War against the Pirate* (Harvard University Press, 1986), 63.

3. CSPCS America and the West Indies, vol. 15, Governor Fletcher to Council of Trade and Plantations.

4. Held in the National Archives under Admiralty Papers 3/15, 1700, and also in Colonial Office, papers 5/680, no. 64.

5. Taken from Ritchie, *Captain Kidd and the War against the Pirates*, 66.

6. Governor Fletcher of New York's letter to the Council of Trade and Plantations, dated 16 Sept. 1697, now filed at CSPCS America and West Indies, vol. 14, which can be found at the National Archives in Kew and at British History Online.

7. Taken from Ritchie, *Captain Kidd and the War against the Pirates*, 72.

8. Ibid., 75.

9. Taken from Richard Zacks, *The Pirate Hunter* (Review, 2003), 33.

10. This whole section on Warren is taken from Ritchie, *Captain Kidd and the War against the Pirates*, 75–8.

11. This is from a letter by John Clarke to the Council of Trade and Plantations, CSPCS America and West Indies, vol. 17.

12. Taken from Ritchie, *Captain Kidd and the War against the Pirates.*

Chapter 6

1. From the account of Captain Kidd filed at Calendar State Papers Colonial Series (CSPCS) America and West Indies, vol. 17, s. 680, part XXV. This can be found at the National Archives in Kew and at British History Online.

2. Taken from Robert C Ritchie, *Captain Kidd and the War against the Pirates* (Harvard University Press, 1986), 89.

3. Taken from Captain Charles Johnson, *A General History of The Robberies and Murders of the Most Notorious Pirates* (originally published 1724; reprinted by Conway Maritime Press, 1998), 35.

4. Information on Johanna is taken from various encyclopedia and internet references on Johanna, including tourist information sites.

5. Taken from Ritchie, *Captain Kidd and the War against the Pirates*, 90.

6. The accounts of both Captain Kidd and William Jenkins allude to the stop at the Island of Mohelia.

7. Taken from Richard Zacks, *The Pirate Hunter* (Review, 2003), 115.

8. Several of the accounts allude to the cleaning – or careening – process being undertaken here. The most notable are those of Captain Kidd and William Jenkins.

9. Zacks has a different account of how the ship was careened. He states that pulleys were attached to the strongest and tallest trees and the rope running over the pulleys used to flip the *Adventure Galley* onto each side.

10. Zacks, *The Pirate Hunter*, 115.

11. The loss of 50 of his crew is referred to by Captain Kidd in his account, filed at CSPCS America and West Indies, vol. 17, s. 680. He tells us that these men died in the space of a week but gives no indication of the likely cause was.

12. Taken from Ritchie, *Captain Kidd and the War against the Pirates*, 91.

13. Johnson, *General History*, 349.

14. From the Journal of Council of Trade and Plantations, Dec. 1698 now filed at CSPCS America and West Indies.

15. Ritchie cites Barlow's Journal, vol. 2, p. 482, originally held in the Indian Office Records, now part of the National Archives at Kew.

16. *Trial of Captain Kidd*, ed. Brooks, 21.

17. Ibid., 19.

18. Taken from Zacks, *The Pirate Hunter*, 126.

19. In the accounts by Kidd and his various crew members, there is very little mention of the time spent in the area of the Red Sea. Kidd skips over it entirely, although some of his crew, such as Hugh Parrot and William Jenkins, do make a brief mention. With the amount of potential shipping carrying both wealthy cargoes and passengers, this entire area would have presented rich pickings. Certainly, if Kidd had encountered any pirates here, he would surely have made claim of such, thereby adding legitimacy to his own innocence to the charge of piracy.

Chapter 7

1. From the deposition of Benjamin Franks signed at Bombay, 10 Oct. 1697, from Calendar of State Papers Colonial (CSPC) America and the West Indies, vol. 15. Held at National Archives at Kew.

2. Zacks in his book *Pirate Hunter*, 129, states that Walker was one of the men who led the assault on the unfortunate crewmates of Captain Parker.

3. Taken from CSCP America and the West Indies, vol.15, s. 733, part II, Deposition by Nicholas Alderson sworn at Bombay, 19 Oct. 1697. In addition to this Ritchie cites a source for this incident: India Office Records, E/3/35, no. 6446, IOR, State Trials, V, 304, 322.

4. This information comes from Richard Zacks, *The Pirate Hunter*, 129.

5. These are some of the items quoted in the transcripts of the trial (3rd Trial, 1st Indictment)

6. Undoubtedly, one of the principal perpetrators of the stories was Commodore Warren.

7. Zacks argues that Kidd's privateer articles would not allow him to order punishment unless he had a majority of the crew in agreement. However, Robert Ritchie states that some men who tried to steal the ship's pinnace were caught and whipped. If the crew were so disenchanted it is hardly likely that they would have agreed to whipping the men who tried to escape.

8. Taken from Robert C Ritchie, *Captain Kidd and the War against the Pirates* (Harvard University Press, 1986), 160.

9. Robert Ritchie cites Indian Office Records, High Court of the Admiralty 1/15, folio 7, State Trials, V, 322–3, as the source for this quote.
10. From CSCP America and West Indies, vol. 16, s. 723, part V, letter from Carwar to Bombay, dated 9 Aug. 1697.
11. This warning and the subsequent departure date is provided by Captain Kidd in his account, filed at CSPCS America and West Indies, vol. 17, s. 680. This can be found at the National Archives in Kew and at British History Online.
12. This verbal exchange and the subsequent events come from the account of Captain Kidd, ibid.
13. Ibid.
14. Taken from Captain Charles Johnson. *A General History of The Robberies and Murders of the Most Notorious Pirates*, introd. by David Cordingly (Conway Maritime Press, 1998). 351.
15. This is according to Ritchie. *Captain Kidd and the War against the Pirates*, 105.
16. Ibid., 103.
17. ibid., 104.
18. From the account of Captain Kidd filed at CSPCS America and West Indies, vol. 17, s. 680.
19. Ibid.
20. Taken from Ritchie, *Captain Kidd and the War against the Pirates*.
21. Taken from *The Trial of Captain Kidd*, ed. Graham Brooks (William Hodge & Co., 1930).
22. Court Transcripts, Old Bailey – 8 May 1701 (1st Trial)
23. Ibid.
24. From Daniel Defoe's *General History of The Pyrates*, ed. Manuel Schonhorn (Dover Publications, 1999).
25. CSPCS America and West Indies, vol. 17, s. 890.
26. Court Transcripts, Old Bailey – 8 May 1701 (1st Trial)
27. This figure of two-thirds comes from Kidd's account, CSPCS America and West Indies, vol. 17, s. 680.
28. Taken from Ritchie, *Captain Kidd and the War against the Pirates*, 106.
29. From the account of Hugh Parrot filed at CSPCS America and West Indies, vol. 17, s. 680.
30. From the account of Captain Kidd, ibid.
31. From the account of Hugh Parrot, ibid.
32. Taken from Ritchie, *Captain Kidd and the War against the Pirates*, 106.
33. Ibid. Ritchie states that the renegade East India Co. employee was Gillam Gandaman.
34. Ibid. Ritchie states that Bradinham's deposition is from the High Court of Admiralty Papers, 1/15 folio 7, Public Records Office, State Trials V, 301–2, 317.
35. From the account of William Jenkins, filed at CSPCS America and West Indies,

vol. 17, s. 680, part XI.

36. Taken from Johnson, *General History of Robberies*.

37. Much of this cargo is provided from the account of Hugh Parrot, CSPCS America and West Indies, vol. 17, s. 680.

38. The treasure that Kidd supposedly found in a chest appears in Richard Zacks. *Pirate Hunter: The True Story of Captain Kidd* (Hyperion, XXXX).

39. From the account of William Jenkins filed at CSPCS America and West Indies, vol. 17, s. 680.

40. Taken from Ritchie, *Captain Kidd and the War against the Pirates*.

41. From the account of William Jenkins and Court Transcripts Old Bailey – 9 May 1701 (4th Trial, 2nd indictment).

42. Taken from Ritchie, *Captain Kidd and the War against the Pirates*.

43. From the account of Captain Kidd, CSPCS America and West Indies, vol. 17, s. 680.

Chapter 8

1. Captain Kidd makes a point of mentioning the name of Robert Culliford in his account, which is filed at Calendar State Papers Colonial Series (CSPCS) America and West Indies, vol. 17, s. 680. This can be found at the National Archives in Kew and at British History Online.

2. From the account of Hugh Parrot, ibid.

3. Taken from Robert C Ritchie, *Captain Kidd and the War against the Pirates* (Harvard University Press, 1986).

4. Ibid. [page ref]. Ritchie uses several different sources for Culliford, including Culliford's own depositions held in the High Court of the Admiralty, papers 1/16, part, 1 folio 5, Admiralty Papers 1/3/3666, folio 100, no. 4, all held at the National Archives in Kew. He also uses testimonies from John Barrett and John Hales which are filed at the National Archives. Richard Zacks states that crew loyal to the captain took the *Josiah* back from Culliford.

5. Taken from Ritchie, *Captain Kidd and the War against the Pirates*.

6. Court Transcripts, Old Bailey – 9 May 1701 (2nd Trial). *The Trial of Captain Kidd*, ed. Graham Brooks (William Hodge & Co., 1930).

7. From the account of Captain Kidd, CSPCS America and West Indies, vol. 17, s. 680.

8. Ibid.

9. Ibid.

10. A piece of eight was also known as the Spanish dollar and was a silver coin minted for use throughout the Spanish Empire after 1497 when Spain was at the height of its power. The coin was used as legal tender throughout Europe, the Americas and the Far East and was the first world currency for trade, right up to the late eighteenth century. It was considered legal tender in North America until 1857. In terms of international trade, it carried the same kind of standing that the US dollar and euro do now.

11. This is taken from Ritchie, *Captain Kidd and the War against the Pirates*, 125.
12. The claim of the destruction of the journals is made at CSPCS America and West Indies, vol. 17, s. 680.
13. This is taken from Ritchie, *Captain Kidd and the War against the Pirates*, 125.
14. Ibid.
15. It is William Jenkins who tells us of the fire on the ship in his account, which is filed at CSPCS America and West Indies, vol. 17, s. XI.
16. From the account of Gabriel Loff, filed at CSPCS America and West Indies, vol. 17, s. 680.
17. In his account, Captain Kidd informs us that he was waiting for five months for a favourable wind.

Chapter 9

1. Taken from Robert C Ritchie, *Captain Kidd and the War against the Pirates* (Harvard University Press, 1986), [page ref].
2. Ibid., citing William Wilson, *A History of British India* (AMS Press, 1966).
3. E/3/53, nos. 6384, 6490, Indian Office Records held at the British Library.
4. E/3/52, nos. 6279, 6311, 6329, Indian Office Records held at the British Library, cited by Ritchie, *Captain Kidd and the War against the Pirates*, 132.
5. This is taken from Ritchie, *Captain Kidd and the War against the Pirates*, 133, citing Indian Office Records E/3/53, no. 6472.
6. This is taken from Ritchie, *Captain Kidd and the War against the Pirates*, 135.
7. Ibid.
8. Copies of two letters to Kidd are held in The Hague, while the log from the *Loyal Merchant* records the capture of the *Margaret*. L. Mar. A., 132, folios 11–12, Indian Office Records.
9. Taken from a letter written to Kidd by Emot, dated 4 June 1698, High Court of the Admiralty papers 1/98, folio 114, now held at the National Archives in Kew.
10. From the account of Captain Kidd filed at CSPCS America and West Indies, vol. 17, s. 680.
11. Ibid., 137.
12. From an entry in the Journal of the Council of Trade and Plantations received on 30 Aug. 1699, now filed at CSPCS America and West Indies, vol. 17, s. 616.
13. Ibid.
14. From the account of Captain Kidd, CSPCS America and West Indies, vol. 17, s. 680.
15. Ibid.
16. Ibid. There has been some dispute, with good reason, over the true ownership of this sloop.
17. Ibid.
18. The spelling Kidd uses for Boulton is different to other accounts that normally spell the name as Bolton. More confusingly we have Burt's name spelt either as Burke or Burk but as he signed a letter as Burt we will go with that spelling.

19. From the account of Captain Kidd filed at CSPCS America and West Indies, vol. 17, s. 680.
20. From the account of Hugh Parrot, ibid.
21. From the statement given by Peter Smith and filed at CSPCS America and West Indies, vol. 17, s. 616.
22. From the account of Captain Kidd, CSPCS America and West Indies, vol. 17, s. 680.
23. From the accounts of Captain Kidd and Gabriel Loff, ibid.
24. From the account of Samuel Wood, ibid.
25. From the account of Richard Barlycorne, ibid.
26. Taken from a letter by Colonel Robert Quary to the Council of Trade and Plantations, filed at CSPCS America and West Indies, vol. 18, s. 300.
27. From the account of John Gardiner, filed at CSPCS America and West Indies, vol. 17, s. 680.
28. Ibid.
29. From the account of William Jenkins, ibid.
30. Let us call it lesser treasure as it doesn't equate to gold and jewels, which he would have feared to lose beforehand.
31. CSPCS America and West Indies, vol. 17, s. 621.
32. CSPCS America and West Indies, vol. 17, s. 528.
33. The letter is filed at CSPCS, vol. 17, s. 680, part V.
34. CSPCS America and West Indies, vol. 17, s. 680.
35. From the letter written by Captain Kidd to Bellomont, ibid.
36. From the account of John Gardiner, ibid.
37. From the accounts of Duncan and Susannah Campbell filed at CSPCS America and West Indies, vol. 17, s. 680.
38. Ibid.
39. CSPCS America and West Indies, vol. 17, s. 726.
40. Taken from a letter from Lord Bellomont to the Council of Trade and Plantations filed in CSPCS America and West Indies, vol. 17, s. 680.
41. From the account of Captain Kidd filed at CSPCS America and West Indies, vol. 17, s. 680.
42. From the account of John Gardiner filed at CSPCS America and West Indies, vol. 17, s. 680.
43. From a statement provided by Theophilus Turner filed at CSPCS America and West Indies, vol. 17, s. 530.
44. CSPCS America and West Indies, vol. 17, s. 530, parts IV and VI.
45. From the account of Thomas Way filed at CSPCS America and West Indies, vol. 17, s. 680.
46. Ibid.
47. From the account of Hugh Parrot, ibid.
48. From the account of Robert Livingston, ibid.

49. CSPCS America and West Indies, vol. 17, s. 633.

Chapter 10

1. Taken from *The Trial of Captain Kidd*, ed. Graham Brooks (William Hodge & Co., 1930), 221.
2. Ibid., 26.
3. Taken from Robert C Ritchie, *Captain Kidd and the War against the Pirates* (Harvard University Press, 1986), 184.
4. Ibid.
5. Ibid., 192.
6. Ibid., 181.
7. From the inventory of goods collected by Bellomont dated 7 July 1699 and filed at CSPCS America and West Indies, vol. 17, s. 680, part XIX. This can be found at the National Archives in Kew and at British History Online.
8. CSPCS America and West Indies, vol. 17, s. 740, part XVII.
9. CSPCS America and West Indies, vol. 17, s. 680.
10. Taken from a letter from Lord Bellomont to the Council of Trade and Plantations filed in CSPCS America and West Indies, vol. 17, s. 680.
11. CSPCS America and West Indies, vol. 17, s. 890.

Chapter 11

1. Taken from Robert C Ritchie, *Captain Kidd and the War against the Pirates* (Harvard University Press, 1986), 192.
2. According to Bellomont, it seems as though there were several hearings in Boston, delayed by Kidd's charade over the writing of the journal.
3. David Cordingly, *Under the Black Flag: The Romance and the Reality of Life Among the Pirates* (Harcourt Brace & Co., 1995), 188.
4. This is taken from Ritchie, *Captain Kidd and the War against the Pirates*, 201.
5. Cordingly, *Under the Black Flag*, 189.
6. This is taken from Ritchie, *Captain Kidd and the War against the Pirates*, 207.
7. Ibid., 209.
8. Taken from *The Trials of Captain Kidd*, ed. Graham Brooks (William Hodge, 1930), 44.
9. Ibid.
10. Ibid., 45.
11. Cordingly, *Under the Black Flag*, 230.
12. Court Transcripts, Old Bailey – 8 May 1701 (preliminary proceedings).
13. Listed in *Trials of Captain Kidd*, ed. Brooks, 69.
14. Ibid., 89.
15. Ibid., 131.
16. Court Transcripts Old Bailey – 3rd Trial, 9 May (1st and 2nd Indictments).
17. Listed in *Trials of Captain Kidd*, ed. Brooks, 167.
18. Court Transcripts Old Bailey – 4th Trial 9 May (1st and 2nd Indictments).
19. Captain Charles Johnson, *A General History Of The Most Notorious Pyrates*

(Conway Maritime Press, 1998), 356.
20. Ibid., 357.
21. Court Transcripts, Old Bailey.
22. Ibid. These are the words that always made a court sanctioned execution legal.

Chapter 12
1. Bellomont makes several references to the gout that eventually claimed his life, e.g. in CSPCS America and West Indies, vol. 17, ss. 621 and 675. These can be found at the National Archives in Kew and at British History Online.
2. With any historical story, an 'unknown factor' always inspires a sense of wonder. Many believe Kidd was bluffing but he does seem to have disposed of many quality items while still at liberty and he had the opportunity of burying a 'rich' hoard, so who knows – only time may tell.
3. This is taken from Robert C Ritchie, *Captain Kidd and the War against the Pirates* (Harvard University Press, 1986), 223. Ritchie uses Lorrain's own account in the *Post Boy* (24 May 1701).
4. This is taken from Ritchie, *Captain Kidd and the War against the Pirates*, 224.
5. Ibid.
6. From various encyclopedia and online sources concerning naval executions.
7. Perhaps Kidd had been the recipient of some divine intervention. In some hangings, mainly for those accused of witchcraft, such an incident was often viewed as a sign from God that the person was innocent.

Chapter 13
1. This is taken from Robert C Ritchie, *Captain Kidd and the War against the Pirates* (Harvard University Press, 1986), 230.
2. Articles of Agreement between Captain Kidd Robert Livingston and Bellomont, clause XI.

Annexes
1. Not paying his crew is something that finally brought Kidd down. His crew took the easy way out in the end and turned pirate.
2. As Kidd's account does not include any reference to the Red Sea, it is implied in that document that this was the date of departure for India.
3. According to many of the accounts available, this act of piracy was committed by some of the crew of the *Adventure Galley* without Kidd's prior knowledge.

Index